More praise for *Simple Steps to Impossible Dreams*

"In the pages of his new book, Steve Scott has captured a very simple but powerful formula for translating one's dreams into reality. The reason this book has so much credibility for me is that I have seen him implement these principles to tremendous success—professionally, with his family, and in all aspects of his life. This is a must-read book."

—HYRUM W. SMITH, Chairman of the Board,
The Franklin Covey Company

"What a tragedy that most adults give up on their dreams early in life. Steve Scott's new book inspires us to dream bigger dreams than ever."

—CONNIE SELLECCA and JOHN TESH

"I need another copy immediately! It was such important information I sent my first copy to my best friend before I finished it. It's EXTRAORDINARY!"

—CHERYL LADD

"In his book, Steve Scott gives us the specific strategies and techniques that we need to learn and use to achieve our most valued dreams. He not only shows us how to make our most impossible dreams possible, he shows us how to make them *probable*!"

—CHRISTIE BRINKLEY

"In our business, we provide the opportunity for helping make people's impossible dreams come true. In his book, Steve Scott now gives the perfect tool, a step-by-step guide for turning even the most impossible dreams into reality. If you read this book it will forever change your outlook. If you live this book, it will forever change your life."

—SANDIE TILLOTSON, cofounder and Vice President,
Nu Skin International

ALSO BY STEVEN K. SCOTT

A Millionaire's Notebook:
How Ordinary People Can Achieve Extraordinary Success

SIMPLE STEPS
to
IMPOSSIBLE
DREAMS

THE FIFTEEN POWER SECRETS OF THE WORLD'S MOST SUCCESSFUL PEOPLE

STEVEN K. SCOTT

Simon & Schuster

SIMON & SCHUSTER
Rockefeller Center
1230 Avenue of the Americas
New York, NY 10020

SIMON & SCHUSTER and colophon are registered trademarks
of Simon & Schuster Inc.

Designed by Irving Perkins Associates

Manufactured in the United States of America

1   3   5   7   9   10   8   6   4   2

Library of Congress Cataloging-in-Publication Data
Scott, Steve, date.
Simple steps to impossible dreams: the fifteen power secrets of
the world's most successful people/Steven K. Scott.
p.   cm.
1. Life skills.   2. Successful people.   3. Success.   I. Title.
HQ2037.S36   1998
646.7—dc21   97-46003
CIP

ISBN 0-684-84868-6

Acknowledgments

First and foremost, my wife, Shannon Smiley Scott. Without your love, faith, and incredible patience, I never could have completed this book.

Bob Marsh. Anyone who knows me knows that you were the turning point in my life. My entire career and my financial success would have eluded me had I not had you as my wise and loving mentor.

Gary Smalley. You have not only impacted every relationship in my life, you taught me the communication skills that my life and success have been built upon.

Jan Miller, you truly *are* the world's best literary agent.

Steven Spielberg, Oprah Winfrey, Bill Gates, Henry Ford, Thomas Edison, Helen Keller, Sam Walton, Mother Teresa, Rich DeVoss, Mary Kay, Phil Knight, Walt Disney, Bob Marsh, Michael Landon, Hyrum Smith, Blake Rooney, and Sandie VanNederveen. Their lives have provided me with wonderful demonstrations of the incredible power of the "Fifteen Power Secrets."

Zig Ziglar, for your friendship, inspiration, and wonderful lessons.

Caroline Sutton, my patient and brilliant editor, and everyone else at Simon & Schuster who have made *this* impossible dream a reality.

Frank Kovacs, for making every production the absolute best, and for being such a wonderful friend.

Jim Shaughnessy, for being the *best* best friend anyone could ever have.

Tom and Marlene Delnoce. For your enthusiastic encouragement on this project.

Hyrum Smith. For your friendship, encouragement, and commitment.

Henry Marsh. Four-time Olympian, American record holder in the Steeplechase, and gold-medal friend, for always being there.

Brett Smiley, Tamme Webb, and Debbie Andersen. For giving me your opinions and input every page of the way.

Contents

PART III
Igniting Your Seven Booster Engines

Foreword

"Steve Scott is the world's expert on making impossible dreams come true. . . . I'm living proof!"

— GARY SMALLEY

IF YOU FOUND Aladdin's lamp and its genie offered to make all your wishes come true, what would you wish for?

> A long, healthy life
> Greater prosperity
> Less weight
> A fulfilling marriage
> Happy, healthy children
> More successful career
> More happiness
> More time
> More control
> More peace
> More fulfillment
> Greater achievements

These "wishes" are, in reality, your dreams. And while Aladdin's genie is only a fantasy, *your* dreams do not have to remain in a fantasy world. Dreams *do* come true—but not by accident and not by luck. Dreams come true as a result of a few, very powerful strategies and techniques that can be easily learned and used by nearly anyone, and yet less than one percent of America's adult population use them. How *powerful* are these strategies and techniques?

Nearly thirty years ago, I had a dream. I wanted to write a book that would teach couples how to have a far more fulfilling relationship.

And yet that dream remained only a hope and a constant prayer for ten years. Then one day I received a phone call from Steve Scott. He asked me if I'd like to write two books on marriage—one for men and one for women. I told him that that had been my dream for nearly a decade.

Three months later, Steve and I had written my first two books: *If Only He Knew* and *For Better or for Best*. Both became best-sellers and enabled me to begin teaching my seminars on relationships. Then, several years later, Steve called me again and asked if I would like to create a video series that could put my seminar in the hands of millions of couples. I told him that would be a dream come true! Within six months, using the Dream Conversion Process, Steve, his partners, and I had not only produced the videos, we were televising and distributing them to millions of people. Does Steve Scott know the secrets of achieving dreams? Absolutely! In fact, he knows more about it than anyone I've ever met. His Dream Conversion techniques have not only enabled me to achieve my dreams, they've enabled me to help countless others. I've seen his techniques turn bad marriages into great ones; I've watched them turn people who didn't have a dime into multimillionaires. I've seen them turn corporate failures into successful entrepreneurs.

Donald Trump said Steve Scott's strategies and techniques are "so specific and easily applied they can empower anyone, from a college student to a small-business owner to the CEO of a Fortune 500 company, to achieve levels of success they haven't yet dreamed of." But don't get the wrong idea: Steve's Dream Conversion Process doesn't just work in business. It can make an incredible difference in *every* area of your personal life as well, including your marriage and family relationships, your friendships, and even the current and future success and happiness of your children.

The Dream Conversion techniques can be applied to every important area of your life, empowering you to reach levels of success that would otherwise be elusive or even impossible. In this book, Steve not only reveals his accessible techniques, he shows you how to *instantly* incorporate them into your daily life. Once you do, you won't have to wait months to see your level of achievement and fulfillment improve. You'll see an instant—and probably a radical—improvement in your level of success and your quality of life. I agree with Donald Trump:

You *will* achieve levels of success you haven't yet dreamed of! What are *your* dreams? If you can't answer that question, don't worry about it. You will be able to by the time you finish this book. You'll not only have a clear vision of your dreams, you'll have a clear-cut way to achieve them.

Gary Smalley

PART I

YOU'VE GOT THE POWER . . .
BUT YOU'RE STUCK ON
THE LAUNCHING PAD!

CHAPTER 1

"A Dream Is a Wish Your Heart Makes"

DREAM CONVERSION CAN MAKE DREAMS COME TRUE IN ANY AREA OF YOUR LIFE.

WHO CAN FORGET the opening line from the love theme in *Cinderella*—"A dream is a wish your heart makes." Even though Cinderella was singing about the kind of dreams you have in your sleep, her description is also true about the dreams we long for as we walk through every stage of our lives. As a boy, I dreamed of becoming an airplane pilot, a cowboy, a fireman, a policeman, a soldier, and a sailor. In college, I dreamed of romance, marriage, and a successful career. Now, I dream of more time and intimacy with my family; more varied and greater achievements, both personal and professional; and greater intimacy with God. Chances are, you're not much different from me. Our dreams may be totally different, and yet, we are alike in that no matter what we have achieved, we still have dreams that have eluded us.

DREAMS STILL COME TRUE . . . FOR AN ELITE FEW

Dreams *do* come true for people like Steven Spielberg, Lee Iacocca, Kathie Lee Gifford, Jane Fonda, and many other "dream achievers" whom I have come to know during my forty-eight years on this planet. People who achieve their dreams tend to be in a tiny minority . . . perhaps one in a million or even one in ten million. On the other hand, the vast majority of American adults not only fail to achieve their dreams, they stop dreaming altogether. Why? Why do some people seem to achieve their dreams, no matter how incredible their dreams may be, while others almost *never* achieve theirs? Is it simply a matter of luck? Of course not! And guess what—it's not a matter of IQ either. Neither is it a matter of education, money, or experience. So what is it?

ARE YOU READY FOR SOME GREAT NEWS?

So the critical question is, "How" do these dream achievers fulfill their dreams? The great news is it's not a mystery; it's an art that they have *learned*. Why is that great news? Because it means that you, too, regardless of your age, inexperience, IQ, education, or financial standing, can achieve your dreams. Incredible dreams . . . wonderful dreams! You can begin to have dreams grander than you have ever had, and see many of them come true. All you have to do is learn and use the same skills that are used by those who *do* achieve their dreams.

I call these skills the "Art of Dream Conversion." An art is simply a skill that enables someone to take a concept, vision, or dream and convert it into reality. Some artists are born with an innate gift that they develop; the art of Dream Conversion, however, is a set of *learnable* skills (strategies and techniques) that anyone can master. For a tiny minority, discovering and utilizing these skills came somewhat naturally and fairly early in life. But the vast majority of adults never even discover these skills, much less use them. *Unless* . . . unless they are taught by someone who has not only discovered them but, more important, has habitually used them and experienced their awesome power and results. I didn't begin to discover these skills until six years after I graduated from college. While those first six years were full of failure and discouragement, the years that followed the implementation of these Dream Conversion skills have been filled with phenomenal success beyond my wildest dreams.

An Important Distinction

Throughout this book I will be referring to the art of Dream Conversion or Dream Conversion and the Dream Conversion Process. When I speak of Dream Conversion or the art of Dream Conversion, I am referring to *all* of the strategies and techniques contained in this book. When I speak of the Dream Conversion *Process,* I am talking about a single strategy or technique that takes a wish or dream, defines it in writing, and creates a specific plan that gives a precise and detailed road map to achieve that wish or dream. This Dream Conversion Process is explained in detail in Chapter 10.

THE BIG IF . . . AND TWO PROMISES

When people first hear my story and the impossible dreams I've seen fulfilled, they often say, "That's you . . . but I'm me." They think "You don't know my background" or "You don't know my circumstances" or "Nothing like that ever works for me." If I looked you in the eye right now and told you, "Your most incredible dreams *can* come true," what would be your first thought? Stop reading and give me your first response right now. And please give it out loud.

Was your response "Great, I can't wait to start seeing my wonderful dreams come true"? Or did you answer with a little more skepticism? Do any of the following responses capture the essence of your response?

"I don't believe you!"
"Give me a break!"
"What dreams?"
"I can't even make ends meet . . . much less achieve my dreams."
"You don't know my husband."
"You don't know my wife."
"You don't know how lonely I am."
"You don't know my situation."
"I'm too old."
"It's too late."
"I'm too tired."
"I don't have time to dream."
"I can't keep up."

Whether you answered with any of these, or gave any other answer, I'm going to make you two promises.

Promise #1: If you read this book, and let these skills and techniques simply remain on these pages and never incorporate them into your life . . . whatever you achieve in your life will only be a tiny fraction of what you *could* have achieved.

Promise #2: If you read this book, learn the few skills that I'm going to show you, and begin to practice them in your daily routine . . . I promise you *will* begin to dream bigger dreams and achieve *more* of those dreams than you would ever have imagined possible.

So, the choice is yours . . . leave these skills on the pages of this book and continue to achieve only a tiny fraction of the dreams you're capable of achieving, *or* lift the skills from the pages of this book and bring them into your life, and begin to achieve dreams you haven't yet dared to dream.

CHAPTER 2

If *My* Dreams Came True, *Anyone's* Can!

How could a corporate failure become a multimillionaire? How could a high school student with no money for flying lessons become a licensed pilot without spending a penny? How could a nonmusician create successful music groups and even direct a symphony? And how could an ignorant, insensitive husband achieve a loving and fulfilling marriage?

Now, maybe these statements sound a little far out, or even impossible. And yet, these "impossible" dreams all came true as a result of utilizing the art of Dream Conversion. My high school dream of getting my pilot's license came true even though I had no money for flying lessons. At the time, flying lessons cost $40 an hour, and I didn't have a dime in savings. And yet the Dream Conversion skills enabled me to receive those lessons and achieve a private pilot's license without spending a single penny.

My college dream of creating two successful music groups came true, even though I knew nothing about music. My dream of directing the "William Tell Overture" with a great symphony came true in the summer of 1994, even though I *still* knew nothing about music. My dreams of succeeding in business and making millions of dollars came true, even though I failed at nine jobs in my first six years after college. And most important, my dream of a loving and fulfilling marriage came true, even though I used to be an insensitive husband who was totally ignorant when it came to knowing how to meet the deepest emotional needs of my wife.

"Yeah, but that's you, not me . . . we're a lot different" might by your first reply. Well, we are different, but *you* are most likely in a better position to make *your* dreams come true than the position I was in a few years ago. Chances are pretty good that you think people who achieve their "impossible dreams" are in a different league from you. That's simply not true. I have known and worked with billionaires, Academy Award–winning actors and actresses, and superachievers from all walks of life and I can tell you: they *don't* have higher IQs; they have *not* been better educated; and they do not have better backgrounds than you. They simply learned and utilized some specific techniques that enabled them to "dream big," and then to achieve those dreams. Instead of just being "dreamers" they became "dream-makers." Everyone in life is a dreamer, a dream-maker, or a dream-breaker. If I had to guess, I'd say 30 percent of American adults are dreamers, 69.9 percent are dream-breakers, and only one-tenth of one percent are dream-makers. Which category do you want to be in? I've been in all three, and I can tell you with all certainty that being a Dream-Maker is infinitely more rewarding.

My goal for this book is twofold: number one, to prove to you that you *can* become a dream-maker, achieve your dreams, and help others to achieve theirs; and number two, to equip you with *all* the specific skills and techniques you need to become a dream-maker.

But first I must prove to you that you can achieve your highest dreams, because if you do not truly believe you can, you won't take the time to learn and practice the very skills and techniques critical to achieving your dreams.

THE NIGHT MY WHOLE LIFE CHANGED

At forty minutes past midnight on December 22, 1971, my life was instantly changed. At that moment I felt a kind of love I had never felt before; not simply *more* of the love I had felt for my wife or my parents, but a completely *different* kind of love. You see, at that precise moment I looked into the beautiful blue eyes of my first child, a brand-new baby girl. As I looked into those eyes, and they looked back at me, I was overcome by a wave of love unlike any I had ever felt before. I wanted to tell my little girl how much Daddy loved her. I wanted to tell her that I would always take care of her, that whatever she needed, Daddy would provide.

But as I began my three-hour drive home from the hospital that night, reality began to set in. How could I even begin to think that I could meet any of my daughter's material needs. I had only been out of college for a little over a year and I was already on my third job. In fact, I had lost my second only four days before my daughter's birth. At the time, my income was less than *half* the national average. As a college graduate with a degree in marketing, I was failing miserably in my chosen field.

About nine months later I was driving to work from the tiny apartment where we lived. As I passed a neighborhood of small homes and saw the backyards with their swing sets and sandboxes, I felt a lump in my throat and tears began to well up in my eyes. I realized that my little girl would never have her own backyard. She would never play on her own swing set. I was sure she would be spending the rest of her life growing up in apartment courtyards because no matter how hard I worked, I simply could not "get ahead." The bills were always bigger than the paychecks, and it seemed as if I couldn't hold a job for more than a few months.

I walked into my office that morning more discouraged than ever. Unfortunately, things only got worse as the day wore on. After lunch my boss called me into his office. He was the senior vice president and the number-two man in the company. He had a beautiful office, and because he was head of marketing, I had tremendous respect for him.

As I entered his office, he looked at me very gravely and I knew I was in trouble. "Steve, you are the single greatest disappointment in my entire career," he said. "You will never succeed in marketing and I've decided to let you go. You have twenty minutes to clean out your desk."

As I walked back to my desk I saw that everyone around was pretending not to notice me. My boss had told the entire department that he was going to fire me after lunch. As I cleaned out my desk, I began to cry. Everyone was sneaking peeks but saying nothing. The last item on my desk was the one that hit me the hardest. It was the picture of my precious little newborn with those great big blue eyes wide open and looking up at me. Daddy had failed again, failed his company, failed himself, and failed his little girl.

Little did I know that I had *six more* jobs to lose in the next four years. I was mastering the art of failing, an art no one likes to dabble in, much less master. Every failure I went through was gut-wrenching, though I later discovered that my dismal failures would become the very foundation for my ultimate success. As you'll see, my story didn't always remain discouraging. In 1996, Simon and Schuster published my first book, *A Millionaire's Notebook,* and they would not have selected that title had my daughter spent her whole life playing in apartment courtyards.

But it's the subtitle of that book, *How Ordinary People Can Achieve Extraordinary Success,* that truly defines what the book was all about. This subtitle confronts one of the most commonly held, achievement-crippling misconceptions in our society today, that people who achieve extraordinary success are in a completely different "league" or "class" from the rest of us! That simply isn't true. In fact, many have risen from far worse circumstances and backgrounds than you have likely experienced. Let me give you three examples.

A MAN NAMED GENE

Gene Orowitz was raised in Collingswood, New Jersey. Because he was a bedwetter into his adolescence, his mother regularly humiliated him by hanging his wet sheets out of his bedroom window for all his friends to see. She told him he would never amount to anything, and his failure in high school seemed to bear her words out—he graduated 299th out of a class of 301. He later told me that the two students who graduated lower than he could barely read and write.

Things didn't get much better for Gene after high school. Because he excelled in track, he was awarded a track scholarship to the University of Southern California, but he lost that scholarship during his freshman year because of a disappointing track season. He had no money to return home, and he ended up sleeping on park benches in Santa Monica, California. His first job was selling blankets door-to-door. And yet, in terms of success rate, Gene went on to become the most successful television writer, director, and producer in television history. I say that because his success batting average was 1,000. In other words, 100 percent of the shows he created were successful. To my knowledge, no other producer in Hollywood history can claim that high a success rate. I knew him as one of the truest and most wonderful friends a man could ever have; you knew him as Michael Landon.

TWO STEVENS

As part of my high school's color guard, I had the privilege of raising the American flag at every home football game. The reward for this duty was a free ticket to each game and a reserved seat with the school's marching band. At many of the games I sat next to a clarinetist who was a lot like me. I didn't know his last name, but his first name was Steven, too. He was skinny, shy, and totally unknown to me and to most of the other students at our high school.

Now, back in the sixties, the last place you really wanted to be at a football game was in the band or the color guard. But with both of us weighing around 120 pounds, the other Steven and I had no chance of making the football team. (Even if we had weighed more, our lack of athletic prowess would have kept us from making any of the sports teams.) Like me, the other Steven never dated anyone from our high school, and neither of us was a great student. In fact, he was a C-minus student in a *good* semester. This other Steven was totally unknown to most of the students and teachers at my high school; you, however, know him because his name has appeared on five of the top ten grossing films of all time. In fact, who in America, or the world for that matter, doesn't know the name Steven Spielberg?

Twenty years after I graduated, my mother phoned me one day and told me that Steven Spielberg was a classmate of mine at Arcadia High School. I told her that was impossible; I knew nearly everyone at Arcadia, and there was no way I wouldn't have known Steven Spielberg. Mom told me to get out my high school annual and look up his name. Sure enough, his name was in the index. When I finally reached the page with his picture, I was shocked. It was the same Steven I had sat next to at nearly every football game. When we ran into each other a few months later, I said, "Steven, if only I had known," and he replied, "Steven, if only *I* had known!"

As for me, I graduated from high school slightly above the middle of my class. In high school, I excelled in nothing "significant." In the first six years after graduating from college in 1970, I flunked out of nine jobs. If I had written my career history in April 1976, here's what it would have looked like:

COLLEGE—CLASS OF 1970

Year	Job & Salary	Duration (in months)	Outcome
1971	1st, $600/mo.	4	quit
1971	2nd, started business	8	failed
1972	3rd, $1,000/mo.	9	fired
1973	4th, $1,000/mo.	9	quit
1974	5th, $1,100/mo.	5	quit
1974	6th, started business	9	failed
1975	7th, $1,000/mo.	4	fired
1975	8th, $1,100/mo.	4	quit
1976	9th, $1,500/mo.	4	quit

As you can see, my income between my second and eighth job rose from only $1,000 per month to $1,100 per month. This was less than half the average income per married household in America. My average length of employment was six months per job. Put it all together and I wasn't even "ordinary," I was "subordinary"!

However, on my tenth job, which has lasted twenty years, I have sold over $1 billion worth of goods, and along with my six partners, I have created numerous multimillion-dollar companies from scratch, creating more than forty millionaires. After I lost my eighth job there was no way you could have convinced me that on my tenth job I would one day earn as much as $500,000 per month. And yet it happened.

SO WHAT HAPPENED?

What took Eugene Orowitz from failure in high school and turned him into Michael Landon? What took Steven Spielberg from unknown, below-average student and turned him into one of Hollywood's all-time greatest directors? And what took Steve Scott from corporate and financial failure and turned him into a successful business builder and multimillionaire? Or, to put it another way: What enabled these three "underachievers" to become achievers beyond their wildest dreams?

The answer is fairly simple. We all learned some critical strategies, skills, and techniques that enabled us to begin to dream bigger than we had ever imagined, and *convert* our dreams into reality. As I've come to know many other men and women who have achieved incredible dreams, I've discovered that like Steven, Michael, and me, they've all employed many of the same strategies and skills that we have. Strategies and skills that are learnable and can be used by *anyone*.

More Than Business Success and Money

These dream-achieving strategies and techniques can be applied to any important area of life. They can enable you to capture your dreams in your relationships, in your hobbies and passions, as well as in your careers, businesses, and personal finances. I have used them to reach my dreams in my relationship with my wife, my relationships with my six children, and my relationships with my friends. I have used them to achieve my dreams in my writing and television directing, my marketing, and in every facet of my business and financial life. I continue to use them every single day.

So why did I bother to tell you the stories of Michael Landon and the two Stevens? To prove to you that ordinary people can achieve their highest dreams. Remember, in many ways, we were way "below average." Right now, you've probably got a much better start on achieving your dreams than Michael Landon, Steven Spielberg, and Steven Scott had on achieving theirs.

"Wait," you say, "that may be true for you three, but that's certainly not true of others." *Au contraire!* As Zig Ziglar points out in his studies of over three hundred historic and contemporary world-renowned men and women, more than 75 percent rose to the heights of human achievement from the depths of disheartening and discouraging circumstances and backgrounds. Almost none rose from an advantageous background or set of circumstances. Thomas Edison had only three months of formal education. By the time he was twelve, he was working full-time on the railroad. He never had a class in calculus or physics, and yet we all enjoy electric lights, movies, and recorded sound because he learned the art of Dream Conversion. Bill Lear dropped out of school in sixth grade, and yet he gave us car radios when high school physics books said "small radios were physically impossible." He also gave us the first airplane "autopilot" and the first business jet, even though the greatest aircraft companies of his time said such advances were impossible because of economic constraints. Oprah Winfrey not only had poverty going against her, she was the "wrong color" in a region of the country where the wrong color created almost impossible odds for any achievement. We could fill volumes with the names of men and women who, through the ages, have achieved their dreams despite their backgrounds and circumstances.

So no matter how you rate yourself, your talents, and your abilities, starting right now, you can begin to embark on a pathway that will lead you into the extraordinary—extraordinary relationships and extraordinary accomplishments, both personal and professional. Whether your dream is to lose fifty pounds, to have the most fulfilling marriage you know of, or to enjoy a rewarding career and income far beyond your wildest imagination, you can have it all by learning and utilizing the art of Dream Conversion.

A FEW PEOPLE WHO BROUGHT ME THEIR "IMPOSSIBLE" DREAMS

- A struggling makeup artist who dreamed of creating her own line of cosmetics.
- A marriage counselor who dreamed of helping millions of marriages instead of only hundreds.
- A college instructor who dreamed of teaching students of all ages how to learn more effectively.
- A hair stylist who dreamed of seeing her hair care products in stores all over America.
- A weight-loss expert who dreamed of helping discouraged overweight people lose their excess weight and regain their health and self-esteem.

These are a few of the people who brought me their dreams but had little or no hope of seeing them come true. And yet, by using the art of Dream Conversion, my partners and I were able to make all of their dreams come true, almost overnight. Makeup artist Victoria Jackson was able to create a cosmetic line with over a hundred products, one million customers, and over $300 million in sales. Marriage counselor Gary Smalley was able to write two best-selling books and create the best-selling video series ever distributed, helping millions of couples achieve their dreams of a more fulfilling relationship.

Dr. Claude Olney saw his little learning seminar turned into a video series, "Where There's a Will There's an 'A,' " that enabled millions of grade school, high school, and college students to learn far more effectively than they had ever imagined possible. Hair stylist Lori Davis saw her hair care products, which she had only been able to sell in her salon, transformed into a hair care line represented by Cher. It is now sold in nearly every retail drug, grocery, and discount store in America. And Richard Simmons saw his "Deal-a-Meal" dream turned into a reality and has helped millions of men and women to lose weight and regain their fitness. And these are just a few of the men and women I have worked with, using the art of Dream Conversion to turn their impossible dreams into tangible realities.

Yes, dreams do come true *if* you know how to *make* them come true!

I love Zig Ziglar. He is not only a great motivator and teacher, he is a great person. He has made a dramatic difference in my life, and I quote him from time to time throughout this book. In his seminars, Zig leads his audience through a very simple, yet liberating and empowering exercise. I would like to do the same thing with you right now by asking you three questions.

1. Do you believe that there is something you could specifically do in the next two weeks that would make your personal life, your family life, or your business life worse? _____ Yes _____ No
2. Do you believe that there is something you could specifically do in the next two weeks that would make your personal life, your family life, or your business life better? _____ Yes _____ No
3. Do you believe that every choice has an end result? _____ Yes _____ No

If you answered yes to all three questions, you got a perfect score. More important, here's what you've agreed to. You just said: "I don't care how good or bad my past has been. I don't care how difficult my circumstances are at this precise moment. There's something I can do right *now* that will make my future either better or worse . . . and the *choice* is *mine!*"

Yes, the choice truly is *yours!* If you choose to learn the principles, techniques, and strategies that make up the art of Dream Conversion, and begin to incorporate them into your daily routine, you will begin to achieve your dreams like never before.

CHAPTER 3

What Prevents *Most* Women and Men from Achieving Their Dreams?

YOU'RE LIKE A ROCKET STUCK ON THE LAUNCHING PAD AND YOUR DREAMS SEEM AS UNREACHABLE AS THE MOON.

IF YOU SAW the movie *Apollo 13,* or if you're old enough to remember watching the Apollo launches, you may remember watching the blast-off of the giant Saturn V rockets that served as the launch vehicles for the Apollo space program. The Saturn V was the largest, most powerful rocket the United States has ever built. It was as tall as a thirty-six-story building. It was powered by five giant engines. Each one of those engines created more than one million pounds of thrust. That's twenty times more powerful than the huge jet engines that power a 747 jumbo jet. Together, these five engines created so much thrust, they could have lifted 3,700 automobiles, stacked on top of each other, off the launching pad.

No matter how I describe the power of these engines, nothing can adequately convey how awesome they truly were or what it was like being near the launch site the day of a launch. When those engines ignited, the noise was as deafening as a continuous wave of a thousand claps of thunder. The earth rumbled and shook for miles. And as that thirty-six-story rocket lifted off the pad, slowly at first and then accelerating faster and faster, it was followed by a massive trail of flame until it soared out of sight. The power of those engines is virtually unimaginable.

Now, for just a moment, visualize in your mind that you are standing right next to that Saturn rocket quietly sitting on its launching platform. As you look up its towering structure, you strain your neck hoping to catch a glimpse of the spacecraft, way up on top, that will carry three astronauts to the moon. Now lower your gaze to those five massive booster engine funnels at the base of the rocket. The rocket is just sitting there, its engines ready to be ignited, all that explosive power just waiting to be unleashed.

My friend, *you* are just like that Saturn V rocket, except you have *seven* giant booster engines, the most powerful engines ever placed into a single vehicle. In fact, your engines are so powerful they're capable of breaking all the bonds of gravity and taking you all the way to the moon and beyond, to a place where your greatest dreams reside, a place that is home to all the truly awesome dreams that have ever been dreamed. Many of these dreams have been found, retrieved, and brought back to earth by those elite dreamers who have learned how to ignite their rockets. It's a place where a little black girl from Mississippi became the most beloved and successful talk-show host in entertainment history. It's a place where a boy who only had three months of schooling lit up the world with an invisible power called electricity. It's a place where a blind and deaf girl became a captivating communicator and an inspiration to millions.

And what kind of dreams are waiting there for you? It's a place where a broken marriage can become the healthy and fulfilling marriage every little girl dreams of. It's a place where a man can become the husband and father his family deserves and desperately needs. It's a place where men and women can create the career or even the business they've always hoped for. This is a place that's full of all the things money can buy, and more important, all the things money can't buy. And here's the great news: This place is *just* as reachable for *you* as it was and is for me. You can go there anytime you want. But you can't get there simply by jumping as high as you can. You can only get there aboard your Saturn V rocket. *And the good news is that your rocket is sitting on the launching pad, all fueled up and ready to go.*

The bad news is that it will just sit there and never get off the ground unless you do two things—two things that more than 95 percent of the adult population of America never do! First, you must recognize that there are six chains keeping you anchored to the launching pad, and if you are ever going to get your rocket off the ground, you *must* sever all six. Second, you must ignite *all* seven of your booster rocket's engines.

Now, don't think, "Oh, great, what happens if I don't have 'what it takes' to cut the chains and 'ignite the engines'?" I promise, you have *everything* it takes to do both! Every day you ignite and harness hundreds of horsepower in your automobile's engine, simply by turning a key in the car's ignition. How gifted, talented, or brilliant do you have to be to do that? You simply need to know *where* the key is located, and *which* way to turn it. I'm going to show you where the ignition switches are located for all seven of your rocket engines, and which way to flip them. As to the chains, how much talent is required to use a pair of chain cutters? All you need to know is where to place the sharp cutter blades. I'm going to show you each of the six chains that are holding you down, and put the appropriate chain cutter in your hand.

When I tell people these two steps, they sometimes ask, "Aren't you oversimplifying this? After all, if it were that easy, wouldn't everyone achieve their dreams?" I respond by telling them that it really *is* that simple . . . but it's not that easy. It's simple in that it's not complex. But it's not easy in terms of effort, because it requires honesty, integrity, and a commitment to learn and begin to use the art of Dream Conversion. Truly, it is simple enough that anyone who genuinely wants to cut the chains and ignite the engines *can*. But it will require that you take the time to learn and make the commitment to utilize the strategies and techniques that I will share with you in the chapters ahead.

One of the most successful oil men of all time was a man named Frank Phillips. Right before the outbreak of World War I, Frank and his brother found enough oil to create Phillips Petroleum and become two of the richest men of their time. And here's the amazing part: Neither one of them was a geologist. In fact, neither one of them even went to college. Frank had been a barber. He married a banker's daughter and went to work at her dad's bank in Iowa. He didn't have the education, training, or ability to find oil and build an incredible oil business, and neither did his brother. But they cut the six chains that held their rockets down, ignited all seven engines, and the rest is history.

Just like Helen Keller and Oprah Winfrey, just like Frank Phillips and Thomas Edison, just like Michael Landon and Steven Spielberg *you, too,* have your own Saturn V rocket fueled up and ready to blast off to the moon and beyond . . . to find your dreams, retrieve them, and bring them back to earth. And just like all the dream-achievers who have gone before you, you are sitting on your launching pad. They cut their chains and ignited their engines. Now it's your turn! T-Minus ten, nine, eight, seven, six, five, four, three, two, one . . . we have ignition. . . .

PART II

CUTTING THE SIX CHAINS

CHAPTER 4

Chain #1: Your Programming for Mediocrity!

YOU'VE BEEN PROGRAMMED FOR MEDIOCRITY FROM YOUR YOUTH.

As A PSYCHOLOGY major in the sixties, a good friend of mine participated in a study in which rats received electric shocks every time they tried to take food from a food tray. They soon completely stopped approaching the food tray because of their fear of being shocked. Then the electricity was turned off and an even more scintillating and desirable food was placed in the tray. The rats still would not approach. As time went on, the rats chose to starve to death rather than take the risk of approaching the tray and being shocked. Can you imagine being so programmed by past events that you would prefer starvation and death rather than confront the *possibility* of encountering the feared event again? And yet that's precisely what happened to these rats. They could have gone back to the tray at any time, eaten better than they had ever eaten before, gained back all their strength and returned to a normal life. But they didn't even try! Oh, the awesome power of negative programming!

The first time I heard Zig Ziglar speak, twenty years ago, he told two stories. The first was about fleas; the second was about elephants. He said if you place fleas in a shallow container, they'll quickly jump out. However, if you put a lid on that container for just a brief period, they'll jump like crazy at first, but they'll soon give up their quest for freedom. When the lid is then removed, instead of instantly jumping out, they will remain in the container . . . and they'll never attempt to leave the container again. Like the rats, they become programmed by past limitations to accept that those limitations will continue to exist in the future.

Well, so much for dumb, tiny animals. An elephant has a big brain and is infinitely smarter than a flea or a rat. And yet circuses used to train baby elephants by tying them to a pole planted securely in the ground. The elephant very quickly learned that when he felt a rope on his neck and a tug on the rope, he could not go any farther. By the time he becomes an adult, he can be tied to a small pole that he could easily rip right out of the ground, but he doesn't even try because he has been programmed to believe that when that rope is around his neck and he encounters the little "tug," he must stop.

Now, as bad as I feel for the fleas and the elephants, I feel even worse for the poor rats. After all, their "programming" resulted in their starvation and untimely death. And yet, as sad as that story is, it can't begin to compare to the tragedy that has been inflicted upon the hundreds of millions of American schoolchildren who have passed through our educational system since the 1940s, including you and me. Like the rats, fleas, and elephants, we were programmed by our teachers, coaches, fellow students, and even our parents to believe that we were average or ordinary kids. And as average, ordinary kids, we began to believe we were only capable of accomplishing average, ordinary achievements. Now, even though *our* programming was totally unintentional on the part of those who programmed us, it was still devastatingly powerful.

By the time most of us graduated from high school, we had been fully programmed for mediocrity, and from that point on we have had a nearly unalterable tendency to accept mediocrity as the best we can do in nearly every area of our lives. We accept marriages and relationships that are okay rather than strive to make them great. We do just what's expected of us in our jobs rather than try to break every performance record in the books. We don't attempt to take risks and convert our ideas into businesses because we truly believe that we are not capable of overcoming great risks and achieving extraordinary success.

While our programming hasn't resulted in starvation, it has had terrible consequences for tens of millions of American adults. How many marriages have ended in divorce because a couple did not have the vision, confidence, and know-how to turn a mediocre or bad marriage into a truly fulfilling one. Or equally tragic, how many couples have continued to live in an unfulfilling relationship for years or even decades because they didn't think they could do anything to change their mediocre, unfulfilling relationship into one where all their highest hopes and greatest expectations are fulfilled? And then there's education. More than half of the students that start college never graduate. They start with a dream, but they give up on it because they've been programmed to believe they don't have what it takes to achieve their ultimate dream. College graduates often earn their bachelor's degree in a field other than one they would really have preferred because they didn't think they were good enough to qualify. And how many people end up in a job, totally unfulfilled, not because they wanted that kind of job but because they believed it was the best they could do in light of their abilities, background, or circumstances. Surveys have shown that 85 percent of the workforce has a job or career that they wish they could change, but like the fleas and the elephants, they are locked into place by their past programming.

I hope you are beginning to see how devastating this chain of being programmed for mediocrity truly is. It keeps you anchored to your launching pad with no hope of ever blasting off and achieving your dreams.

Now, before you get too depressed, let me tell you that everyone I've ever met has been anchored by this same chain, at least for a while! Lee Iacocca, Steven Spielberg, Michael Landon, and Steve Scott were all programmed for mediocrity. You see, in high school, we are all judged by our teachers, parents, coaches, peers, and, worst of all, ourselves by only three standards of measurement: grades, popularity, and athletic abilities. If we didn't graduate with straight A's, if we weren't with the "in crowd," and if we were not star athletes, we thought of ourselves as average or ordinary, or maybe a little above or a little below average or ordinary. And from that point on, we continued to accept that assessment of ourselves. We don't even *attempt* extraordinary achievements. We set goals that are low because we believe that is all we are capable of achieving.

The result: We place our destiny in the hands of others, whether it's our employer, our banker, or our mate. We think the Rolls-Royces and mansions are reserved for the other guys—the Steven Spielbergs, Bill Gateses, and Lee Iacoccas. We think the great marriages are reserved for men and women who marry the geniuses and the beauties, not for those of us who married ordinary people. We think that medical school or law school or engineering school are for the people with high IQs, certainly not for us or our children. We think that the great companies are built by brilliant businessmen with the right backgrounds, circumstances, and luck, that we could never build a multimillion-dollar business from scratch.

My dear friends, these are lies, lies, lies, and more lies. Yet we've believed these lies for a long time and allowed ourselves to be programmed by them. Even athletes, medical researchers, and scientists have had their performances severely limited by negative or false programming. Runners were told by scientists that it was physically impossible for a human being to run a mile in under four minutes. As a result, for years, runners would run the mile just to the four-minute mark but no lower. After all, it was physically impossible. Then one day a man named Roger Bannister ran a mile in under four minutes. Once the word got out that someone had broken the four-minute mark, runners all over the world began doing it. Had they all discovered a magical pill or a steroid that gave them superhuman speed? Were their bodies redesigned to break that "impossible" barrier? Not at all. They had simply deprogrammed themselves. They threw away the mental programming that had limited their performances for their entire athletic careers.

American aeronautical engineers had all determined that a small corporate jet could not be prototyped for under $100 million, so they didn't even try! Then Bill Lear built a prototype for $10 million. He hadn't been programmed like the engineers of the giant aerospace companies.

Medical researches said polio was unconquerable, but a doctor named Jonas Salk threw that programming away, and made polio a disease of the past. Equally important, as a result of Dr. Salk's breakthrough, medical researchers have learned "Never say never."

As I said earlier, *all* of us have been programmed for mediocrity. But like Roger Bannister, Bill Lear, and Jonas Salk, we've learned how to cut the devastating chain of mediocrity, and to keep cutting it every time it appears.

So the question now becomes, How can *you* sever this devastating chain . . . and keep cutting it every time it appears in your life? The great news is that it's a lot easier than you think. All it takes is a conscious awakening to a reality that has long been hidden from you, a corresponding adjustment of your attitude, and setting aside a few minutes a week to engage in one of the most powerful activities you'll ever take part in.

AN AWAKENING AND AN ATTITUDE ADJUSTMENT

An Awakening

The first step in cutting this chain is an awakening. I'm not talking about a spiritual event but simply waking up. First, you must wake up to the fact that you, too, have been programmed for mediocrity. Isn't it true that when you think of the super successful, whether in business or in marriage or in any other area, you think of someone other than yourself? Realizing that you have been programmed for mediocrity is the first step in the awakening I'm talking about.

> **EVEN THOUGH YOU'VE BEEN PROGRAMMED FOR MEDIOCRITY, YOU WERE DESIGNED AND CREATED FOR *EXTRAORDINARY* ACHIEVEMENT.**

The next step is even more important. You must wake up to the fact that even though you may be an average, ordinary person, you are capable of *extraordinary* achievement. In fact, God did not create you for mediocrity. He created you for extraordinary, awesome achievement—in *all* areas of your life. You may not believe this is true, but it is! Let me explain what I mean by "extraordinary achievement," and then show you how you have been equipped for it.

ACCURATE MEASUREMENTS OF EXTRAORDINARY ACHIEVEMENT: In your past, true extraordinary achievement was not accurately measured by the grades you received in school, by how popular you were with your classmates, or by your athletic accomplishments. Today, extraordinary achievement is not accurately measured by your income or the material things you possess. While these may be general indicators of achievement, they are not accurate measurements of the height or degree of accomplishment.

We've already seen that, measured by their grades in school, Steven

Spielberg and Michael Landon were failures as students. And yet, I will tell you that they were incredibly successful students when they are *accurately* measured. They both "studied" off campus at movie theaters and became great scholars in the art of storytelling and movie composition. The accurate measure wasn't a grade they received in school but rather what they were able to accomplish later in life using the lessons they had learned through their observations at the movies. By that *accurate* measure, they were incredibly successful students.

Mother Teresa made very little income and never had a lot of material possessions, and yet her achievements far surpassed those of the world's richest men. The true measure of her success could only be found in the loving and appreciative eyes of the dying men, women, and children she nourished and cared for throughout her life. My wife is a homemaker and a wonderful wife and mother. Her achievements in the raising of our children are far more extraordinary than anything I have ever accomplished in business. Her success is measured by their sense of security, love, and respect for others.

In such cases, extraordinary achievement is not measured by wealth. Even for people such as Steven Spielberg and Oprah Winfrey, who have been financially successful, the true measure of their achievements is the impact they have had on the lives of so many people.

Day in and day out, whether she's felt like it or not, Oprah has shown up at the studio and has walked onto the stage. She has been a constant and dependable companion, friend, and encourager, not only to those closest to her but to millions of strangers who spend an hour with her each day.

Steven Spielberg has provided millions with a source of entertainment, and has also made an incalculable contribution to the future of our world with his film *Schindler's List*.

So how do we accurately define "extraordinary achievement"? Simply stated, *extraordinary achievement is achievement that brings an extraordinary amount of benefit or fulfillment to us or to others.* Two people who have a relationship that truly meets the other's deepest emotional needs have achieved an extraordinary relationship. Parents who raise children who are truly motivated by their love of others, who take responsibility for all that they do, who demonstrate tremendous character qualities such as loyalty, courage, dependability, and trustworthiness, are extraordinary parents.

All of this is to say that the true measure of *your* achievement is the amount of fulfillment you are able to bring to others and to yourself. I have known many people who have accomplished extraordinary things in one or two areas of life and failed miserably in others. How many multimillionaires have failed in marriage and parenting? How many successful parents have failed in their careers and businesses? Well, the good news is that we can accomplish extraordinary achievement in *every* area of life that is important to us. We don't have to sacrifice success in one to achieve it in another.

Now, before you can believe that *you* can achieve your loftiest dreams in every important area of life, I must first prove that you have been *equipped* to do so. If I told you that you are capable of flying faster than the speed of sound, but I only equipped you with a hang glider, I would be a liar, and you would be a fool to believe me. If, on the other hand, I made that same statement and equipped you with a supersonic jet aircraft and a pilot, you would have everything you need to accomplish the task and more. The incredible "on-board computer" that God placed between your two ears is the best proof I can offer to show that you have been adequately equipped to accomplish your biggest dreams.

THE WORLD'S MOST ADVANCED COMPUTER: A friend of mine was one of the handful of engineers who developed the most advanced scientific computer in the world back in the 1970s. At that time, he told me that this computer could receive one billion inputs or bytes of information per second.

Now, as incredible as that was, this "supercomputer" could only receive those bytes of information *one* at a time. Your brain, on the other hand, receives four million bytes of information *simultaneously* just from your eyes! At the speed of light, your brain processes those four million bytes of information, creates a picture of your surroundings, and perceives that picture in three dimensions with color and motion. And it does that every moment you are awake! At the same time, your brain also receives hundreds of millions of other bytes of information from your other senses, organs, and nerves; processes that information at the speed of light; and sends out millions of commands, also simultaneously! I hope you're thinking "Wow" right now. (If not, close this book and give it to someone else.)

Are you awesomely equipped or what! If every floor of the Empire State Building were filled with mainframe and personal computers, and they were all wired together, they *still* could not accomplish what your brain automatically accomplishes on a moment-by-moment basis.

Now, just as man did not create computers in order to accomplish mundane, mediocre tasks, our Creator did not equip us with our phenomenal "on-board computer" just so we could complete simple mundane, mediocre assignments. He gave us the most advanced computer in the universe so we could do things that are *truly* awesome and extraordinary.

If you were broke, and I deposited $10 million in your checking account and told you about it, but you did not believe me, what would happen? Absolutely nothing! Even though you would be $10 million richer, you would continue to live and behave as if you were broke. And even though the money would be in your account, neither you nor anyone else would gain any benefit whatsoever from your wealth. The only way you would ever benefit would be to (1) believe that I had made the deposit, and (2) begin to act accordingly and write checks against it. The same is true right now. You *are* fully equipped to achieve extraordinary things in every area of life that is important to you, *but* . . . you must first believe that you've been so equipped, and then you must behave accordingly.

An Attitude Adjustment

So now that you have been awakened to the fact that you are truly capable of achieving your dreams, of achieving extraordinary things in every important area of your life, you need to make a definite attitude adjustment. Go back to my example of the $10 million deposit and imagine how tragic it would be if you never invested or spent a dime of that money because you had been programmed to pinch pennies and you had never adjusted your attitude to that of a responsible steward of $10 million. Without that attitude adjustment, you would continue to act as someone who was broke. Think of all of the good things your family, friends, charities, and society in general would be deprived of, simply because you maintained the attitude of a penny-pincher.

BETTER THAN A $10 MILLION DEPOSIT TO YOUR BANK ACCOUNT!

While I have not deposited $10 million in your bank account, God has given you a mind that is worth far more than that. And it's up to you to be grateful for its endowment, to be excited about learning how to use such a gift to achieve your dreams, and to help others achieve theirs. If you can adopt this attitude and commit yourself to exploring and pursuing all the incredible opportunities that await you, the activities and techniques revealed here will empower you to achieve things you have not yet dared to dream.

This means that your past levels of achievement will *not* determine or limit your *future* level of achievement! Even your greatest failures need not limit your future accomplishments. On the contrary, they will likely serve as your greatest teachers and the springboards to extraordinary success. If you can accept these truths and adjust your attitude accordingly, well . . . get ready for the ride of your life.

IF YOU ONLY REMEMBER THREE THINGS FROM THIS CHAPTER, HERE'S WHAT THEY SHOULD BE:

1. You've been programmed for mediocrity by false standards of measure—grades, popularity, athletic abilities, level of income, and amount of material possessions. These are not the true measures by which you should judge yourself. If you have only achieved ordinary success as measured by these standards, you most likely view yourself as an ordinary person capable of only ordinary things.

2. You were designed and created to accomplish extraordinary things in every area of life that's important to you. You must wake up to the fact that your past programming has anchored you to the launching pad, and acknowledge that such past programming need no longer keep you anchored.

3. You must begin to gain the attitude of one who has been given the greatest computer in the universe and become committed to using it to achieve your dreams and to help others achieve theirs.

POWER SECRET #1:
Reprogramming Your On-Board Computer

AT THE END of this and the remaining chapters you'll find the most important pages of this book. These sections contain exercises that will enable you to take the strategies and techniques from each chapter and incorporate them into your life and the pursuit of your dreams. As you will discover, these exercises are not "work"; rather, they are a lot of fun, because they are about *you* and about achieving *your dreams!* If you complete one of these sections per month, you will, in fifteen months, radically change your level of achievement. If you complete one of these sections per week, then in fifteen weeks you will radically change your life. But if you complete them any faster than two sections per week, they will be nearly ineffective. Set your own pace, from two sections per week to one per month, but set it and stick to it.

You will need two loose-leaf notebooks, paper, and section dividers to complete these exercises and those in the other chapters. One notebook will be used to record your answers to the questions; the second will serve as your Dream Conversion Journal. This journal will ultimately be your road map and planning guide to achieving your most important dreams, even those you have considered impossible. If you would like a preprinted notebook and a preprinted Dream Conversion Journal that includes all the forms you need, you can order a set at 1-800-246-1771.

Remember, these exercises are for *your* benefit, so answer them honestly and realize that they are going to provide the foundation you need to achieve your short-term and long-term dreams. Answer the following in your notebook.

1. List what you consider to be your personal strengths.
2. List what you consider to be your personal weaknesses.
3. List what you consider to be your business or professional weaknesses.

4. List what you consider to be your business or professional strengths.
5. List the things you really love to do and the things you do well (your passions, hobbies, work projects, etc.).

CHAPTER 5

Chain #2: Your Fear of Failure

CONSCIOUS OR SUBCONSCIOUS FEAR OF FAILURE SHORT-CIRCUITS YOUR ABILITY TO ACHIEVE YOUR DREAMS IN EVERY AREA OF YOUR LIFE.

OF THE SIX chains that keep people bound to their launching pads and prevent them from achieving their dreams, fear of failure is the strongest and hardest to cut. It is a chain that begins to form and take hold in childhood and is usually fully developed and firmly anchored by the time you graduate from high school. It not only prevents you from achieving your dreams, it can be so oppressive and destructive that it can cause you to willingly set aside your dreams before you even make the slightest attempt to achieve them. In fact, it often trains you to *stop* dreaming altogether.

The fear of failure literally stunts your emotional growth and convinces you to accept mediocrity in nearly every important area of life. Your vision, your hope, and consequently your achievements are suppressed and all but destroyed by this merciless tyrant. And here's the surprising part: Many of you have lived with your fear of failure for so long that it has moved into your subconscious. Thus, most of the time you are *not even aware* of its presence, and yet it exerts its moment-by-moment influence on every aspect of your personality and decision-making process.

THE FEAR OF FAILURE IS HIGHLY CONTAGIOUS, AND IS UNWITTINGLY PASSED FROM GENERATION TO GENERATION.

For parents, here is the scariest part of all. As long as your visions, hopes, and achievements are disfigured and impaired by your fear of failure, you will unintentionally limit and destroy the visions, hopes, and achievements of your children. This debilitating fear and its consequences are highly contagious, and are passed from generation to generation. Therefore, you *must* sever this chain, if not for your sake then for the sake of your children and everyone else you truly love. Your goal must be to break its relentless grip and sever its hold in such a way that it will never seriously restrict you again. To do this, you must: (1) gain a true and clear understanding of the two component parts, *fear* and *failure;* (2) see this chain in its true light; and (3) learn a technique for recognizing it and destroying it every time it reappears.

> **FEAR:** An *emotion* that can be: (1) very healthy, helpful, and even lifesaving, *or* (2) very destructive, emotionally paralyzing, and even deadly.

Good fear teaches you your natural limits from your earliest childhood. It taught you not to touch a hot stove (a second time). It taught you not to stay under water too long or jump off something that was too high. As you grew older, it taught you not to pick fights with someone who could beat the snot out of you. It taught my father to be a great combat pilot and saved his life and the lives of his crew because it taught him not to assume *anything* and to check and double-check *everything* before he began his roll down the runway.

Good fear has taught most of us to obey those in authority and stay within the boundaries of the law in our activities. So good fear has kept many of us from being arrested and thrown in jail. All of this to say that good fear is a natural positive factor in our lives that brings with it positive outcomes. And for Jews and Christians alike, the Torah and the Bible teach that the "fear of God is the beginning of wisdom." (Who doesn't want to be wise?) So, this good or friendly fear is a lifelong friend and not to be ignored or disregarded.

Then there's the other kind of fear, bad fear or *fear your enemy.* This fear causes you to focus on the very things you should not fear but do. It brings with it devastating consequences that can create emotional paralysis, even death. For some people, this fear results in terrible phobias that make them virtual prisoners of their fears. For most, however, bad fear is more subtle; yet its consequences are no less damning. It literally stops you from doing a lot of very good things and achieving phenomenal success. In fact, it can keep you from even attempting to do things. In Little League, you didn't swing at a good pitch because you were afraid you might miss and strike out. In school, you didn't try out for a sports team or the school play because you were afraid you wouldn't make the cut; or you didn't raise your hand to ask a question because you were afraid it might be a "stupid" question. In college, there were a lot of girls I never asked out because I was afraid they would say no. Adults don't ask their spouses to do things that may be very important because they are afraid their spouses might say no—or even worse, ridicule or criticize them. They don't share their ideas with their bosses because they are afraid they will be rejected. They don't even try to start their own businesses because they are afraid they will fail and lose everything they've worked for.

One of my former bosses was playing tennis with a good friend of his when, in the middle of the game, he collapsed with a heart attack. The paramedics came and tried to revive him in the ambulance, but they were too late. Shortly after the ambulance arrived at the hospital, my boss died. An angry emergency room doctor asked my boss's friend why he didn't administer CPR on the tennis court. The friend replied, "I was afraid I'd break his ribs." Frustrated and disheartened, the doctor replied, "People can live with broken ribs!"

This is a perfect example of how bad fear works and the kinds of consequences it can deliver. This man's fear had caused him to focus on the wrong thing (the possibility of breaking ribs) and blinded him to the reality of the situation (my boss—his friend—was dying). It also blinded him to the possibility of achieving an extraordinary accomplishment, saving his friend's life. And the consequences of his fear were devastating. A man lost his life, a wife lost her husband, and seven children lost their father. Whether or not my boss would have survived if CPR had been administered on the tennis court will never be known. But we do know that he *didn't* survive without it.

While fear may not ever cost you your life or the life of someone you love, it *will* rob you and your family of many wonderful things that you would otherwise accomplish and enjoy.

So the question is, How can we distinguish between good fear and bad fear? Good fear advances, protects, or preserves that which is truly in your best interest or the best interest of others. Bad fear prevents you from doing what is good and right and keeps you from achieving that which is best for others and yourself. Good fear usually focuses on the long-term consequences of doing that which is right and good, while bad fear usually focuses on short-term consequences. For example, bad fear tells me not to ask a question because I might look stupid to my peers and superiors. Good fear, on the other hand, tells me if I don't ask the question I may not learn, and therefore won't be able to achieve in the future. So the source of bad fear tends to be the desire for immediate gratification or the fear of short-term or immediate loss. I share all of this so that you can remove the mystic of fear and deal with it effectively.

Now that you can begin to distinguish good fear from bad fear, the question becomes, How do we detect bad fear when it's more subtle than obvious, and once it is detected, how can you diffuse or defeat it?

HOW TO DETECT THE SUBTLE FEARS THAT DIVERT YOUR PATH

What do you *really* want? If you could accomplish anything you desire—in a relationship, a job, a career, or a business—what would it be? This is the first question that can help determine the subtle fears that divert your path from extraordinary achievement to mediocre or ordinary achievement. Once you clearly define what you want, make a list of the obstacles that keep you from achieving it. Once you've defined the obstacles, ask what is keeping you from confronting or overcoming them. This is where your fears will usually be uncovered.

For example, perhaps your answer to the question "What do you really want in your marriage?" might be "To have a relationship where my deepest emotional needs are consistently fulfilled." Your next question is "What are the obstacles to achieving that kind of marriage?" Your answer may be, "My spouse doesn't know how to meet my deepest needs, or for that matter doesn't care."

Now comes the moment of truth—identifying your subtle fears with the critical question: "What keeps me from confronting or overcoming this obstacle?" It may be your fear of being rejected or criticized if you were to talk about it with your spouse. It may be your fear of discovering he or she cares even less about your needs than you thought. It may be a fear of not being able to adequately communicate how you really feel. Whatever your subtle fears in any given area may be, the first step to overcoming them is to clearly identify and define them. Once you identify a fear, the next step is to diffuse and defeat it.

EXAMPLES OF DETECTING FEARS

Desire	Obstacle	Fear of Confrontation
Great marriage	Husband doesn't care about my feelings.	He'll get mad, criticize, or reject me and my concerns.
More fulfilling job	Not qualified for better job.	May fail to get qualified and lose all hope. May lose current job in the process.
Have my own business	Not enough money for start-up.	May be turned down for loan or fail to repay the one I get; may lose everything I have.

HOW TO DIFFUSE AND DEFEAT BAD FEARS

Once you've detected a fear that has subtly or overtly guided your behavior or caused you to accept mediocrity in place of the extraordinary, it's fairly easy to diffuse or defeat it. When you diffuse a fear, it becomes like a diffused bomb: totally impotent and powerless to affect or harm you in any way. And once you've diffused it, you defeat it by simply moving forward as if it didn't exist. I have diffused many of the bad fears that have subverted my way through a very simple exercise. The first step is to see that fear in its *true* perspective. Oftentimes, you have magnified your fears way beyond their true stature. Put fear into its true perspective by asking three questions:

1. What's the worst that can happen if that which I fear came upon me?
2. What's *more likely* to happen if that fear were realized?
3. What's the *best* outcome possible for me and for others if we acted contrary to or in spite of our fear?

These questions usually put a fear into its proper perspective and that, in itself, diffuses most bad fears. The chart below shows how to use this exercise to diffuse the fears from an example in the previous chart.

PUTTING FEARS INTO PERSPECTIVE

Fear	Worst Case	Likely Case	Best Case
He'll get mad, criticize, or reject me.	Another disappointment; things will stay the same.	He won't get *that* mad, and maybe he'll hear me and things will improve.	He will understand what I'm saying and feeling, and things will get a lot better.

You will not necessarily eliminate a fear when you take it through this exercise, but you will put it into proper perspective so you can accurately weigh the risks versus the benefits. That in itself will relieve the stress that builds up when you bury your fears and hide from them. This exercise will also uncover some of your weaknesses, which you can then focus on and strengthen.

UNDERSTANDING THE OTHER COMPONENT . . . *FAILURE*

The primary goal of this chapter is not to eliminate every bad fear in your life (although that would be wonderful). Rather, the goal here is to equip you with a means of diffusing and defeating a particular type of fear that seems to invade every area of life and often severely limits your level of achievement—namely, your *fear of failure*. As I mentioned earlier, the first step in achieving this goal is to understand the component parts: fear and failure. While fear is an emotion, failure is an event.

When Zig Ziglar wrote his review of my first book, *A Millionaire's Notebook,* he wrote, "Steve Scott is living proof that failure is an event, not a person." Boy is that the truth. As I mentioned in the first chapter, I mastered the art of failure by the time I was twenty-seven. By then I had failed in two businesses that I had started and had lost seven jobs with other companies. And as if that weren't enough, I was failing in my marriage as well. I had no idea what my wife's greatest needs were, much less how to meet them.

Through all of my personal and professional failures, I discovered the true meaning and nature of failure, its benefits and detriments. And I learned how to use failure to my advantage rather than being a victim of its tyranny and allowing it to dictate my future. This is my definition of failure:

> FAILURE: An *event* in which you did not achieve your desired outcome.

But more important than the definition is the *role* failure plays in your life.

> FAILURE'S ROLE: Any failure you experience can be: (1) a great teacher, even a powerful mentor to your future success, *or* (2) a tyrannical dictator that can drastically limit or even destroy all hopes of future success.

Is this good news or bad news? In fact, it's *great* news! I say that because the role failure takes in each of your lives is *your choice*. Its role is never forced upon you. You can choose to assign it the role of teacher and mentor to your future success, or you can assign it the role of a dictator that drastically limits or even destroys your future success. There is no middle ground. It will be either one or the other! If you assign your past failures the role of teacher, they become your best friends and mentors. If you assign them the role of dictator, then you run away from them and become fearful of future failures. Nobody ever feared their favorite teacher, and no sane person ever loved a dictator.

Unfortunately, most people assign failure the role of dictator. Failure is so painful at the time they experience it that their natural inclination is to run away from it as fast as they can. Consequently, they never allow a failure to become their teacher and mentor. They view failure as a tragedy. And because they run away from or bury it, all they gain is pain, bitterness, and anger. Then, because they only remember the pain, they do all they can consciously or subconsciously to avoid future failures. The best way to avoid failure is to avoid risk.

And the only way to avoid risk is to attempt to achieve only that which you are positively sure you are able to achieve. So you set sub-conscious or conscious goals that are mediocre at best. And medi-ocrity is what you get—in relationships, in job and career, and in any other areas of life where the pain of past failures dictates your goals.

Thus, the *fear of failure* takes its unrelenting hold on your mind and emotions and becomes the single greatest limiting force in your life. That's the bad news. The good news is that you can easily eliminate the fear of failure and its devastating hold on you.

First you must choose to assign all past and future failures to the role of being your teachers and mentors. You do this by simply revisiting them after the initial pain has subsided, and learning all you can from them. You not only try on your own to discover all the hows and whys behind your failures, but you seek the advice and counsel of others, asking them to help you discover the reasons why you failed. You will be amazed at all you will learn. And if you write down what you learn, and review it before you attempt your next goal in that area, your chances of success increase dramatically. If you don't revisit your failures, learn from them, write down what you've learned, and review it, you will repeat the same mistakes over and over again.

The other way you can break the hold fear of failure has on your future is to follow the same exercise I gave earlier in this chapter for dealing with your other fears. Write down the failure you fear; then write the worst possible outcome should that failure become reality. Then write down what you think is the most likely outcome if that particular failure is realized. Finally, write down the greatest possible benefit you could realize if you succeed rather than fail. Usually, this reduces the possible failure to its true perspective, and in most cases will eliminate your fear of it.

THE FINAL CRITICAL STEP IN PUTTING A FEAR INTO THE *RIGHT* PERSPECTIVE

The last step in putting a fear or a fear of failure into proper perspec-tive is one of the most important steps of all. It not only will give you the right perspective, it will likely help you avoid an "unavoidable" failure or achieve an unbelievable level of success. This step is to seek the views and advice of *qualified* advisers. To be *truly* qualified, these people should either be experts in the area you are fearful of, or they should have done that which you are fearful to do. For example, if you are thinking about starting your own business but are afraid you may fail, don't limit the advice you seek to loved ones, relatives, and coworkers. Don't ask someone who has worked in a corporate environment all of his or her life. Rather, seek out people who have started their own businesses, both those who have succeeded as well as those who have failed. The former will tell you how they overcame obstacles, and the latter will show you the obstacles that caused their failure. If you seek qualified advice from those who have succeeded and those who have failed, you'll gain the good fears that will help protect you from disaster and you'll discard the bad fears that would otherwise steal your dream.

I have experienced terrible failures and tremendous successes. Although I would always choose to experience success (I'm not an idiot), I can tell you that I have learned very little from my successes. On the other hand, my failures have been some of my greatest teachers. In fact, my failures ultimately provided a strong and secure foundation upon which most of my greatest successes have been built. While I know the enormous value of failure, I still begin every significant effort with a natural fear of it. But I have learned that dealing with my fear of failure in the ways I have shared in this chapter has always liberated me from the strong grip of these fears, and it has enabled me to take the necessary risks to achieve extraordinary outcomes in the areas of life that are so important to me. Put these techniques to the test, and they'll do the same for you. Use your past failures as a springboard to future success instead of using them as an excuse for accepting mediocrity.

POWER SECRET #2:
Overcoming Fear of Failure

I. DETECTING SUBTLE FEARS

1. TAKE ANY AREA of your life (your career, your marriage or any other relationship, a hobby, finances, etc.) and write down the answer to this question: If you could have anything you want happen in that area, what would it be?
2. List any or all of the obstacles that prevent you from seeing that wish fulfilled.
3. Now list any fears that keep you from confronting that obstacle and trying to overcome it.

II. DIFFUSING AND DEFEATING BAD FEAR

Take any of the fears you've listed above and answer the following three questions:

1. What's the *worst* that can happen if that which I fear came upon me?
2. What's *more likely* to happen if that fear is realized?
3. What's the *best* possible outcome for me and others if the fear isn't realized and I overcome the obstacle?

III. PUTTING FEAR OF FAILURE INTO PERSPECTIVE

If you can identify any fears of failure that have kept you from pursuing a wish, a dream, or a project, answer the same three questions from section II above as they relate to that particular fear of failure.

IV. MAKING YOUR PAST FAILURES YOUR STRONGEST ALLIES

1. List any personal or business failures that you can recall that were hurtful to you (a failed marriage or relationship, a failed project or business, a rejected idea, etc.).
2. Using that list, write down all of the possible reasons that caused or contributed to each failure.
3. Looking at those causes, write down the general lessons or principles they demonstrated.
4. Are you currently ignoring those lessons and repeating those factors in any relationship or project in which you are currently involved? If so, write them down.

If you have a hard time answering any of these questions, seek answers from those who may have been involved or can help you learn the lessons of those failures.

5. List any similar relationships or projects in which you are currently involved, in which these failures could be repeated.
6. List the actions you can take to prevent repeating the lessons of past failures in your current similar situations.

CHAPTER 6

Chain #3:
Your Avoidance of Criticism

**YOUR CONSCIOUS OR SUBCONSCIOUS EFFORTS TO AVOID CRITI-
CISM SUBVERTS AND SUFFOCATES YOUR CREATIVE THINKING
AND SABOTAGES YOUR LAUNCH BEFORE YOU EVEN *ATTEMPT*
TO ACHIEVE YOUR DREAMS.**

"I TOLD YOU so!" "I can't believe you did that!" "What the heck were
you thinking about?" "You *always* do that!" "You *never* do that!"
"Don't be ridiculous!" "Are you *crazy?*" "I knew that would happen!"
"Why don't you *listen* to me!" "Don't be so sensitive!" "You look like
you're gaining weight! You've really got to start watching what you
eat."

Criticisms, criticisms, criticisms. Criticism is not a four-letter word,
but it should be. Criticism can come in any form—a statement, a
sarcastic question, even with a condescending look or sigh. No one
wants it, and yet everyone gets it. And even though you hate getting it,
you have no problem giving it. Receiving criticism is one of the hardest
experiences you have to deal with on a daily basis, and yet giving
criticism is as natural and easy as breathing.

Can you remember anything you were criticized for when you were
growing up? Think about it for a minute. What were some of the
criticisms you received from your teachers, friends, parents, brothers
or sisters, girlfriends or boyfriends? I was told I had a big nose. I was
told I had terrible handwriting, that I was sloppy, that I was too
possessive, that I was stupid—and those were just a few from my
youth. Can you think of any yet?

Now try to remember any criticisms you received during the past thirty days. Do any come to mind? Now try to remember some of the criticisms you handed out during your childhood. Chances are the criticisms you received are a lot easier to remember than the ones you handed out. Why? The answer is that criticism hurts you far more deeply than you think it does. It hurts so deeply that your brain never turns loose of it, even decades after you stopped thinking about it.

In fact, criticism is so distasteful, disheartening, and painful, that by the time you graduate from grade school, you do everything you can to avoid it. You constantly adjust your behavior, not to achieve what's in your best interest and the best interest of others but rather simply to avoid being criticized. And the more you care about someone or the higher you regard a person, the more devastating and painful is the impact of their criticism. And in this case, pain *isn't* gain!

The pain of criticism causes people to withdraw from relationships that might otherwise be a source of tremendous joy. It causes them to stop doing or saying things that could help them and others. For example, you don't begin an exercise program, because if you quit, someone will say, "I knew you wouldn't stick with it." Or, you don't voice your opinion on how to improve a relationship or a project because someone might say, "Don't be ridiculous" or "That will never work." What a tragedy!

How many relationships and families could have been saved if help had been freely offered instead of withheld for fear of criticism. How many great ideas and innovations that could have made lives better, have never been realized for fear of criticism. Criticism is one of the most destructive forces in your personal and professional life and in society in general. That's the bad news. The good news is that there is a way that you can completely overcome the negative impact of *anyone's* criticism and completely defeat any negative consequences it might have in your life. A way that can liberate you from your self-imposed restraints and enable you to be all that you really are and achieve what you are truly capable of achieving.

The way to defeat the negative impact of criticism, and to stop avoiding it, is to risk facing it. Don't ignore or become callous to it. Don't even learn how to defend yourself against it. The only way to defeat the negative impact of criticism is to learn the *right* way to deal with it. And there's only *one* right way to deal with criticism. You see, any criticism you receive can be your best ally or your worst enemy, depending upon three things: its source, its accuracy, and your response to it. And whether it becomes your conquering enemy or your supportive ally is *your* choice. Even though it may come to you as an enemy, intent on hurting you, you can convert it into an ally that can help you enormously.

TURNING THE ENEMY

Ask anyone who has ever fought in a war or been involved in intelligence work, and they'll tell you it's a lot easier to kill an enemy soldier or a foreign spy than it is to turn them. But they'll also tell you that when you are able to turn the enemy into an ally or into a double agent, the positive consequences of your action are infinitely greater. Killing a soldier or a spy only reduces the negative impact he can have on you. Turning him into an ally not only eliminates his negative impact on you, but it also provides a tremendous positive in the overall battle with your enemy.

The same is true with criticism. Avoiding it, defending yourself against it, or becoming callous and ignoring it only limits its negative impact upon you. But such actions do nothing to advance you, your personal growth, or your level of achievement.

On the other hand, turning criticism into your ally will have a tremendous positive benefit to you and to your growth and your level of achievement. Its ability to hurt you will be reduced to almost nothing; instead, it will provide a stronger foundation for your personal and professional advancement. Sound too good to be true? Well, it is true. And the good news is that it's not that difficult. It simply requires that you make a specific choice every time criticism comes your way. As you make that choice, criticism becomes your ally instead of your enemy and you will soon lose all fear of criticism. And as you lose your fear of criticism, you'll stop consciously and subconsciously adjusting your words and behavior to avoid it. You'll be free to do whatever it takes to improve any situation or relationship in your life, regardless of the risk. So, what choice must you make when you are confronted with criticism? You must choose *not* to react or defend, not to withdraw or attack, but rather to *turn* the enemy into an ally.

How does one do this? By being like a wise judge, and saying to yourself, "I'll take that into consideration." This is a very important line that you should memorize, so say it out loud right now: "I'll take that into consideration." That's not the only step in turning the enemy, but it is the first step, and you must say it to yourself every time a criticism is launched at you, or it will defeat you. So, the first step is not to react, defend, or attack but to "consider." The next step is the two things you are to "consider": the source of the criticism, and the accuracy of the criticism.

CONSIDER THE SOURCE

First consider the source: Who said it and why it was said. Is the person qualified to make such a criticism? Does he know all the background necessary to make a wise and valid criticism? Did he fully understand what you were doing or saying or the true intentions behind what you said or did before he criticized? Or was he simply reacting to what he *perceived* as your intentions? You should always ask yourself, "Was the criticism based on emotions, past experiences, or failures (yours or his), lack of understanding, 'conventional' thinking, or was it based upon logic and/or the realities of the situation?" You should also consider if your critic truly *meant* exactly what he said. For example, if your wife says you are never considerate of her feelings, she doesn't mean "never." She means in *this* situation you weren't considerate of her feelings in the way she would have liked you to be, and there have been other times when you haven't been considerate of her feelings in the way she wanted you to be. If your husband says you always put everyone else's needs above his, he doesn't really mean "always" and he doesn't mean everyone. He means you did in this circumstance, and you have at other times in the past.

My former boss told me I was the single greatest disappointment in his entire career and that I would never succeed in my chosen field. Although he was brilliant and had achieved the level of senior vice president, he wasn't qualified to make that kind of prediction about my future. He wasn't a fortune-teller, and he certainly wasn't God, so how could he possibly predict my future? So, while the first part of his criticism may have been valid, the second part was totally invalid, because the source wasn't credibly qualified to make an accurate criticism about my future success.

I never cease to be amazed at the incredible weight adult daughters give the childish criticisms of their mothers. I have seen women wiped out for days by a single motherly comment. Ladies, consider the source! Your mother may be a saint, but she's probably not a child psychologist, a housekeeping expert, a world-renowned cook, or a trained marriage counselor. She's your mother, and she probably loves you dearly. She wants the absolute best for you, and she thinks she knows what that is. Know that she is motivated by her love and by her desire to continue to be your mother. But also know that she isn't God and she isn't an expert in everything. You need not defend, attack, or withdraw from her or her criticisms; you simply need to *turn* them. Considering the source, their qualifications, and their intention and motivation is the first step in "turning" a criticism from an enemy into an ally.

CONSIDER ITS ACCURACY

The next step in turning a criticism into an ally is to consider its accuracy. All criticism is like a bucket full of water. At the very bottom of the water is a little bit of sand, and sometimes, hidden in the sand, is one or more gold nuggets. Whenever someone criticizes you, they are throwing this bucket of water into your face. Now, your natural inclination will always be to do one of three things: duck and run, throw up your arms and defend, or get angry and attack.

While these are all natural inclinations, they are all wrong reactions. It's *only* a bucket of water, not a bucket of cement. No one has ever been critically injured being splashed with a bucket of water. And yet some people react by pulling out a gun and shooting the person criticizing them. Yes, the water in the face is cold and uncomfortable for a few moments, but it's still only water. Grab a towel and dry off. As far as the sand goes, if a little gets in your eyes, it will momentarily distort your vision and cause your eyes to tear. It *will* cloud your judgment. So, clear the sand out of your eyes and take the matter under consideration by looking at the source and accuracy of the criticism. Do not instantly react. And now comes the good part: As you consider the accuracy of the criticism, you'll often find a gold nugget of truth hidden in the sand. When found, that nugget can be turned into cash by using the truth to make an improvement in your behavior, attitude, or words. An improvement that will raise your level of achievement and fulfillment.

When I wrote my very first commercial script in 1976, I couldn't wait to show it to my boss. I had been working on it for days and I thought he was going to love it and really be proud of me. I was with him at his home when I finally pulled it out and showed it to him. He carefully read it and then looked up at me and gave a single criticism. He said, "There's no hook; nothing grabs my attention and makes me want to watch the rest of the commercial." After all my work and excitement, I was stunned when the bucket of water hit my face. Now, I could have reacted by saying, "Do you know how long I worked on that script? It's a great script." I could have attacked him by saying, "How many great scripts have you written?" I could have defended it by saying, "Well, what about this line, or that line," or "Why do you find the *one* fault with my script instead of looking at all the good things about it."

Had I reacted, attacked, or defended, I would have missed a valuable gold nugget that later would make me millions of dollars. You see, there really was no hook. I didn't even know what a hook was. So I said, "What do you mean." He told me that no one has a natural attraction to a television commercial. When a program goes to a commercial break, the viewer's attention is instantly turned to something else, so you have to hook their attention and bring it back to the commercial. A few minutes later I came up with a great hook. That commercial launched our company and generated more than $20 million in sales our first year in business. More important, I learned a lesson that I have used in more the than eight hundred commercials that I subsequently wrote and directed—that produced over $1 billion in sales. I am so thankful that I learned to find the gold nuggets in criticisms.

There is nearly always a little gold in even the most painful criticisms. But sometimes the gold is in the form of dust rather than nuggets, so you have to look behind the criticism. When my former boss said, "You're the single greatest disappointment in my entire career," there was a lot of water, a reasonable amount of sand, and a little gold dust. He was obviously disappointed in me, but how could I possibly be the "greatest" disappointment in his career when I was only a junior manager? He was obviously exaggerating with the hope of inflicting pain in retaliation to the disappointment I had brought to him. As young and impressionable as I was at the time, the sand landed in my eyes and stung like heck for a few days. But when I was able to separate the emotion I felt at his criticism from the logic, my vision was fully restored and I found gold dust, even in this harsh criticism. His disappointment in me was a result of my mediocre performance and what he perceived to be my disloyalty. If I wanted to experience greater success in my next job, I would have to discover specific ways to raise the level of my performance and demonstrate my loyalty to my boss and my company.

Now let's look at a criticism that a lot of us hear these days, namely, "you're getting too fat." Now, that bucket may have a lot of sand. You rarely need a criticism like that, because you are the first to realize you're putting on too much weight. The gold in that criticism is it confirms and reinforces your own opinion that you are putting on too much weight, and if you let it, it can motivate you to take responsibility to begin to eat in a way that's in the best interest of your long-term health instead of your instant gratification, and to begin to give your heart and body the consistent exercise it so desperately needs. That exercise can add years to your life, health to your quality of life, and needed energy to your daily routine. So instead of defending, attacking, or retreating from a criticism like that, find the gold nugget of truth and cash it in by acting upon it.

Right now, take a little break from reading, and think about a recent criticism you received from someone you care about. Think about how you reacted. Did you run away, defend, or attack? Consider the source, and the accuracy of that criticism. And then look for the nugget of truth and think about what you can do to apply that nugget to your life.

YOUR RESPONSE TO CRITICISM

The third and final step in turning criticism into your ally is your *response* to it. I've already shown the three wrong responses and the one right response. So, criticism becomes your best friend or worst enemy depending upon its source, its accuracy, and your response to it. All of this is wonderfully illustrated in a story I once heard.

One Saturday morning, a couple decided to go to a pet store and look for a dog. As they walked into the store, they were greeted by a loud, obnoxious parrot on a perch by the door.

"Hey, buddy," the parrot said.

"Yeah," the man answered.

"You're stupid, and your wife's ugly," the parrot said.

"What did you say?" the man angrily asked.

"I said, 'You're stupid and your wife's ugly!' "

Well, the man became furious and his wife started to cry. He quickly found the store manager and began to rant and rave.

"My wife and I get all excited about coming out and finding a pet, and then your stupid parrot greets us with his obnoxious message. Look at my wife . . . ruined her day."

"I can't believe he did that again," said the manager. The manager then put a glove on one hand and walked over to the parrot. He grabbed him and smacked him on the side of the head two or three times. Well, the man and his wife felt vindicated, looked around for a dog, and finally decided to leave. On their way out, they started to walk past the parrot, when the parrot said, "Hey, buddy." The man quickly looked at the parrot and said, "Yeah?" The parrot replied, "You know!"

I tell this story to illustrate my three points. Who was smarter, the parrot or the couple? Obviously it was the parrot. The man and his wife would not have had their morning ruined by the parrot's criticism had they simply considered the source, its accuracy, and taken control of their response to it. It was a parrot, not a college professor or the owner of a modeling agency. So how valid could his criticism be when it comes to one's intelligence or beauty. His criticism couldn't be totally accurate. And finally, had they simply taken his criticism under consideration rather than react to it, they would have laughed and said to themselves, "What does a stupid parrot know anyway." But judging from their response, the man was a little stupid and the wife probably wasn't great-looking. So they could have found a nugget of truth, and the man could have cashed it in by taking a "verbal advantage" course and the woman could have looked for a new hair stylist, or maybe started a new exercise program.

Gary Smalley and I were once on a flight from Dallas to Chicago, and we were surrounded by members of the Dallas Cowboy Cheerleaders. Gary asked one of them to rate her appearance on a scale of one to ten. He purposely picked a cheerleader both he and I thought to be a perfect ten. She said, "Oh, I'm about a seven." Gary and I both said in unison, "Why would you say that." "Look at my nose," she said. Then she pointed to one of her friends and said, "Now *she's* a perfect ten." Gary instantly said, "There's *nothing* wrong with your nose, why would you say that?" "Oh, you're wrong," she said. "Just look at it. When I was a teenager, my very first boyfriend told me that I would be a perfect ten if it wasn't for my nose."

Isn't that tragic? She had never gotten over that criticism. What kind of beauty expert was her boyfriend? Was he a "nose expert"? She should have considered the source, its accuracy, and laughed at his criticism. He was a "parrot."

The world is full of parrots—people who freely give criticism who aren't qualified to do so. But that's not your responsibility or mine. Our responsibility is to take control of how we respond to each and every criticism that comes our way. Let them throw their buckets of water at you. Step back, consider the source and the accuracy, wipe the sand out of your eyes, and look for the gold nuggets. Do this, and criticism will become one of your best friends, providing you with added wisdom, and faster and more mature personal and professional growth and advancement. In the beginning, you'll have to work hard not to react and to instead respond correctly. But if you work at it for a few months, then responding correctly to criticism will become a positive habit and ally that will serve you for the rest of your life.

POWER SECRET #3:
Turning Criticism from Foe to Friend

1. MAKE A LIST of some of the more memorable criticisms that you have received either at home or at work.
2. By each of the criticisms, determine how qualified the person was to give such a criticism. Put a V for *very* qualified; an S for *somewhat* qualified, and an N for *not* qualified.
3. By each criticism, write down as many of the following reasons as may have been the basis of the person's criticism.

> E—*emotionally* based
> PE—based on your or their *past experiences* or past failures
> LU—based on their *lack of understanding* or fully comprehending your goal, intention, or vision
> CT—based on their *conventional thinking* rather than creative thinking
> L—based on *logic*
> RS—based upon the *realities of the situation*

4. What was the motive of the critic? Was it love, his concern for you or the project, his genuine concern for others, or was it selfishness, jealousy, fear, animosity, hurt or anger, or his own immaturity?
5. Looking back, how accurate was his criticism?
   - Define the "water" in the criticism—that which was exaggerated, absurd, or meaningless.
   - Define the "sand" in the criticism—that which was most irritating or hurtful (specific words, tone of voice, spirit of criticism, etc.).
   - Determine the "gold" in the criticism—the truths that can be drawn from the criticism that can help you better perform in the future.
6. How did you respond to the criticism? Was it with anger, defensiveness, denial, blame, attack, withdrawal? Or did you listen, acknowledge, thank, or give the critic an explanation that helped him to better understand you or your action?

7. How could you have responded that would have been better for you, for your growth, and for your relationship with the critic?
8. Write down the best ways you believe you could respond to criticism in the future.

CHAPTER 7

Chain #4: Your Lack of Clear and Precise Vision

IF YOU DON'T HAVE A CLEAR PICTURE OF YOUR DESTINATION AND A PRECISE MAP TO GET THERE, YOU WON'T EVEN BEGIN THE TRIP.

IMAGINE FOR A moment that you live in New York City. One day the mailman knocks on your door and hands you a certified letter. You open it up and you discover that it is a personal letter from my friend Dick Clark. In this letter he tells you that he wants you and a guest to come to Hollywood and be his guests for one week. He's going to put you into a beautiful suite in the finest hotel in Beverly Hills. He will give you $5,000 a day for spending money each day you are there. You will have a limousine at your disposal twenty-four hours a day. You will be Dick's personal guest at the Academy Awards, and you will be dining with your favorite movie star one night, and your favorite recording star the next. Following the week in Hollywood, you and your guest will be flown first class to Hawaii, for a ten-day vacation of a lifetime.

As you approach the end of this letter, you are so excited you can hardly see straight. You then come to the last paragraph, which reads as follows:

> The only catch is that you must drive from your house in New York to my house in the Los Angeles area, and you must not use any map at any time. Furthermore, you cannot ask ANYONE for any directions whatsoever. In fact, my friend Ed McMahon will be at your door momentarily to escort you on your trip to make sure you are not tempted to use

a map or ask directions. Finally, you have one week to reach my house and claim your prize.

You read that paragraph and your response might be, "That's ridiculous! There's no way on earth I could get from New York City to Los Angeles, and then to Dick Clark's house without a map and without asking directions. It's totally impossible!"

Well, if this was your reaction, you would be right. If you had all the time in the world, you might make it from New York to L.A. You'd waste a lot of time and gas, and it might take months or years. Then, once you arrived in L.A., you'd still be looking for Dick's house in the greater Los Angeles area. And finding his house without a specific address, map, or asking directions would take you even longer. After all, there are 3,500 square miles in the greater Los Angeles area. Would you even attempt to start the trip? Of course not. It would be a total waste of time and there would be absolutely no chance of seeing your dream fulfilled.

Now, suppose the last paragraph of Dick's letter was a little different. Suppose it said you can't use any existing map, and you can't ask any directions along the way, *but* before you start on the trip, you could make one call to Dick's office and get his specific address and a complete set of directions that would tell you every road, highway, and turn to take, right from your front door to his.

Now here's the critical question: When the time came to call Dick's office to get his address and those onetime precise, detailed directions, would you have a pen and a pad of paper ready to write down every detail? Or would you simply listen to the directions and trust your memory? The answer is obvious: Of course you would write them down. Receiving your dream vacation would depend upon it. You would then create your *own* map. And once you began your trip, you would consult your map and notes every step of the way to make sure you stayed right on track all the way to your destination. By simply defining your destination, writing down the address and directions, and creating your own simple map, you would arrive at Dick's house in plenty of time to claim your dream vacation.

I give you this story to illustrate several points that you must understand if you ever want to get your rocket off the launching pad and begin to achieve your most awesome dreams. The first point this story makes is how impossible it is to reach a destination, no matter how great the reward, without first getting an address, writing down directions, creating a map, and precisely following that map each step of the way.

The second point of the story is this: If you would be willing to take all of these simple steps—defining your destination, writing down the directions, creating a map—just to achieve your dream vacation, how much more should you be willing to do the same thing to achieve your dreams in the most important areas of your personal and professional life? After all, isn't your life and what you accomplish with it worth infinitely more than a seventeen-day dream vacation? What you accomplish in your marriage, with your children, on your job, and in your future career are *all* far more valuable and lasting than even the finest vacation money could buy.

And yet, if you are like the vast majority of American adults who will never launch their rockets, chances are you haven't yet clearly defined your dreams in writing. And if you haven't defined them in writing, you certainly haven't written down the directions or charted a map on how to achieve those dreams. And I will promise you, that if you *don't* define your dreams in writing and chart a map to reach them, you will *never* achieve them.

Your first reaction may be: "It sounds so hard and would take so much time," or "I don't even know what my dreams are." Well, the good news is that once you begin to think about your dreams, you'll find that defining them is not only easier than you think, it's a lot of fun. And it doesn't take a lot of time. Initially, it may take a few sittings of fifteen to thirty minutes each, but after that, you'll only need a few minutes per week. You'll learn the right ways to do this in the chapters ahead, so don't even worry about it now. Just realize that the Grand Prize for defining your dreams and mapping a course of action to achieve them will make this the most rewarding activity in your life.

HOW TO GAIN A CLEAR VISION AND CHART A PRECISE MAP TO ALL OF YOUR DREAMS

Of the six chains that keep you anchored to the launching pad, this one is the easiest to cut. Your cutting tool can be a notebook and pen, a day planner, or your computer. The procedure itself is so simple, it may be hard for you to believe that it will actually work. Our goal here is not to begin the trip, but simply to get a specific address for each dream and to define it in writing. In Chapters 10 and 11 I will show you how to use the Dream Conversion Process to create a map and plot a course for each dream you choose to pursue. You'll then have a map in hand with which to pursue your dream, and a very specific, plotted course on which to measure your progress every day, week, and month of your journey to that dream. Later chapters will show how, when you run into an obstacle—a canyon without a bridge or a hill that's too steep to climb—you can make adjustments to your course or recruit help to overcome the problem. You'll be amazed at how fast you'll arrive at your destination. But in this chapter, I will show you how to take the first step in creating your map—that is, how to clearly define your dreams, in writing.

The first thing you need to do in defining your dreams is to create, on a single sheet of paper, a simple list of the most important areas in your life, starting with the most important and working down. For example, my list of important areas is:

> My relationship with God
> My marriage
> My children
> My family's health, happiness, security, and future
> My health
> My business and career
> My extracurricular activities and passions

After you have created your list, take a sheet of paper for each item and write that item at the top. On each page (you may need several pages for each category), write as many *dreams* as you can think of for that particular category. They do not have to be prioritized; just write them down as you think of them, and be as general or as specific as you like. I will share a page of mine under the category "My extracurricular activities and passions." I am choosing this category because the others are too personal (as yours will be).

My Extracurricular Activities and Passions— Defined Dreams

1. To provide a complete Dream Conversion Kit with audio- and videotapes and a loose-leaf manual that would enable me personally to coach my family, friends, and anyone else in every strategy and technique they need to learn and apply the art of Dream Conversion to every area of their lives.
2. To train others to become trainers and mentors in the art of Dream Conversion.
3. To create a Dream Conversion program that can be taught in high schools and colleges.
4. To finish my novel *Dirty Tricks, Inc.* and see it become a number-one national and worldwide best-seller.
5. To spend more time skiing, relaxing, and writing at our mountain home.
6. To spend more time speaking publicly, encouraging audiences to utilize the art of Dream Conversion.
7. To promote Dream Conversion through press interviews on radio and television as well as newspapers and magazines.
8. To build a file of the people who write to me with their stories of how they used Dream Conversion to achieve their specific dreams.
9. To begin my next screenplay.
10. To begin my next novel.

I share this page to show you how easy it can be. It took less than ten minutes for me to uncover, define, and write these dreams down. Now remember, this is a page about my dreams in the category that represents number seven in my order of priority. My dreams in some of the higher priority areas such as my marriage and my children are more extensive and detailed. I have a "dream" page for each of my six children that relates my dreams for my relationship with each of them, our times together, and what we do in those times.

After you have created your dream page in any area, go back and number each of those dreams according to its priority. For example, on the page I've given, the first item happens to be my number-one priority, and the fourth item is my number-two priority. So following the statement of dream number one, I would write a large number one, and following the statement of dream number four, I would write a large number two. In only a couple of minutes, all of the dreams in this area have been prioritized. Writing your dreams down and prioritizing them is like creating an address book for your dreams. You've defined them and placed them in order of importance. Once you've done this, you'll be ready to use the Dream Conversion Process to create a map and chart an efficient route to each of your most important dreams. And with these maps in hand, you'll be amazed at how quickly you will be able to begin to achieve dreams you've never dared hope to achieve.

POWER SECRET #4:
Gaining a Clear and Precise Vision

THE FOLLOWING EXERCISES should be recorded in the notebook you've titled "Dream Conversion Journal."

1. Using your section dividers, create one section for each of the most important areas of your life. Number and place the sections in order of their importance.
2. Beginning with your first and most important section, make a list of your dreams for that area (see example on page 76).
3. In each section, create and title one page for each dream you've listed in that section.

This exercise is the first stage of the Dream Conversion Process. You will be adding information to each of these pages as you complete the exercises at the end of each of the remaining chapters.

CHAPTER 8

Chain #5: Your Lack of Know-How

YOU CAN'T FLY YOUR ROCKET TO THE MOON IF YOU DON'T KNOW HOW TO FLY! DISCOVER A FLIGHT PLAN THAT GIVES YOU EVERYTHING YOU NEED TO KNOW TO ACHIEVE YOUR DREAMS.

"I DON'T KNOW how!" "I wouldn't even know where to start." "I could never do that, I don't even have a clue how to do it." These statements represent a roadblock everyone confronts—namely, lack of know-how. It is without a doubt the single greatest perceived obstacle to extraordinary achievement for the vast majority of American adults. It affects every area of your personal and professional life. How many men and women give up on relationships because they simply don't know what to do when it comes to figuring out what their partner needs or wants, or how to take a relationship that isn't working and make it work a whole lot better?

How often do salesmen lose a sale because they don't know what to do to overcome a client's objection? How many parents give up on a rebellious teenager because they don't know how to handle the child? Nothing is more discouraging or frustrating than to face a situation in which you simply "don't know what to do" or how to do it.

The majority of adults surrender or retreat when confronted with a situation that reveals their lack of know-how. Even though everyone lacks know-how in some area or other, in reality, this is usually only a *perceived* obstacle. In fact, the one-tenth of one percent of American adults who are dream-achievers view *their* lack of know-how as nothing more than a temporary inconvenience. When dream-achievers are confronted with a situation that reveals their ignorance, they hear a call to action and creative thinking.

Do you think Thomas Edison had know-how when he began to

pursue his dream of creating electric light? He had *no* know-how! That's why it took over ten thousand attempts before he finally achieved his dream. Or how about Oprah Winfrey, when she agreed to host her first talk show? Having never hosted a talk show before, she certainly lacked know-how. Lack of know-how is as common to human experience as breathing. And yet, the vast majority of adults view it as Mount Everest in a blizzard—an impossible obstacle to overcome. And because it's *perceived* this way, no attempt is made to climb or conquer it.

A SECRET KNOWN ONLY TO THE WORLD'S MOST SUCCESSFUL ACHIEVERS

Here is a secret that blew me away when I discovered it. Instead of being an insurmountable obstacle, lack of know-how in any situation can become a *springboard* to unimaginable success and achievement. In fact, I usually have far greater success in areas where I have absolutely *no* know-how than I ever could in areas where I have a *little* know-how. Why? Because when I honestly face a problem where I have no know-how, I immediately look for an expert who has more knowledge in that area than I will ever have. I have directed over eight hundred television productions, many filmed on stages with spectacular sets. If I had a little knowledge in set design and set building, and were tempted to design and build my own, it would take me thousands of hours, and the results would be at best only mediocre. However, because I know my limitations in designing and building sets, I don't waste my time even trying. Instead, I hire my favorite set designers and builders, and they deliver incredible sets in a fraction of the time it would take me to create a terrible one.

Steven Spielberg is one of the most gifted storytellers and directors ever to make a movie. And yet he could no more create the amazing special effects that fill his movies than you could. He doesn't even try. When a scene calls for a special effect, he hires the best effects people in the business to create it for him, usually George Lucas's company, Industrial Light and Magic. When he needs a model dinosaur he hires the best live-action model maker in Hollywood, Stan Winston. Instead of being an insurmountable obstacle, Steven's lack of know-how becomes his springboard to unimaginable success.

You and I (and everyone else) have a *limited* number of strengths, talents, and abilities, and yet we have an *infinite* number of weaknesses and inabilities. Said another way, what we *do* know and *can* do is much less than what we *don't* know and *can't* do. If we can't find a way to convert our weaknesses and inabilities from obstacles into springboards, we will never achieve anything beyond mediocrity. The major difference between dream-achievers and the vast majority of adults is that dream-achievers recruit others to make up for their lack of know-how, while the vast majority of adults simply surrender to it. Even worse than surrendering is to ignore it and proceed into a situation as if you know it all. Know-it-alls will never achieve a fraction of what they could achieve if only they would face their weaknesses and inabilities and follow the dream-achiever's example.

So if you want to graduate from the masses who rarely achieve their dreams, you must first admit that you only have a few strengths, talents, and abilities, and lots of weaknesses and inabilities. That's the first step. The second step is to *identify* your strengths, talents, and abilities, and your weaknesses and inabilities. In addition to using your own mind to identify these, ask for help from those who know you the best. They will help you identify areas you would otherwise completely overlook. This is the reason I asked you to create a written list of your strengths and weaknesses at the end of Chapter 4. These lists will become part of the foundation you will build upon in later chapters.

DISCOVERING YOUR PERSONALITY TYPE—A KEY TO OPENING THE DOOR TO YOUR DREAMS

Why do you tend to consistently act the way you act, from situation to situation? Why is it so easy for some people to talk to anyone about anything and so hard for them to listen? Why is it so hard for some people to be confrontational and so easy for others?

My wife and I discovered that one of our maintenance workers had consistently overcharged us thousands of dollars on various projects that we had entrusted to his care. We were both deeply hurt, and knew we would have to confront him. The thought of initiating that confrontation was terrifying to my wife. I wasn't looking forward to it either, but it certainly didn't worry me. When I confronted him, he tried to deny and lie his way out of it. He even tried to blame my wife. I knew the only option was to dismiss him. Even though my wife was in complete agreement, had I asked her to make that phone call to "fire" him, she would have panicked and fretted for days before she could make the call. For me, it was a piece of cake. Why was it so easy for me and so hard for my wife? It's not because she's a woman and I'm a man. In fact, if the same thing had happened to my best friend, he would have had just as much trouble placing that call as my wife. It's a matter of personality. My personality type never has a problem firing someone who has proven to be dishonest. My wife's and best friend's personality type find it next to impossible to place such a tough phone call.

At the same time, my best friend will listen to someone tell her tale of trouble for hours, while I zone out after only a couple of minutes. I want the person to give me the facts, just the facts; then I'll give a quick solution. Once again, it's not that my way is better than his (necessarily). But the way one acts and reacts to situations is often-times strongly influenced, if not outright dictated, by one's personality type. And each personality type has tremendous strengths and significant weaknesses. Once you understand your type and its natural inclinations, you can begin to play to your strengths, strengthen your weaknesses, and partner with people whose personality types complement yours. In the remaining pages of this chapter, I give a five-minute test that will help you determine your dominant personality type, and then help you to focus on the wonderful ramifications of knowing your strengths and weaknesses. All of the material on this subject is taken and condensed from my good friend Dr. Gary Smalley.

THE FIVE-MINUTE PERSONALITY TEST

Refer to the table on page 83. The four letters at the top of each section represent the four basic personality types. On each line, put the number 4 next to the word that best describes you in that line, a 3 next to the word that describes you next best, a 2 beside the next best, and a 1 by the word that least describes you. On each horizontal line

The Five-Minute Personality Test

L		O		G		B	
1. ___	Likes authority	___	Enthusiastic	___	Sensitive feelings	___	Likes instructions
2. ___	Takes charge	___	Takes risks	___	Loyal	___	Accurate
3. ___	Determined	___	Visionary	___	Calm, even keel	___	Consistent
4. ___	Enterprising	___	Very verbal	___	Enjoys routine	___	Predictable
5. ___	Competitive	___	Promoter	___	Dislikes change	___	Practical
6. ___	Problem solver	___	Enjoys popularity	___	Gives in to others	___	Factual
7. ___	Productive	___	Fun-loving	___	Avoids confrontation	___	Conscientious
8. ___	Bold	___	Likes variety	___	Sympathetic	___	Perfectionistic
9. ___	Decision maker	___	Spontaneous	___	Nurturing	___	Detail-oriented
10. ___	Persistent	___	Inspirational	___	Peacemaker	___	Analytical
___	TOTAL "L"	___	TOTAL "O"	___	TOTAL "G"	___	TOTAL "B"

Each horizontal line above has four words. In each of the ten lines, place the number 4 next to the word that best describes you in that line; a 3 next to the word that describes you next best; a 2 by the next best word, and a 1 by the word in that line that least describes you. In each line only use each number once. After completing all ten lines, add the numbers for each of the four vertical columns. The column with the highest total score is your dominant personality type, and the column with the next highest score is your subdominant personality type.

of words you will then have one 4, one 3, one 2, and one 1. For example, my choice for the first line would be:

(3) Likes Authority *(4)* Enthusiastic *(2)* Sensitive Feelings *(1)* Likes Instructions

This is one test you can't flunk.

As you work through each horizontal line, you may find it hard to decide which words are more like you than others. You may even feel like all of the words describe you, or none of them do. Don't panic. Just make your best guess as to which word is most like you and which word is least like you. Put a 4 by the one which is most like you and a 1 by the word that is least like you; then make your best guess between the two remaining words. Even if you make a few inaccurate choices your total score will not be significantly affected. Be honest, and you'll discover both your dominant and subdominant personality type. No one is totally one type, but rather a unique combination of all four, with one or two usually being stronger or dominant over the others.

Now add the numbers for each vertical column.

Each column represents a specific personality type. The column with the highest score is your dominant personality type, while the column with the second highest number will be your subdominant type. While you are a combination of all four personality types, the two with the highest scores reveal the most accurate picture of your natural inclinations, strengths, and weaknesses.

What Does All of This Mean?

After you've taken the test, do you want to know what it means? An individual's personality type reveals his or her natural inclinations, strengths, and weaknesses, and determines how he or she will *naturally* respond in most situations. The higher your score in any column, the more dominant will be the traits of that personality type. Gary Smalley likens the four personality types to animals because it makes them a little easier to visualize and remember than the numbers, letters, colors, or technical terms that are more commonly used to label personality types. I agree with Gary, so I, too, will use his animal analogies.

L = Lions

Lions are leaders. They are usually the bosses at work . . . or at least they think they are! They are decisive, bottom-line folks who are observers, not watchers or listeners. They love to solve problems. They are usually individualists who seek new adventures and opportunities. Lions are very confident and self-reliant. In a group setting, if no one else instantly takes charge, the Lion will. Unfortunately, if they don't learn how to tone down their aggressiveness, their natural dominating traits can cause problems with others. Most true entrepreneurs are strong Lions, or at least have a lot of Lion in them.

Natural Strengths	Natural Weaknesses
Decisive	Impatient
Goal-oriented	Blunt
Achievement-driven	Poor listener
Gets results	Impulsive
Independent	Demanding
Risk-taker	May view projects more important than people
Takes charge	
Takes initiative	Can be insensitive to the feelings of others
Self-starter	
Persistent	May "run over" others who are slower to act or speak
Efficient	
Driven to complete projects quickly and effectively	Fears inactivity, relaxation
Competitive	Quickly bored by routine or mechanics
Enjoys challenges, variety, and change	

BASIC DISPOSITION: Fast-paced, task-oriented

MOTIVATED BY: Results, challenge, action, power, and credit for achievement

TIME MANAGEMENT: Lions focus on "now" instead of distant future. They get a lot more done in a lot less time than their peers, hate wasting time, and like to "get right to the point."

COMMUNICATION STYLE: Great at initiating communication, not good at listening (one-way communicator)

DECISION MAKING: Impulsive, makes quick decisions with goal or end result in mind; results-focused, needs very few facts to make a decision

IN PRESSURE OR TENSE SITUATIONS: Takes "command" and becomes autocratic

GREATEST NEEDS: Needs to see results, experience variety, and face new challenges; needs to solve problems and wants *direct* answers

WHAT THE LION DESIRES: Freedom, authority, variety, difficult assignments, opportunity for advancement

O = Otters

Otters are excitable, fun-seeking, cheerleader types who love to talk! They're great at motivating others and need to be in an environment where they can talk and have a voice in making major decisions. The Otters' outgoing nature makes them great "networkers"—they usually know a lot of people who know a lot of people. They can be very loving and encouraging unless under pressure, when they tend to use their verbal skills to attack. They have a strong desire to be liked and enjoy being the center of attention. They are often very attentive to style, clothes, and flash. Otters are the life of any party, and most people really enjoy being around them.

Natural Strengths	Natural Weaknesses
Enthusiastic	Unrealistic
Optimistic	Not detail-oriented
Good communicator	Disorganized
Emotional and passionate	Impulsive
Motivational and inspirational	Listens to "feelings" above "logic"
Outgoing	Reactive
Personal	Can be too talkative
Dramatic	Excitable
Fun-loving	Avoids drudge work

BASIC DISPOSITION: Fast-paced, people-oriented

MOTIVATED BY: Recognition and approval of others

TIME MANAGEMENT: Focus is on the future, has a tendency to rush to the next exciting thing

COMMUNICATION STYLE: Enthusiastic and stimulating, often one-way (talking rather than listening), but can inspire and motivate others

DECISION MAKING: Intuitive and fast, makes lots of right calls—and lots of wrong ones

IN PRESSURE OR TENSE SITUATIONS: The otter *attacks,* can be more concerned about popularity than about achieving tangible results

GREATEST NEEDS: Social activities and recognition, activities that are fun, freedom from details

WHAT THE OTTER DESIRES: Prestige, friendly relationships, opportunity to help and motivate others, the chance to share ideas

G = *Golden Retrievers*

One word describes these people: loyal. They're so loyal, in fact, that they can absorb emotional pain and punishment in a relationship and still stay committed. They are great listeners, incredibly empathetic, and warm encouragers. However, they tend to be such pleasers that they can have great difficulty being assertive in a situation or relationship when it's needed.

Natural Strengths	Natural Weaknesses
Patient	Indecisive
Easygoing	Overaccommodating
Team player	May sacrifice results for the sake
Stable	of harmony
Empathetic	Slow to initiate
Compassionate	Avoids confrontation even when
Sensitive to feelings of others	needed
Tremendously loyal	Tends to hold grudges
Puts people above projects	Fears change
Dependable	Ignores or sacrifices own needs
Reliable	
Supportive	
Agreeable	

BASIC DISPOSITION: Slow-paced, people-oriented

MOTIVATED BY: Desire for good relationships and appreciation of others

TIME MANAGEMENT: Focus is on the present and devotes lots of time to helping others and building relationships

COMMUNICATION STYLE: Two-way communicator, great listener and provides empathetic response

DECISION MAKING: Makes decisions more slowly, wants input from others—and often yields to that input

IN PRESSURE OR TENSE SITUATIONS: Gives in to the opinions, ideas, and wishes of others, often overly tolerant

GREATEST NEEDS: Security, gradual change and time to adjust to it, environment free of conflict

WHAT THE GOLDEN RETRIEVER DESIRES: Quality relationships, security, consistent known environment, own "area" or specialty, a relaxed and friendly environment, freedom to work at their own pace

B = Beavers

Beavers have a strong need to do things right and "by the book." In fact, they are the kind of people who actually *read* instruction manuals. They are great at providing quality control in an office, and will provide quality control in any situation or field that demands accuracy, such as accounting, engineering, and so on. Because rules, consistency, and high standards are so important to Beavers, they are often frustrated by those who do not share these same characteristics. Their strong need for maintaining high (and sometimes unrealistic) standards can short-circuit their ability to express warmth in a relationship.

Natural Strengths	Natural Weaknesses
Accurate	Too hard on self
Analytical	Too critical of others
Detail-oriented	Perfectionistic
Thoroughness	Overly cautious
Industrious	Won't make decision without "all"
Orderly	the facts
Methodical and exhaustive	Too picky
High standards	Overly sensitive
Intuitive	
Controlled	

BASIC DISPOSITION: Slow-paced, task-oriented

MOTIVATED BY: The desire to be right and maintain quality

TIME MANAGEMENT: Tend to work slowly to make sure they are accurate

COMMUNICATION STYLE: Good listeners, communicate details, usually diplomatic

DECISION MAKING: Avoids making decisions, needs lots of information before making a decision

IN PRESSURE OR TENSE SITUATIONS: Tries to avoid pressure or tense situations, can ignore deadlines

GREATEST NEEDS: Security, gradual change and time to adjust to it, environment free of conflict

WHAT THE BEAVER DESIRES: Clearly defined tasks, stability, security, low risk, tasks that require precision and planning

GREAT NEWS ABOUT *YOUR* PERSONALITY TYPE

As you focus on your dominant and subdominant personality type, it is critical that you understand that these traits are *natural* inclinations. The weaknesses and negative inclinations can be strengthened, balanced, compensated for, or even eliminated by *choosing* to do what is right and best in a situation rather than simply letting your personality's "natural inclination" dictate behavior. For example, Lions have an easy time talking and a hard time listening. As a Lion, I find listening neither natural nor easy. So my natural inclination is always to talk rather than to listen, but I can *choose* to keep quiet, and make a choice to *listen* even when I don't feel like it. You can choose to cultivate the strengths of the other personality traits, and choose to utilize them rather than yielding to your natural weaknesses. Once you know that you have a natural bias or tendency to act in a certain way, you can be on the alert and balance your natural tendency by modifying your behavior.

I have included this information on personality types for two reasons: first, to help you identify some of your hidden strengths and weaknesses so you can play or strengthen them, and second, and equally important, to enable you to use them as a springboard to recruit those with complementary personalities whose strengths will balance or compensate for your weaknesses.

As is the case with your lack of know-how, your natural inclination will be to view your weaknesses as difficult or even insurmountable obstacles standing between you and your dreams. What this chapter has tried to do is to change your view of your weaknesses from insurmountable obstacles to springboards to super achievement. As you learn to use your weaknesses, inabilities, and lack of know-how as springboards, the fifth chain that has kept you anchored to your launching pad will be completely and permanently severed. In Chapter 12 you'll see how the recruiting of outside resources is itself a massive rocket engine. One so powerful that, by itself, it can break the bonds of gravity and enable you to achieve dreams that you would never have dared to attempt before.

POWER SECRET #5:
Overcoming Your Lack of Know-How

1. ON EACH DREAM Page that you've created in your Dream Conversion Journal, write any ways in which your lack of know-how could prevent you from achieving that dream. For example, if one of your dreams is to meet your spouse's deepest emotional needs, but you do not know how to do this, you would write that down underneath that dream.

2. Beneath each lack of know-how that you've listed under each dream, list the types of outside experts who could help you overcome your weaknesses in that area. Using the example from item one above, you would list: marriage counselor, author/expert on marriage, minister, or maybe even a "friend who has a great marriage."

3. On each Dream Page, write down how your personality strengths or traits can help you achieve that dream. Then write down how your weaknesses might work against your achieving that dream. Finally, write down the personality types of the other people you might need to recruit to help you achieve that dream. For example, if you are an Otter who wants to start your own business, you would need to recruit a Lion to raise your chances of success, and a Beaver or the services of a Beaver to handle details.

CHAPTER 9

Chain #6: Your Lack of Resources

You can't launch your rocket all by yourself. Failure to recruit the right outside resources makes getting off the ground totally impossible.

"I WOULD *LOVE* to do that, but I don't have the money!" "I would love to start my own business, but I'm not a good salesman!" "Where does the day go? There just aren't enough hours in the day!" "I know I need to start exercising, but I just don't have the time!"

These are just a few of the statements I have heard from friends during the past few weeks. They all reflect the same problem, the same *chain* that keeps most adults anchored to their launching pad their entire adult life. These statements reveal a "lack of resources" that these people believe they need to overcome in order to achieve a goal or fulfill a dream. This chain is right next to lack of know-how in its strength and the consequences it produces. Like the lack of know-how, lack of resources appears to many as insurmountable obstacles. When lack of resources stands between people and their dreams, their normal response is to turn around and walk away from those dreams.

The comment "I would love to do that, but I don't have the money!" points to the one resource no one ever feels they have enough of: *money*. No matter how much you have, it's never enough. Barbara Walters asked billionaire John Malone, of TCI Cable, why he still works fourteen hours a day, seven days a week, when he could "walk away from it all with a billion dollars in his bank account." He paused for a moment and replied, "Because I guess I realize it could all go away!" Bill Gates is the richest man in America, but the company he owns—Microsoft—still borrows money from the bank. Steven Spielberg has hundreds of millions of dollars in the bank, yet he still seeks outside financing for his films. I have personally known many multi-millionaires, some worth *hundreds* of millions. Yet I've never heard even one of them say "I've got enough." Money represents a "limited" resource to all of us.

"I would love to start my own business, but I'm not a good salesman," reveals another limited resource that plagues us all: talent and ability. Oprah Winfrey has incredible talent whether it's in front of a live audience on her daily show or in front of a movie camera. And yet she would be the first to tell you that there are innumerable talents and abilities that she sees in her various guests each week that she herself does not possess. Bill Gates is obviously talented, and yet a recent article in *Forbes* says Microsoft would be only a fraction of what it is today if it wasn't for the talents and abilities of his partners.

In my first book, *A Millionaire's Notebook,* I pointed out that I only have four significant talents: I know how to type reasonably well; I know how to effectively and persuasively communicate; I know how to direct on-camera talent; and I know how to market products and ideas. That's it! Are my talents and abilities limited? Absolutely! I can't play a musical instrument; I can't understand accounting spread sheets; I can't understand anything mechanical; and I have no athletic ability whatsoever. I can't understand computers or computer programs, and I can't even understand my sixteen-year-old's math problems. So all in all, I only have four significant talents; I lack *all* others! And yet those four talents have created over one billion dollars in sales and myriad companies with products ranging from insurance to cosmetics. Do we all have limited talents and abilities? *Yes!* Does that mean we have to let them keep us from achieving our dreams? *Absolutely not!*

"Where does the day go? There just aren't enough hours in the day" and "I know I need to start exercising, but I just don't have the time" are two statements that represent the most precious limited resource we all possess: time! No matter how rich and powerful someone may be, she is still limited to twenty-four hours in every day, seven days in every week, and fifty-two weeks in every year. Time is more limited and precious than any other resource you possess, and yet it's the one you pay the least attention to and squander the most freely. When you squander your money, even if you lose every dime, you have the potential to gain it back. Donald

Trump built a billion-dollar empire and came close to losing it all, yet today he is worth more than ever. Sam Walton lost everything when his Ben Franklin Five-and-Dime stores went broke, and was close to bankruptcy himself when he started Wal-Mart. He not only gained back all the money he lost, he went on to become the richest man in America by the time he died.

If you fail to use your talents today, you can always begin to use them tomorrow. They are always at your beck and call. But when you squander *time*, you can never get it back, not a single minute. No matter how much money you have, no matter how talented you are, once time has passed it is gone for good. Even worse, your time in the future is equally limited, and becomes *more* limited with every passing day. Yet time, the most limited and precious commodity on the entire planet, more limited and precious than gold, rubies, or diamonds, is wasted as freely as the water you flush down the toilet.

In August 1994, my father was diagnosed with terminal cancer. The doctors thought he had eleven or twelve months to live. During that time I occasionally set aside my business obligations and took a few days to spend time with him. He lived six hundred miles away, and visiting him usually involved a lot of advance planning. A little over six months after he was diagnosed, he started going downhill faster than expected. Yet I still acted as if we would have more time later. I took him to the hospital one weekend and, as I was leaving, told him I'd be back in three weeks. He died two and a half weeks later. Like every adult who loses a parent, I have since wished a million times that I could get just one more hour with my dad. I would trade every dime I have in the bank for that hour, without a moment's hesitation. And yet I can't have him back for even a moment. Not a hug, not a kiss, not a smile. I miss him so much that at times I find myself physically aching for his presence. And yet, while he was alive, I could have had hundreds of those hours . . . I just didn't realize how fast and irrevocably time was passing.

In the second chapter of this book I related the night in 1971 when my whole life changed with the birth of my first child, my daughter Carol. I wrote a song for her sixteenth birthday and had an L.A. band record it. I gave it to her and we danced to it at her "sweet sixteen" party. The first verse and the chorus went like this:

Looking down . . . at those eyes . . . so blue, not even an hour old;
And yet they are looking back at me . . .
How can it be? Never felt so good.
But the years . . . how they flew . . .
Pigtails and braces gave way to books and boys,
And daddy's girl is all but grown . . .
And now I look at you . . . at your "Sweet Sixteen."
Little Girl, Daddy's girl, oh I can't believe your smile;
Little Girl, Daddy's girl, you've grown up in just a while.
Seems like only yesterday when I held you on my shoulders;
Now I'm watching. . . . And you're dancing, are you really that much
   older?

Today, Carol is twenty-five and has just received her master's degree in counseling. I'm sure that anyone who has children in their twenties will agree with me that time really does fly. While my first three children were growing up, I was living in Philadelphia and working most of the time in Los Angeles. I missed countless activities and events throughout their childhoods; not only school plays and baseball games but, more important, hundreds of dinners and bedtimes. I lost some of the most wonderful times of their lives, times that can never be regained. The times I missed during their childhoods is a regret that will always be one of the biggest in my life. Back then, I just didn't realize how precious and fleeting time was. I share this because it is my hope that by the time you finish this book, you will have a much greater awareness and appreciation of all your limited resources, especially your time, so that you might guide your behavior in a way to make the absolute *best use* of *all* of your limited resources.

THE SILVER LINING IN YOUR CLOUD OF LIMITED RESOURCES

Your limited resources never have to be viewed as insurmountable obstacles to your dreams and goals. Instead, like your lack of know-how, they can become a springboard to achieving your loftiest dreams. In college, I loved music but had absolutely no musical talent or ability. Whenever I sang in the shower my roommates would pound on the door and yell at me to stop. Once they even threw a wastebasket full of ice cubes and ice water on me as I was hitting a high note.

One day I thought it would be really awesome to create a choral group of singers and instrumentalists. When I told my roommates about it they laughed. One said, "You don't know anything about music!" And yet, within seven days, I had recruited a group of seventeen singers and eighteen instrumentalists, most of whom were music majors. A few weeks later, I recruited the best choral director in the state (and probably the best in America) to be our director. A few months later, we were performing almost weekly, receiving standing ovations at every major performance. We continued to perform together until we graduated two years later. Had I viewed my inability as an insurmountable obstacle, thirty-five musicians, the director, and I would have been robbed of a wonderful experience. By the way, the director's little girl, who used to attend our rehearsals, went on to become one of America's all-time favorite gospel singers. She has won a phenomenal thirty-seven Gospel Music Awards and five Grammys. Her name is Sandi Patti.

When I was recruited by my partner to start our TV marketing business, I had never written or directed a single commercial. I knew nothing about television or television commercials. And yet, four months later, I wrote and directed my first commercial. A two-minute commercial that cost us $4,200. It generated over $20 million in sales and launched our company. Within a few months my partner (and mentor) Bob Marsh brought his two sons and two sons-in-law into the company. Look at their qualifications: one was a twenty-four-year-old printing estimator; one was a twenty-four-year-old oil field worker; one was a twenty-eight-year-old dog trainer; and one was a nineteen-year-old convenience-store clerk who had just been fired from his job for incompetence. Do you see any expertise in television marketing, media purchasing, manufacturing, or any other appropriate talents necessary to build a group of media and marketing companies? It was literally nonexistent. And yet we went on to build myriad multimillion-dollar companies from scratch, selling over a billion dollars' worth of products. You see, we learned early on that our lack of talent and ability were *not* insurmountable obstacles at all. Rather, they were green lights that signaled us to get busy and learn what we could, and to recruit people with the talents and abilities that we not only lacked but couldn't learn.

In later chapters you'll discover booster engines that can overcome a lack of resources. You'll also learn how to accomplish more of what you really want in life in less time than you would ever imagine possible.

NO SUCH THING AS A SELF-MADE MILLIONAIRE

Over the years, many men and women have been introduced to me as "self-made millionaires." On my book tour in 1996 for *A Millionaire's Notebook,* countless radio and television hosts introduced me to their audiences as a self-made multimillionaire. In my case, I always corrected them by saying they could describe me as a "homemade" millionaire but certainly *not* self-made. For if I had not joined forces with six great partners, and had I not been mentored by an entrepreneurial genius, I definitely would not be in the financial position I'm in today. And I can honestly say the same is true of every millionaire and even every billionaire I've ever met. They all had mentors, partners, advisers, counselors, financiers, and so on. I know of *no* exceptions. And for those who have achieved their other dreams in life, whether in their marriage, family, relationships, careers, or hobbies, you will find that those dreams would never have been achieved without the benefit of outside resources.

My marriage and personal life, my friendships and other relationships would not be nearly as happy or as fulfilling had I not received the wisdom, advice, and mentoring of Dr. Gary Smalley. Simply stated, we can never achieve any extraordinary dreams or accomplishments without recruiting the advice, counsel, and help of others. But recruiting the *right* mentors, partners, advisers, counselors, and financiers is next to impossible *unless . . .* unless you use the techniques and strategies that will be enumerated later.

THE DAILY BATTLE BETWEEN THE GOOD AND THE BEST

Because limited resources are so valuable, you should realize that most adults rarely make the best use of their resources. It is not that one's resources are used in a bad way but that they are simply used in a "good" or expedient way. In other words, the *best* use of your resources is usually sacrificed and replaced by a simple "good" use. During the years I was living in Philadelphia and working in L.A., my television production activities represented a good use of my time, maybe even a great use of my time. But those activities, as good as they were, robbed me and my children of the *best* use of my time, which would have been better spent with them. One of my dreams for this book is to empower you to start trading the *good* use of your limited resources for the *best* use. The worst use of limited resources is accepted in place of the best use only by the most foolish. So I expect that you'll rarely if ever make that trade. But daily, the vast majority of adults accept good uses in place of best uses; when you learn how to stop making that trade, your level of accomplishment and fulfillment skyrockets to heights you never imagined possible.

POWER SECRET #6:
Overcoming Your Lack of Resources

1. YOUR THREE MOST limited resources are time, talent, and money. On each of your Dream Pages in your Dream Conversion Journal, write down if your lack of any of these resources is an obstacle to your achieving that dream. For example, going back to the dream of fulfilling your spouse's deepest needs, lack of time to visit a counselor or read a book could be a significant obstacle. Or if your dream is starting your own business, lack of time, talent, and money could all be significant obstacles.

2. You can expand your limited resources by seeking outside help. You can expand your time by delegating work and duties; you can expand your talents by recruiting those who have the expertise you lack; and you can expand your money by arranging for help from banks, investors, financiers, and so forth. On each of your Dream Pages, if time is an obstacle, write down any of your current activities that could be delegated to someone else so as to free up more of your time. If your lack of talent is an obstacle, write down the kinds of talents you need to find in others. If money is an obstacle, write down the possible sources you might recruit to gain the money necessary to achieve that dream.

3. At the end of Chapter 16, you will take an "inventory" of how you currently spend your time. You will find entire time blocks you are currently spending on "good" uses rather than on "better" or "best" uses. This will enable you to replace those "good" uses with the "best" uses, which will reflect your priorities for achieving your most important dreams.

PART III

IGNITING YOUR
SEVEN BOOSTER
ENGINES

CHAPTER 10

Engine #1: "Henry Ford Productivity"

AN AWESOME HABIT ANYONE CAN ACQUIRE

HENRY FORD DID *NOT* INVENT THE AUTOMOBILE, HE DID SOMETHING FAR MORE INGENIOUS!

WHEN I WAS a child, I thought that Henry Ford had invented the automobile. To my surprise I have discovered that a great many adults *still* think Henry Ford invented the automobile. If you are one of those adults, I am sorry to be the one to inform you that he did not! The first automobile was invented in 1769 and was powered by a steam engine. The first gasoline-powered auto was built in 1885 in Germany by Carl Benz, eighteen years before Henry Ford sold his first car. You should not, however, feel bad for Mr. Ford; what he passed on to America and the world was far greater than any *single* invention, save the wheel. He created a way for a car—and just about anything else—to be manufactured in greater numbers and at lower cost than anyone had ever imagined possible.

You see, Henry Ford had a dream: to see to it that every family in America could own their own car. When he first had this dream, it was truly an impossible one! Cars were far too expensive for average families to afford, for they were built one at a time. Only the very rich could afford a car. But Henry Ford had a dream . . . and he converted that dream into reality by developing the moving assembly line. When he created his Model T assembly plant in 1908, there were 250 other car manufacturers in the United States. With this assembly line, he could assemble 100 cars in one day, more than most other factories could assemble in a month. By 1914, he could make nearly 1,000 cars a day, more than most other manufacturers could make in an entire year. The result of this productivity breakthrough was enormous for Ford. Between 1908 and 1928, he made nearly seventeen million cars, more than *half* of the world's automobiles. His secret was to create workstations where a group of workers did the same task to every car as it arrived at the station. He divided the labor so that each worker became a specialist who concentrated on a single activity in the production of each car. Before long, other American manufacturers followed his example, and American industry became the most productive in the world.

The creation of the modern assembly-line production plant resulted in an *infinite* leap in productivity, not only for Ford's company but for every industry in America, and ultimately throughout the world.

WHAT THE ASSEMBLY LINE DID FOR HENRY FORD AND THE INDUSTRIAL WORLD, THE DREAM CONVERSION PROCESS WILL DO FOR YOU!

In this book, I would like to give you my definition of personal productivity. In either the corporate or industrial world, personal productivity refers to the amount of goods or services an individual is able to produce in relation to time and costs. This is not what I mean when I refer to your personal productivity. The word "productivity" is very cold and mechanical, but it's the only word I can think of that adequately conveys what I want to convey.

> YOUR PERSONAL PRODUCTIVITY: The degree and quantity of significant accomplishments you are able to achieve in a limited amount of time that reflect your true values, dreams, and goals.

As you consider this definition, you should start with the word "significant." In Chapter 4, I redefined "extraordinary achievement" as something that couldn't be accurately measured by grades, popularity, or athletic abilities in our school days, by amounts of money or material possessions or job titles in our adulthood. Rather, the true measure of achievement is the amount of benefit or fulfillment that an achievement brings to you or others. As you can see, there is a great difference between how most of us are programmed to measure achievement and its *true* measure. The same can be said for the concept of "significance."

You have been programmed to think that significance can be measured by the same false standards people often use to measure achievement. By these standards, nonworking moms who spend their days chasing after toddlers, running errands, and performing chores that keep a house and family running smoothly accomplish nothing significant. Nothing could be further from the truth. What could be more significant than the physical safety, emotional security, and well-being of one's children and family as a whole? How many divorces, trips to the therapist, and teen drug addictions and suicides would be avoided if marriage and family relationships were well nurtured and produced emotionally fulfilled and secure families?

My wife is a homemaker and manages our family and all of our personal affairs. Occasionally she has said she sometimes feels she isn't accomplishing anything significant with her life. She looks at my activities and professional achievements, or the achievements of others, and compares them to hers. But, it is *as* important for me to see Shannon achieve her dreams as it is for me to achieve mine. So when she makes statements like these, I don't downplay her feelings; rather, I try to help her define her short-term and long-term dreams and goals and map out a plan to achieve them. At the same time, however, I realize that it is critical that she sees the *true significance* of what she is accomplishing with our children and me every single day. She has three wonderfully happy and emotionally secure children at home who love being around her. She gives them boatloads of love, encouragement, and hope. She is giving them the emotional and spiritual foundations upon which their lives will be built. Lives full of honor, respect, joy, peace, hope, love, and compassion.

How significant are my wife's daily activities? More significant than she could ever calculate! Yes, I want her to do and achieve all the things she dreams of, all the things she considers significant. But at the same time, I don't want her to buy into the pervasive misconception that only that which can be measured by money or the world's applause is significant. The *true* measure of significance is the long-term impact an activity or accomplishment makes on a life. Thus, the greater impact an activity or accomplishment has on people's lives, the more significant is that activity or accomplishment.

With this true understanding of the meaning of significance, let's look at the working definition of your personal productivity once more: The degree and quantity of significant accomplishments you are able to achieve in a limited time that reflect your true values, dreams, and goals. With this definition, I can promise you that the Dream Conversion Process, by itself, will make as big a difference in your personal productivity at home and in business as Henry Ford's concept of the assembly line made in the productivity of industry. When consistently utilized, the Dream Conversion Process will empower you to achieve a far greater degree and quantity of significant accomplishments that reflect your true values and goals than would otherwise be humanly possible.

Simply stated, the Dream Conversion Process is:

> Defining a dream in writing
> Converting that dream into specific goals
> Converting each goal into specific steps
> Converting each step into specific tasks
> Assigning a projected time or date to complete each task

As you can see, the Dream Conversion Process is a very simple technique. And even though it does not appear to be an earth-shattering concept, if you begin to use it consistently it will have earth-shattering results in your life. It is the first and most important single engine aboard your Saturn V rocket. And yet, even though it is such a powerful engine and requires only a minimal amount of effort and time to ignite and maintain it, most Americans (and, I'm afraid, most of my readers) will never ignite and utilize this enormously powerful engine. I hope that you will be the exception. To help you, I'm going to lead you through this process step by step, using my own experiences as an example. But first, I want to help you understand the foundation upon which your Dream Conversion Process must be built.

THE FOUNDATION OF YOUR DREAMS

George Washington had a dream, one that was shared by Thomas Jefferson and the others who signed the Declaration of Independence. Their dream was based upon their *personal values,* and they drew upon their *personality types* and their *strengths* to fuel their efforts to achieve their dream of creating an independent democratic nation. They compensated for their individual personal weaknesses and limitations by partnering with one another, drawing upon one another's strengths to overcome their own limitations and weaknesses. Their dream was converted into reality, and you and I and our families are the direct beneficiaries of that dream.

Adolf Hitler, Benito Mussolini, and Hideki Tojo also had a dream, based upon *their* personal values, personality types, and personal strengths and weaknesses. Their dream not only resulted in their premature deaths (suicide, hanging, and stoning), but infinitely worse, their dream became a nightmare for their own nations, sacrificing the lives of men, women, and children, and almost bringing one group to the verge of annihilation. At the same time, their dream caused the deaths of men, women, and children from other nations and spawned the development of nuclear weapons that threaten future generations.

The difference between the outcome of Washington and Jefferson's dream and that of Hitler, Mussolini, and Tojo's was a function of *one* thing: the difference in their personal values. Whether we like it or not, every dream ever pursued is based upon someone's personal values. If those values are greed and self-aggrandizement, the dream may become other people's nightmares. On the other hand, when a dream is based upon personal values that are virtuous, the achievement of that dream can bring incalculable benefit to generations.

In case you can't identify with Washington and Jefferson, let's take another case in point: a man who was a barber in Nashville in the 1950s. His daughter had grown up living with his in-laws in her early childhood, and then with her mother in her early adolescence. She spent her early adolescence in and out of trouble, and at fourteen she finally went to live with her father. He had a dream for his daughter: namely, to see her turn her wayward life around and follow a more virtuous path. The foundation of his dream was his personal values, which stressed the importance of discipline and education. The conversion of his dream into reality not only resulted in turning his teenage daughter around, it also provided a foundation on which she could achieve her dreams. We can all be grateful that Vernon Winfrey built his dream for his daughter Oprah upon a foundation of his virtuous personal values.

WHAT PERSONAL VALUES DO YOU WANT TO BUILD *YOUR* DREAMS UPON?

The strategies and techniques in this book are so powerful that, when you begin to utilize them consistently, you will begin to achieve dreams as never before. That's the good news. The bad news is that these strategies and techniques are universally effective and non-discriminating in regard to the types of dreams they can be used to achieve. In other words, if you use these strategies to achieve dreams that reflect faulty values or misplaced priorities, they will still be effective in achieving those dreams, but you may discover that even when you've achieved those dreams, you still lack happiness and fulfillment. If you use these techniques to gain tremendous success in business, but don't use them to strengthen your family and personal relationships, your success will turn out to be hollow in terms of personal happiness and fulfillment. My hope is that you will first clarify your own priorities and values, and then use them to achieve your dreams, and that the end result will be true fulfillment and joy to you and to all those with whom you interact.

Ty Cobb dreamed of being the greatest baseball player that ever lived. He achieved that dream and set more records in professional baseball than anyone who has ever played the game. He dreamed of gaining fame and fortune, and he did. In addition to his baseball fame, his investment in the first public offering of the fledgling Coca-Cola Company earned him more wealth than he could have spent in a dozen lifetimes. He achieved his impossible dreams, and yet only three people attended his funeral. Not even his children showed up—they had come to despise him. He had gained success, fame, and fortune during his lifetime, yet he was devoid of love, joy, and personal happiness.

There was nothing inherently bad or wrong with Cobb's dreams to be the best baseball player in history or to make a personal fortune. Had those dreams been founded upon the right values and priorities, he would have been a happy and fulfilled man, even if he didn't achieve them. His life would have been filled with the joy that comes from loving relationships with his family and friends. And the pursuit of his dreams would have been much more fulfilling. But instead, he lived and died an unhappy man who was known for his anger, rancor, and bitterness. At the time of his death, he still possessed more than ninety major league baseball records and had millions of dollars in the bank. Yet he was totally bankrupt in the most important areas of life: love, family, friends, happiness, fulfillment, and inner peace. How tragic it would be if you were to gain your loftiest dreams only to discover they brought little or no happiness because, like Cobb's, they had been built upon faulty values.

My purpose here is not to preach certain values to you, or to even suggest that my values should be your values. My goal for this section is simply to help you identify and prioritize your values so that you can pursue and achieve your most important and rewarding dreams, and delay or set aside those that don't reflect your true values. For example, if you value your husband or wife and your children more than anything else in life, do you want to pursue a dream that might ruin your marriage and devastate your children—both now and in the future? I have known countless men who truly loved, and yet destroyed, their families in pursuit of their business and career dreams. And how many magazine articles have appeared telling of women who are deeply discouraged because they sacrificed having a family while pursuing a career? My friend, it doesn't have to be this way. You can have a wonderful family life and a fulfilling career at the same time. But to do so, you must first define and clarify your values and then prioritize them. After you have done this, you will be in a position to prioritize your dreams.

In Chapter 7, I asked you to make a list of the most important areas of your life, starting with the most important area and working down to the least. If you haven't yet done that, turn back to page 78 and follow through on this exercise ASAP. It's the first step in the Dream Conversion Process and provides the foundation for each of the steps that follow. That list not only reveals what is most important to you, it reflects your *core values*. And you may have to do a little soul search-ing to discover the core values each important area reflects. For example, if your mate is high on the list, it could reflect core values of love, loyalty, and commitment. Or it could reflect a core value of selfishness, if you simply value your mate as someone whose impor-tance to you is based upon how well she or he gratifies your base needs.

All of this is to say that it is critically important to look at all your priorities and dreams in order to gain an understanding of how important each may be to you and what underlying values they are based upon. So, as you think about the most important areas of your life, write down what you consider to be the core values that make that area so important.

My good friends John Tesh and Connie Sellecca are two people who passionately pursue their individual and mutual dreams. And because those dreams are based upon virtuous core values, the pursuit itself has added to their joy and the joy and benefit of others.

Return to your list and make sure that each area and dream you've included reflects your true core values. When you do this, it may be necessary to change the priority you assigned to certain areas or dreams.

MISPLACED PRIORITIES ARE MORE COSTLY THAN YOU CAN POSSIBLY CALCULATE!

When my business began to boom in 1977, I began to visualize all the dreams that my booming business could fulfill for my children. They would be able to grow up in a nice house instead of a tiny apartment. They would be able to have good college educations without having to incur debt. They would be able to choose careers based upon their passions rather than their financial needs. The fulfillment of these dreams for my children was a driving force behind my pursuit of success. And yet my pursuit of success kept me away from home up to 160 days a year in the early years, and 300 to 330 days a year in the later years. Yes, my children all grew up in a nice home. Yes, they've had quality educations. But looking back, was achieving those dreams worth giving up all of the time and activities with my children that I had sacrificed? If I had completed the exercise I've just asked you to complete, I would have still enjoyed a good level of success (though maybe not to the degree that I have), but I would not have sacrificed the unbelievable amount of time that I gave up with my children.

Reevaluating your important areas and dreams based upon your core values and then reprioritizing them when necessary will ensure that those things that are truly *most* important to you are not sacrificed to achieve things that are less important. Once you have prioritized your important areas and dreams based upon your core values and true priorities, you will then be ready for the next step in the Dream Conversion Process.

THE DREAM CONVERSION PROCESS: THE MAGICAL KEY OF THE TOP 3 PERCENT OF AMERICA'S MOST SUCCESSFUL PEOPLE

When my daughter was eleven years old, Michael Landon asked her what she wanted to be when she grew up. Without a moment's hesitation my daughter instantly answered, "The first girl on the Philadelphia Phillies baseball team." My daughter could give Mike such a quick and precise answer because she had discussed it with me just a few days earlier. Philly pitcher Steve Carlton had signed her baseball glove two weeks earlier, and she had decided that he was so cool, she wanted to play ball on his team. She told me her dream that same night. Fortunately, a few months earlier, Zig Ziglar had told me to be a dream-maker rather than a dream-breaker with my kids, even when they brought me ridiculous or impossible dreams. So, when Carol told me her dream, I didn't react by telling her, "Girls can't play major league baseball and therefore you'll never make the Phillies." Instead, I told her that when you have a dream, you have to convert that dream into goals. So she decided that her goals would be to become the best hitter and fielder on her softball team.

Next, she had to convert these goals into steps. So we decided that to become the best fielder and the best hitter on her team, she would have to begin to regularly practice hitting, throwing, and catching. And finally, she would have to convert those steps into tasks. So we agreed that I would come home before sundown three days a week to practice throwing and catching with her, and that I would take her to the batting cage or to a field to practice hitting on Saturdays. That is a very simple example of the Dream Conversion Process. And because we had gone through the process, when Mike asked her that question, she gave her answer with authority because she truly believed she was going to see her dream come true.

Carol never made the Phillies, because by the time she was thirteen, her dream had changed. However, she saw such improvement in her fielding and hitting that she helped take her team from the worst record in league history (all losses and no wins) to the league championship the next year, without losing a single game. Same girls, same coach. The only difference between the worst team and the championship team was Carol and a few of her teammates who had discovered the power of the Dream Conversion Process.

Converting Your Dreams to Goals

As in the example above, once you have clearly defined and prioritized your dreams, the next step is to take each important dream and convert it into specific, tangible goals. Ask yourself, "What specific goals need to be achieved to accomplish this dream." For example, in Chapter 7, I shared some of my Defined Dreams in the Extracurricular Activities and Passions area of my life. The first dream I listed involved my dream for mentoring others in the art of Dream Conversion. I defined this dream as follows:

DEFINED DREAM #1

To provide a complete Dream Conversion Kit with audio- and video-tapes and a loose-leaf manual that would enable me to personally coach my family, friends, and anyone else in every strategy and technique they need to learn and apply the art of Dream Conversion to every area of their lives.

After reviewing this dream I came up with the goals that I needed to accomplish to make this dream a reality.

GOALS

1. Produce a Dream Conversion Kit with video- and audiotapes and a loose-leaf manual.

2. Form a partnership with a company that will be able to distribute the Dream Conversion Kit to millions of people through their existing distribution channels.

Another one of my clearly defined dreams is to be the absolute best husband my wife could have ever hoped for. This is one of my highest priorities because my wife is not only the most incredible person I have ever known, but she has given me the most wonderful gift anyone could ever give me, herself. When I converted that dream into specific goals, here are the ones I came up with.

DEFINED DREAM #2

Be the absolute best husband my wife could have ever hoped for.

GOALS

1. Learn what Shannon's deepest needs and desires are—emotionally, physically, psychologically, and spiritually.
2. Learn how she thinks each of these needs and desires can be most effectively and consistently fulfilled.
3. Learn what Gary Smalley (my favorite relationships expert) says about a woman's deepest needs and desires, and gain any insights I can from him on how to best fulfill these needs and desires.
4. Begin to consistently focus my time and attention on fulfilling her needs and desires.

As you can see from these two examples, setting specific, tangible goals is a fairly easy yet critical step in the Dream Conversion Process for dreams in all areas, both personal and professional. Right now would be a perfect time for you to take just one of your clearly defined dreams and convert it into the specific goals you need to accomplish to achieve your dream.

Converting Goals into Steps

The next step in the Dream Conversion Process is converting each of these goals into specific steps. Going back to my earlier examples, here's how I converted some of my goals into specific steps.

GOAL #1

Produce a Dream Conversion Kit with video- and audiotapes and a loose-leaf manual.

STEPS

1. Determine the content needed for a manual and video- and audiotapes to effectively coach a person step by step through each strategy and technique in the art of Dream Conversion.
2. Determine what it would take physically and financially to produce the manual and video- and audiotapes.
3. Create a precise timetable and budget for the production of the manual and tapes.
4. Write the manual.
5. Write the scripts for the audio- and videotapes.
6. Set aside or acquire the funds to produce and duplicate the kit.
7. Create artwork for the manual and tapes.
8. Print the manual.
9. Record the master video- and audiotapes.
10. Duplicate and package the video- and audiotapes.
11. Package the Dream Conversion Kit.

GOAL #2

Form a partnership with a company that will be able to distribute the Dream Conversion Kit to millions of people through their existing distribution channels.

STEPS

1. Make a list of the publishers and other distribution companies that might be possible candidates for distributing the Dream Conversion Kit.
2. Prioritize companies according to their ability to market and distribute the kit.

3. Have my literary agent call each company to determine their level of interest.
4. Schedule meetings with the highest-priority companies that have expressed the highest levels of interest.
5. Select the best offer from the company that has the largest distribution network and is willing to make the biggest marketing commitment.
6. Sign a contract with the distribution partner and create a marketing plan.

Converting goals into steps is a very simple exercise. In fact, this may seem so easy that you are tempted only to do it in your head and not in writing. Believe me when I say that it is critical that *every* step of this process be put in writing. If you don't remember and perform each step you have written, you will render the entire process null and void. Remember that you are creating a detailed road map to achieving your dreams. You may think you will remember the route you want to take, but without a written map you'll waste a lot of time and may even get lost. Now would be the ideal time to take one or more of your written goals and convert them into steps.

Converting Steps into Tasks

The next stage in this process may be one of the hardest, but even this stage is not too difficult. Simply stated: Convert each step into specific tasks and assign a specific date to complete each task. Some steps are so simple they do not need to be broken down into detailed tasks, but rather only need to be assigned a completion date. To achieve other steps, multiple tasks may be required. Those tasks should be stated and given completion dates. Here are a couple of examples.

GOAL #1

Produce a Dream Conversion Kit with video- and audiotapes and a loose-leaf manual.

STEP

1. Determine the content needed for a manual and video- and audio-tapes to effectively coach a person step by step through each strategy and technique in the art of Dream Conversion.

TASKS

1. Write a general outline for the manual—*May 1*
2. Write a very detailed outline for the manual—*May 7*
3. Write a general outline for each video- and audiotape—*May 14*
4. Write a very detailed outline for each video- and audiotape—*June 14*

GOAL #2

Form a partnership with a company that will be able to distribute the Dream Conversion Kit to millions of people through their existing distribution channels.

STEP

1. Make a list of the publishers and other distribution companies that might be possible candidates for distributing the Dream Conversion Kit.

TASKS

1. Create a list of the publishers and other companies I think might be distribution candidates—*May 1*
2. Ask my literary agent to submit a list of publishers and other companies she thinks might be best distribution candidates ASAP—*May 1*
3. Create a combined list of possible candidates with our comments about each candidate—*May 3*

As you can see, this, too, is a simple step in the Dream Conversion Process. The only difficulty here is assigning a date for completing the task.

The Final Stage in the Dream Conversion Process

Once you have defined your dream in writing, converted that dream into specific goals, converted those goals into steps, and converted those steps into dated tasks, you will have completed a detailed written map to achieving your dream. Now all you have to do is follow that map and begin to complete each task. It's that easy. "Wait," you say. "What happens when I reach a step that I cannot take because of a lack of know-how or a lack of resources?" What a great question! You *will* arrive at steps that you are simply not equipped or able to take. For example, my sixth step under goal number one was, "Set aside or acquire the funds necessary to produce and duplicate the Dream Conversion Kit." If I want to produce a quality kit and distribute it to hundreds of thousands or even millions of people, I do not have the funds necessary to take this step. So I will have to recruit an outside resource to provide those funds—a step that is critical to achieving my goal and, therefore, critical to fulfilling my dream.

Anytime you begin the Dream Conversion Process to achieve a dream that is truly worthwhile, you will arrive at steps and tasks that are totally impossible for you to complete by yourself. Don't be surprised or discouraged when you reach such an impasse. That is confirmation that your dream is truly worthwhile. Instead, let this be a signal to you that it's time to ignite the third booster engine in the art of Dream Conversion. An engine that must be ignited for you to achieve your loftiest dreams. I call this booster engine "Steven Spielberg Partnering," and igniting it is what Chapter 12 is all about. You will discover that this engine is by far the most powerful of your seven booster engines. It is the engine that by itself will break the bonds of gravity and propel you toward whole new worlds of achievement. But before you learn how to ignite that engine, you must ignite the second engine, and that is the engine we will look at next. I call it "Babe Ruth Power" because it adds tremendous power to the Dream Conversion Process, and it will enable you to have bigger dreams than you ever dared to dream before.

POWER SECRET #7:
Achieving Infinitely More in a Fraction of the Time

1. IN YOUR NOTEBOOK, make a list of what you consider to be your most important core values and prioritize that list (integrity, love, spirituality, health, responsibility, financial security, family relationships, friendships, personal security, family security, personal happiness, family happiness, etc.).
2. Using your prioritized list of core values, review in your Dream Conversion Journal how you prioritized the most important areas of your life and each of your dreams within those areas. Do the priorities really reflect your most important core values? Should any of those areas or dreams be reprioritized?

THE DREAM CONVERSION PROCESS

The following exercises should be completed in your Dream Conversion Journal.

1. Starting with the most important area of your life, and the most important dream in that area, create a page entitled "Dream to Goals." On that page, write down all the specific goals you can think of that need to be accomplished to achieve that dream. After you have done this move on to the next dream in that area; follow the same routine for each dream in each important area. You can tackle one dream at a time or start on as many as are truly important to you (for examples, see pages 112 and 113).
2. For each goal that you have stated, create a page entitled "Goal to Steps." On each of these pages, write down all the steps you need to take to achieve the goal. Once again, start with your highest-priority dreams (for examples, see pages 114 through 115).
3. For each step that you've listed, create a page entitled "Step to Tasks." On each of these pages, list the specific tasks that need to be accomplished to take that step. Assign a target completion date for each task *after* you have listed all the tasks (for examples, see pages 115 through 116).

4. Review the tasks necessary to complete each step of each goal and circle those you *cannot* achieve on your own because of your lack of know-how, lack of resources (time, talent, or money), lack of adequate ability, or lack of certain personality traits.
5. For each circled task, write down the type of person, company, or outside resource you need to recruit to accomplish that task. Later in the book, you'll learn the specific strategies and techniques you'll need to recruit these outside resources.

CHAPTER 11

Engine #2: "Babe Ruth Power"

A TREMENDOUS STRENGTH ANYONE CAN GAIN

HITS ARE GOOD, HOME RUNS ARE GREAT!

BABE RUTH BEGAN his professional baseball career as a pitcher, and overnight became the best left-handed pitcher in the American League, winning 89 games in his first six seasons. He set a pitching record of 29⅔ scoreless innings in the 1918 World Series, and that remarkable record remained unbroken for forty-three years! Babe Ruth also had more strikeouts in his career than any other baseball player in history. And yet, when you hear the name Babe Ruth, you don't think of his awesome pitching feats or his embarrassing number of strikeouts. No, the "Babe" is synonymous with one thing and one thing alone: home runs! He not only hit more home runs in the number of games and innings played than anyone else in history, but his "slugging" percentage—.847 (the number of bases reached divided by the number of at bats)—is a record that has never even been approached much less equaled. The great Bambino had learned how to add power to his swing and distance to his hits like no one before him and no one since.

Most people go through life just hoping to get on base. Whether it's in their marriage, their relationships with their children, or in their business or career pursuits, they just want to avoid the strikeouts and get on base. They think just like my first Little League coach. He was so afraid whenever I came up to the plate that I would swing at bad pitches and strike out, he would yell, "Steve, a walk's as good as a hit!"

Hogwash! Anyone who's ever hit a baseball and made it to first base knows that a walk is *never* as good as a hit. And as good as a hit feels, a home run feels a thousand times better.

The greatest hitters of all time played pro ball when Ruth was playing. But none of them were credited with saving major league baseball or building a team into the most financially successful baseball team in history. In 1920, Ruth hit more home runs than any entire *team* in the major leagues (except one). That year more than one million fans turned out to watch the great Bambino knock the ball out of the park at the Yankees' home games. That was more fans than had ever watched any team in a single season, and the irony is, the Yankees didn't even have their own ballpark. They played in the Polo Grounds, home of the New York Giants. The Yankees' owner made so much money, he built the finest ballpark in America, and in 1923 the Yankees' played their first game in Yankee Stadium. The stadium that became known as "the House That Ruth Built." And that was no exaggeration. Oh, the thrill of hitting home runs!

WHY DO MOST PEOPLE SETTLE FOR WALKS OR SINGLES?

If everyone loves home runs, why do people settle for walks or singles in nearly every area of their lives? Believe it or not, there are only four reasons:

- We don't realize we are capable of hitting home runs.
- We don't know *how* to hit home runs.
- It's less risky to take an easier swing and settle for a hit.
- We don't have enough power in our swing to get the ball over the fence.

I dealt with the first three in earlier chapters when I focused on cutting the chains of past programming, fear of failure, lack of know-how, and lack of resources. In this chapter I'm going to focus on reason number four and show you how to bring so much power into your swing that the ball nearly always sails over the fence. Solving this problem will in itself provide the key to totally solving the other three problems. I'm going to show you how to add so much power to your swing that you'll immediately realize that:

- You *are* capable of hitting home runs.
- You'll know *how* to hit a home run.
- You will want to take the risk of swinging for the bleachers.

Simply hoping for walks or hits will become a thing of the past.

So, what does all of this mean to you? Leaving the baseball analogy, it means that instead of settling for a good marriage, you're going to strive (and achieve) a great one, in which all the deepest needs and desires of you and your spouse are consistently fulfilled. It means instead of accepting a job where you live paycheck to paycheck, where you simply show up and do time, you are going to swing for a career in which you far surpass your employer's highest expectations. You are going to become a shooting star instead of a falling star. The number and level of significant accomplishments at home and at work are going to skyrocket!

CONVERTING YOUR HITS INTO HOME RUNS!

As you discovered in the last chapter, the Dream Conversion Process is a very simple method to produce life-changing results in every area in which it is utilized. It is a value-based, goal-setting program that can take nearly any dream, no matter how abstract or how lofty it might be, and convert it into a tangible reality. The technique I call "Shooting for the Moon," takes the Dream Conversion Process and powers it into a league as far above other goal-setting programs as the stars are above the earth. Its driving strategy is literally the opposite of a primary tenet of every other goal-setting program I have ever read or heard about. I have listened to countless motivational speakers and looked at various goal-setting programs. Every one I've looked at to date has been excellent, and if followed would make a significant difference in the life of anyone who has never used an effective program.

In fact, according to various studies, only 3 percent of the population uses a goal-setting program at all, and yet that 3 percent earn more than double what the other 97 percent make. And according to one source, as a group, they are happier, healthier, and have far better relationships than those who don't have an effective goals program. With this in mind, I would never belittle any effective goals program.

THE CRITICAL WOUND IN MOST GOAL-SETTING PROGRAMS

And yet, as good as other goal-setting programs are, they all have one severe limitation. And with this limitation, while these goals programs can double or triple a person's income and accomplishments, they rarely multiply a person's income or accomplishments by a hundred- or thousandfold.

The limitation I am referring to is in every goals program I've looked at and is usually stated: "Make sure the goals you set are realistic and achievable." You are warned ahead of time that if your goals are unrealistic, you won't achieve them, and you will become frustrated and discouraged, possibly to the point that you will abandon the goals program altogether.

Now, all of this makes perfect sense. It's perfectly logical. I'm sure that many people have become frustrated and discouraged and have even abandoned their goal-setting programs because they set unrealistic, unachievable goals, so I can understand the concern of most of America's motivators and trainers. However, if you follow this rule in any goal-setting program, including the Dream Conversion Process, you may significantly improve your batting average, but you won't become a home-run hitter. You may hit a few doubles or triples, but that's about it. On the other hand, if you want to start hitting home runs, and hit them consistently in every important area of your life, then you should abandon this rule once and for all and never return to it. Setting realistic, easily achievable goals is the only weak link, the only severe limitation in any goals program. It's okay if your desire is only to reach above-average achievement. But it will keep you from making extraordinary achievements a regular occurrence in your life.

Imagine if Thomas Edison had only set realistic, achievable goals. We would only be reading under bigger and better kerosene lamps. We would be cleaning our floors with brooms instead of electric-powered vacuum cleaners. We would all live in homes without air-conditioning. There would be no recording industry and we would never see a movie. Our entire way of life would be radically different.

Or how about our friend Henry Ford? Where would we be if he had not set an impossible goal of building a thousand cars a day? Only the rich would be driving cars, everyone else would be riding in buggies. I could fill volumes showing how our lives would be radically different if the dream-achievers of the past had set only realistic, easily achievable goals. Thank God they never heard of this modern rule of goal setting.

Setting realistic, achievable goals is like reaching for apples on top of a two-foot wall. They are easy to reach, and there's virtually no risk of falling or failing when you reach for them. If you set ten apples on a two-foot wall, you will be able to successfully reach ten out of ten every time. That's good; it's certainly better than not getting any apples at all. But apples on top of a two-foot wall are also easily accessible to dogs, worms, and rats. While apples that have been gnawed at by dogs or infested by worms may be better than no apples at all, they aren't really *that* tasty or satisfying when you eat them. Realistic and achievable goals are just as good as those apples, they'll keep you from starving, they'll even provide a reasonable amount of energy, but that's about it.

On the other hand, apples hanging on the tree twenty feet off the ground are not accessible to dogs, worms, and rats (or even to teenagers or rug-rats). They are unspoiled, untouched, tasty, and juicy, and they are wonderfully satisfying when eaten. "Wait a minute," you say, "I can't reach a branch twenty feet off the ground!" You're right. In fact, Michael Jordan can't even reach that branch, no matter how high he tries to jump! Dreams and goals that are twenty feet high are both unrealistic and unachievable—at first glance! That's the bad news. The good news is that even my four-year-old can reach that twenty-foot branch—all he needs is a stepladder. That's what all of the strategies and techniques that make up the art of Dream Conversion give you: a ladder you can use to climb whatever wall is keeping you from reaching your most unrealistic, unachievable, and impossible goals.

When you become skilled at using these strategies and techniques, achieving impossible goals will become a part of your daily experience. But to reach such goals and dreams, you must first break the habit of setting goals on the two-foot wall and start looking to the top of the twenty-foot walls—and that's what the technique of Shooting for the Moon is all about.

SHOOTING FOR THE MOON: THE TECHNIQUE THAT SUPERCHARGES THE DREAM CONVERSION PROCESS

In Chapter 2, I said there were three types of people: dreamers, dream-breakers, and dream-makers. I defined a dream-maker as someone who dreams big and achieves those big dreams. I said they represent at best about one-tenth of one percent of America's adult population. I have personally known a number of America's most renowned dream-makers and read about many others. To date, everyone I've come to know and everyone I've read about shoots for the moon when they set their goals. In a sentence, Shooting for the Moon means setting goals that are beyond your reach, even impossible for you to achieve on your own. Years ago, when I was setting my goals on a project, a close friend told me, "Always shoot for the moon, if you miss, you'll still be high." I began using that philosophy when I set my goals, and it radically changed everything. I began attempting what I believed was impossible, and to my amazement I began achieving it.

Said another way, Shooting for the Moon is starting with goals that are twenty feet high and only lowering your sights when you fail to achieve the highest goal. So you start at the top and work down, rather than starting at the bottom with easily achieved goals.

For example, whenever I begin a new project and have to determine which celebrity I want to sign as an endorser, I have a choice. I could create a list of celebrities who I think are within my budget who are willing to appear in commercials. I could start by calling the ones I think I have the best chance of signing. This would not only be the easiest path to follow, it would be the safest and the least time-consuming because I would probably be able to sign the first person on such a list. This would follow the conventional approach in a goals program of setting reachable, achievable goals.

Or, I could shoot for the moon. I could ask myself, "Who would be the absolute best celebrity in the world to endorse this particular product." If I could have anyone in front of that camera when it's rolling, whom would I pick? And if I can't sign that person, who would be the next best, and so on. *This* is the Shooting for the Moon approach that I and every other dream-maker or dream-achiever I have ever known has used. As a result, I have been able to sign such great endorsers as Michael Landon, Cher, Jane Fonda, Charlton Heston, Tom Selleck, Chuck Norris, Kathie Lee Gifford, Ted Danson, Larry Hagman, Holly Hunter, and seventy other "A"-list celebrities during the height of their careers to appear in my company's projects and endorse our products.

Many of the celebrities I signed were never willing to appear in a commercial until I approached them. For example, when I needed an endorser for an educational product, I felt Michael Landon and John Ritter would be the absolute best endorsers. Both were starring in prime-time shows and each was totally committed to education. Michael had struggled in school and had succeeded in spite of his learning difficulties, and John had been president of the student body at the University of Southern California and was married to a former teacher. I couldn't afford either one of them, but I knew they were the absolute best—the top of the "A" list.

As it turned out, both signed on at various stages of the project. Because of their involvement, "Where There's a Will, There's an 'A' " became the best-selling educational series in history, helping millions of grade school, high school, and college students raise their learning skills and get better grades. It even became the "study-skills" program of many of America's most prestigious universities. Had I simply tried to sign a "B" or "C" celebrity, the program may have never been rolled out, and if it had, it would have only reached thousands of students instead of millions.

The Shooting for the Moon approach to goal setting is so powerful that when you use it, two outcomes are likely. First, you will achieve a much higher level of accomplishment and fulfillment than you would ever have thought possible, and second, the impact will very likely spill over to those around you, and its ultimate impact may be felt for generations. One of my favorite examples of this took place in the 1840s in the life of an individual named Nicholas Trist. You may not have heard of him, but your life and the lives of your parents and your children have been radically affected by his decision to shoot for the moon.

In 1847, President James Polk dispatched Nicholas Trist to Mexico to negotiate a peace treaty to end the Mexican-American War. Shortly after Trist began the negotiations, he decided to shoot for the moon by asking for extraordinary concessions from Mexico at a bargain-basement price. Concessions that others (including the president) considered totally impossible to achieve. Polk was shocked and hor-rified that Trist would be so bold as to ask for so much for so little. In fact, Polk was so upset by Trist's proposal that he fired Trist and demanded his immediate return to Washington.

But Nicholas Trist was intent on shooting for the moon, and in February 1848, on behalf of the United States of America, which he no longer officially represented, Trist signed the treaty along with the Mexican government that ended the Mexican-American War. The concessions on which Trist had set his sights and achieved were so remarkable and beneficial to the United States that President Polk and the Senate ratified the treaty without hesitation. For even though the president had only set his sights on a "realistic, achievable goal," Nicholas Trist had decided to take the risk and asked Mexico to concede the areas of present-day California, Arizona, Nevada, Utah, and New Mexico and parts of Colorado and Wyoming for less than five cents an acre! How many acres of California gold and oil, Arizona copper, and Colorado silver would *you* buy for five cents an acre? To the amazement of everyone in Washington, Trist gained the conces-sions he asked for at the price he offered!

How much have those states been worth to the prosperity and security of our country? No dollar amount is high enough, and there is certainly no other way to estimate the incredible worth of what we acquired through Trist's treaty. If he had simply set his sights on the "attainable goals" of the president, the United States might be a lot smaller today. In fact, it is very likely we would have lost World War II for lack of the vital oil and mineral resources these states provided. So, not only do we owe a great part of our nation's prosperity to Mr. Trist's decision to shoot for the moon, but the entire free world may also owe him their thanks.

But we don't have to look as far back as Nicholas Trist to see the power and impact that an individual's Shooting for the Moon can have on people. If Lee Iacocca didn't shoot for the moon, Ford would never have been revitalized by the creation of the Mustang, Chrysler would have gone bankrupt, and millions of families would still be cramming their kids into station wagons instead of minivans. But Lee has filled his professional life with setting impossible goals, then doing whatever it took and recruiting whoever was necessary to achieve those goals. Steven Spielberg has set "impossible" goals in nearly every project he has ever attempted since he began his film career. Goals that were impossible for him to achieve by himself became achievable through his brilliant direction and his ability to recruit the outside resources he needed to convert his dreams into reality.

Where the Rubber Meets the Road

The Shooting for the Moon approach can and should be applied to every dream you want to achieve, personally as well as professionally. It is just as powerful and valid in the personal arena as in the professional one. For example, I once asked my friend Sue if she could have any dream come true in her marriage, what would it be? "I would *love* for my husband to just stop criticizing me" was her reply. She went on to say, "A day doesn't go by that he doesn't openly criticize me or something I've done. I just get so tired of it, I'd give anything if he would just stop."

Can you see the tragedy in this? While it's obvious that Sue's husband's constant criticism was extremely painful to her, the real tragedy was that she set her sights so low. I then asked her, "Instead of just wanting an end to his criticism, how about wanting the criticism not only to end but to be replaced by his consistently realizing how valuable you are and all of the things you do; and have him actually replace all of his criticism with appreciation and praise and encouragement?"

Her reply was, "That would be a dream come true all right, but he would never do that!" I then went one step further. I said, "How about he not only ends his criticism and begins to appreciate and praise you, but he begins to meet all of your deepest emotional needs?" "That's *really* impossible" was her instant reply. And yet that is exactly what the Shooting for the Moon approach would aim for. If she shoots at *that* goal and misses, she will still end up with a heck of a lot more than if she merely aims at reducing his criticism. Instead of her relationship just becoming more tolerable, it would have the potential to become far more intimate and fulfilling! On the next page I've put into diagram form Sue's current reality, her reachable goal, her dream, her

impossible dream, and her revised dream after applying the Shooting
for the Moon approach. If you were Sue, would you settle for her
reachable goal, or would you try for her dream, her impossible dream,
or her revised dream after applying the Shooting for the Moon approach?

Revising Dreams and Shooting for the Moon

(A) SHOOTING FOR THE MOON REVISED DREAM—Marriage
where husband meets wife's deepest emotional needs.
(B) IMPOSSIBLE DREAM—Replace criticism with appreciation,
praise, and encouragement.
(C) DREAM—End constant criticism
(D) ACHIEVABLE GOAL—Reduce frequency and severity of hus-
band's criticism
CURRENT REALITY—Husband's constant criticism

"BUT I DON'T HAVE WHAT IT TAKES TO *HIT* THE MOON!"

This was Sue's first reaction when I went through this exercise with
her, and it may be yours. And the truth of the matter is, Sue is right
and so are you if this is your reaction. Nobody has all the know-how
or resources within them to hit the moon when they shoot for it! Not
Steven Spielberg, not Bill Gates, and not even Oprah Winfrey. And if
they relied upon their own limited know-how and resources, they
would not only miss the moon they wouldn't even get off the
ground! And because they know this, they don't even think of just
relying upon their own know-how and resources. The fact that they
don't have what it takes to hit the moon doesn't stop them from
shooting for it—they still set their sights at the moon and beyond.
They simply know that before they begin their countdown, they are
going to have to recruit all the outside resources necessary to create a
clear and precise map.

If you told Steven Spielberg he was going to have to produce his
sequel to *Jurassic Park* without recruiting anyone else to do his special
effects or model making, lighting or set building, he would tell you he

would have to walk away from the project. You see, Steven isn't interested in just making another movie; he wants to make it even better than *Jurassic Park*. He wants it to be as awesome and yet believably realistic as possible. To achieve that kind of impossible dream, he *must* recruit the absolute best resources possible. The result will not only be an incredible movie that will make hundreds of millions of dollars, it will be so good it will make everyone who sees it want to see it again and again. And guess what? At the end of the film, you will see a very long list of credits. Credits that include the most talented resources Steven Spielberg could recruit.

One of my neighbors is a wonderful lady named June Morris. June loved to travel, and one day she decided to start her own travel agency. Several years after doing so, she noticed that the fares between Salt Lake City and Hawaii were extremely high. She decided to begin to charter jets from airlines and provide regularly scheduled low-cost flights from Salt Lake City to Hawaii. Her idea was so successful that she began offering regularly scheduled low-cost flights between Salt Lake and other destinations popular with Utah residents, such as Los Angeles, San Francisco, Phoenix, and Las Vegas. After running her charter service very successfully for seven years, she decided to shoot for the moon and start her own airline.

Starting an airline involved a lot more risk than running a charter service. She would have to buy and lease jets each worth tens of millions of dollars. She would have to meet volumes of regulations not applicable to charter services and take on liability concerns that would make most entrepreneurs cower in a corner. She would be facing enormous marketing, administrative, and expense challenges. And she would be competing against America's largest and most successful airlines every day of the week. Airlines with far deeper pockets than hers that could afford to reduce their fares below costs in an attempt to quickly force her airline out of business.

To make matters even worse, she decided to start her airline at a time when nearly every major airline in America was hemorrhaging millions of dollars a month. The year June Morris started her airline, America's other airlines lost more money than all of the profits America's airlines had made in all the years since the airline industry had begun. Was June crazy? Absolutely yes—if she had tried to do it by herself! But she and her brilliant son recruited all the resources and talent they needed to pull it off. She was shooting for the moon at a time when everyone else in the airline business was just trying to survive. Every other airline (except one) that had started up since deregulation had gone out of business. The airline industry had boldly predicted that no new airline would ever again be successfully started and survive.

It would have been much easier and safer for June to have set a reachable, achievable goal of simply expanding her charter service. She could have added more destinations and more flights to her schedule. And yet she chose to shoot for the moon.

The result was June Morris, her son Rick, and their partners not only launched Morris Air, they made a $16 million profit during their first year of operation—a year when nearly every major airline (including June's strongest competitor) lost hundreds of millions of dollars *each*. And yet June was flying twenty-two 737s on 168 flights a day to 23 cities. And she was doing it *profitably*. After being in the airline business for only two years, June sold her fledgling airline for more than $130 million to Southwest Airlines. Not bad for a business that was only two years old! If she had simply set reachable, achievable goals, she would not have been able to sell her charter service for one-twentieth of that amount!

WHEN SHOULD *YOU* SETTLE FOR SETTING ACHIEVABLE GOALS AND WHEN SHOULD YOU SHOOT FOR THE MOON?

So now let's talk about you and your dreams and goals. Should you always shoot for the moon, or are there times when you should simply set reachable, achievable goals? In my opinion there are lots of unimportant low-priority endeavors where you need not shoot for the moon. I love to snow ski, but I have no desire to become a great skier. I just love to get to the top of a beautiful mountain and cruise down at an enjoyable pace. This is one area in which I do not shoot for the moon.

Personally, I apply the Shooting for the Moon approach to all of my important priorities and endeavors. You should apply this approach to those areas of your life and to those projects that you consider to be vital or at least important to your happiness and fulfillment or to the happiness and fulfillment of those you love.

A simple rule of thumb is: In areas where you only desire ordinary accomplishments or outcomes, set achievable goals; but in those areas where you want *extraordinary* achievements and outcomes, you should use the Shooting for the Moon approach to Dream Conversion.

SHOOTING FOR THE MOON IS GREAT, *HITTING* THE MOON IS AWESOME!

The real power to "hit" the moon once we shoot for it comes from two forces. The first is our determination to "strive for excellence"; the second is our ability to ignite our third engine (which I call "Steven Spielberg Partnering"). However, before we move on to that engine, we must first focus on our determination to strive for excellence.

I have never met a dream-achiever who settled for mediocrity in his or her pursuit of dreams. To the contrary, every dream-achiever I've ever known has had an overpowering inner drive for achieving excellence. When these people gain a vision for a project, you never have to wonder if the project will be performed or achieved at merely a satisfactory level. They always strive for excellence and nearly always achieve it. Even when they fail, it won't be because they gave it only a halfhearted try. When they fail, they fail *greatly*, and when they succeed, they succeed greatly.

As common as this trait is in dream-achievers, it is equally uncommon in the general population. According to one survey I read several years ago, 85 percent of those surveyed admitted that when they go to work, they do only what is expected and little else. "Just enough to get by" is how one commercial builder described the attitude and jobs of his subcontractors. Although the pervasiveness of this attitude in our society is bad news for our nation, it's great news for you. It means that you can rise to the top 15 percent in almost any line of work or activity, just by doing a little more than is expected. And that means that if you make a commitment to strive for excellence, not only will you pass the 85 percent, you will quickly pass the next 10 percent and move into the top 5 percent in whatever company or endeavor you undertake.

How Can You Truly Strive for Excellence?

This is one of the easiest prescriptions I'll give in this entire book. It's also one of the easiest to follow. There have been entire books written on this subject, and I could probably write one myself. But even if I were to write a three-volume treatise on this subject, everything I would write beyond the simple prescription I'm about to give would add only about 5 percent more in terms of power and effectiveness. In other words, I believe that this simple prescription will give you what you need to achieve at least 95 percent of the level of excellence you are capable of achieving. If you follow this prescription and continue to follow it weekly, monthly, and yearly, you will not only strive for excellence, you will achieve it. In fact, you will learn to achieve it as routinely and as easily as those around you achieve mediocrity. Here's my prescription.

Rx for Excellence

1. Begin to use the Dream Conversion Process in any area or on any project in which you want to strive for excellence and achieve extraordinary outcomes.
2. Add the Shooting for the Moon approach to your Dream Conversion efforts.
3. Add the magic of "Steven Spielberg Partnering" to your Dream Conversion efforts.

If you only do these three things and nothing else, you will reach levels of excellence and achievement that place you into the top one percent of those around you. As you strive for excellence and begin to achieve it, you will experience more passion in your pursuit of your dreams than you have ever felt or experienced before.

Don't Forget, You Will Come Up Short

When you are rightly applying the Shooting for the Moon approach to Dream Conversion, even when you are striving for excellence, you will not have all the mental, physical, and financial resources necessary to reach the moon. You will need to recruit outside resources. This is not something to be feared. As I mentioned, the third booster engine, "Steven Spielberg Partnering," which focuses on this opportunity is the most powerful rocket engine you possess. Without it, no matter how often you shoot for the moon, you will never hit it. You won't even break the bonds of gravity. But if you ignite this third engine, there will be no limit to the dreams you will be able to achieve.

POWER SECRET #8:
Dreaming and Achieving Impossible Dreams

1. REVIEW ALL THE dreams you have defined on your Dream Pages and ask yourself if each dream is simply an achievable dream or does it reflect Shooting for the Moon? Then determine if that dream should be revised to reflect the Shooting for the Moon approach. If so, on the same page, write your revised dream.
2. For each of your revised dreams, check each of your goals, steps, and tasks and see if any need to be revised.
3. Make a revised list of outside resources you need to recruit to achieve your revised dreams.

CHAPTER 12

Engine #3: "Steven Spielberg Partnering"

A MULTIPLYING SKILL THAT ANYONE CAN DEVELOP

REMOVE THE LIMITS OF YOUR LIMITED RESOURCES AND MULTIPLY YOUR POTENTIAL—INFINITELY!

DURING MY 1996 book tour for *A Millionaire's Notebook,* there was one question that kept coming up over and over again: "What is the *single* most important key to success?"

When asked this question, I would quickly say, "There isn't a *single* key but rather a group of keys; a group of strategies and techniques that can be used by anyone to achieve levels of success that are totally impossible to achieve without these keys." But for most reporters, that answer (as accurate as it was) was not good enough. They wanted that *one* secret . . . that one single "magic bullet." Now, even though I truly believe that the best and fastest way to achieve extraordinary success in any area of life is to ignite all *seven* rocket engines, if I were allowed to ignite only *one* in my attempt to reach my dreams, the engine I would choose to ignite is the one I call "Steven Spielberg Partnering," and between you and me, if you lost the rest of this book in a fire and were only able to save this chapter, you would still have a marvelous chance of breaking the bonds of gravity and reaching your most coveted dreams.

I can say this because this engine is not only the most powerful of our seven booster engines, it is the one that was ignited at the beginning of my tenth job, and it became the turning point of my entire life. At the same time, I can honestly say that had I ignited the other six engines but not this one, I would never have achieved the level of success that I have.

Does that mean the other engines aren't very powerful? Not at all! Does it mean that you only need to ignite this engine to achieve your dreams? Of course not. Each of the other six engines are incredibly powerful and deliver over a million pounds of thrust. But *this* engine is located right in the center of the other six, and it delivers more than two million pounds of thrust. It not only puts a lot more power at your disposal, it brings added stability and endurance to everything you do. You see, in addition to providing awesome power, it can also prevent the six anchor chains we discussed earlier from ever exerting their power over you again.

The Magic of Spielberg

To say that I am an admirer of Steven Spielberg is a massive under-statement. We grew up in the same neighborhood, we went to the same school, and we sat next to each other at football games. When I think of what he has achieved in his life I am blown away. He not only raised the level of moviemaking to unparalleled heights, he has forever ensured that the story of the Holocaust will be permanently burned into the minds of the world's youth, both now and for generations to come. Steven is one of the most gifted and imaginative storytellers ever to hit Hollywood. To call his directorial abilities genius is also an understatement. He has entertained us and challenged us like no single moviemaker in history. And yet all his talents combined do not equal the most important skill he has mastered: the skill of effective partnering.

Effective partnering is like a brilliant fiery ten-carat diamond. It has numerous individual facets that each reflect and refract light to pro-duce brilliant colors within that facet. And yet, as wonderful as each facet is by itself, it is the incredible combination of them that magnify the splendor, brilliance, and depth of the diamond as a whole. When I speak of partners, I am not just speaking about legal or technical partners. I am talking about official and *unofficial* partners, as well as mentors, advisers, counselors, financiers, investors, consultants, key employees, and outside experts.

When I talk about effective partnering, I am actually talking about two separate skills. The first is the skill of identifying and recruiting the right people. The second is the skill of effectively utilizing and motivating these people once they've been recruited. Steven Spielberg is a true master at both of these skills, and it's their combination that makes him so masterful in the art of effective partnering.

Important Definitions

I believe that my "working definitions" of partners and effective partnering are so important that they should be reiterated and highlighted.

PARTNERS: Official and unofficial partners; mentors, advisers, counselors, financiers, investors, consultants, key employees, and outside experts.

EFFECTIVE PARTNERING: The combination of two learnable skills:
(1) the skill of identifying and *recruiting* the right partners; and
(2) the skill of effectively *utilizing* and *motivating* the partners.

BAD NEWS, GOOD NEWS

The bad news is that you are not born with these skills, so critical to achieving your loftiest dreams. And they do not come naturally or easily to most people. Consequently, this most powerful seventh engine is never ignited by the vast majority of adults.

The good news is that both of these skills *are* teachable and learnable, and therefore can be effectively utilized by anyone. You *can* ignite this engine in the near future, and when you do, you'll go faster and further toward achieving your dreams than you have ever gone before.

WHY IS THIS ENGINE SO CRITICAL?

This engine is critical to your success because it provides the *only* way for you to overcome the roadblocks created by your lack of know-how and resources.

How would you like an eighty-hour day or a thousand-day year? How would you like instantly to gain those talents and abilities that you've always wanted but never had a prayer of attaining? How would you like to have more money at your disposal than you could ever earn in a lifetime? This one engine can perform all of these "miracles" and more. It is the only way of removing the limits of your limited resources.

As we discovered in Chapters 8 and 9, lack of know-how and lack of resources are obstacles that seem insurmountable to most people. When your lack of know-how and lack of resources stand between you and your dreams, you quickly surrender, turn around, and walk away. You truly believe you don't know what you need to know, or have what you need to have to ignite this engine. And, if you don't ignite this engine, you will forever remain anchored to your launching pads.

As I mentioned in those earlier chapters, dream-makers and dream-achievers never let their lack of know-how or their lack of resources keep them from attempting and achieving their dreams. Instead, because they have learned how to ignite the engine of effective partnering, they genuinely view their shortcomings as opportunities to achieve levels of success they could never have hoped to achieve by themselves.

Another reason why this engine is so critical is that it provides the *only* way we can reach the moon when we shoot for it.

In the last chapter I revealed that Shooting for the Moon was the secret to success that is used by the top one-tenth of one percent of America's most successful adults. If these people had not learned to ignite this engine, they could shoot for the moon all they wanted, but they would never hit it. Without this engine it is impossible to break free of the bonds of gravity. Yet *with* this engine, hitting the moon is not only a possibility, it's a probability!

HOW TO IGNITE THIS ENGINE

Now that you understand why igniting this engine is so critical to achieving your dreams, and the awesome power it provides, it's time to move on to where the rubber meets the road. How can *you* begin to ignite this engine in the most important areas of your life, and how can you keep it burning until you've reached your loftiest dreams? Once again, this isn't an inborn talent, but it is a learnable skill. And while it's not hard to learn, it does take a little time both to learn and to utilize. Still, the time and effort you invest into mastering this skill will be the most profitable investment you'll ever make.

STEP #1: IDENTIFYING THE KINDS OF PARTNERS YOU NEED

The first step in igniting this engine is identifying the kinds of partners, mentors, advisers, counselors, and so on that you need to recruit to convert each dream into reality, especially those in which you are Shooting for the Moon. To do this, you must: (1) have a clear and precise vision of your dream; and (2) have an accurate assessment of your strengths and weaknesses, abilities and inabilities that relate to achieving that dream.

For example, one of my dreams was to become successful in my own business. I am fairly strong in my marketing abilities but terribly weak administratively (in fact I'm totally bankrupt in that department). I am very optimistic and see the upside in almost any opportunity. I get so excited about the upside potential, I rarely notice (much less focus) on the downside. I am good at seeing the big picture and getting a job completed in record time, but I'm terrible at follow-through and the detail work. So if I want to fulfill my dream of building a successful business, I will desperately need a partner who is a great administrator, who is alert to the downside risk in any opportunity, who is great on follow-through and detail work. If you don't have an honest and accurate assessment of your weaknesses, you will not be able to identify the partners you need to recruit to achieve your dream.

If you fully realize the ramifications of this principle, you will no longer have to deny your weaknesses. You will no longer have to hate or fear them. They can become your allies in identifying the people you need to achieve your dream faster and better than would otherwise be possible.

As I've mentioned previously, another one of my dreams is to be a great husband. One of my strengths is that I'm a good learner. My weakness is I'm a man. In other words, I do not have the inborn knowledge, talent, or sensitivity to become the kind of husband my wife needs and deserves. So I desperately need a mentor who can teach, advise, and counsel me while I acquire the talent and sensitivity that I need to become a great husband.

For years, another of my dreams has been to conduct a full symphony orchestra in the performance of the finale of the William Tell Overture. I had grown up watching the "Lone Ranger," and was given a record of the William Tell Overture when I was in the eighth grade. During high school and college, I would put on a set of headphones, crank the volume up, and pretend to conduct this overture over and over again.

In 1994 the opportunity to fulfill this lifelong dream was staring me in the face. I was at a charity event for the Utah Symphony. They were auctioning off the right to conduct the symphony in a live performance of the 1812 Overture. I asked an official if I won the bidding, could I conduct the William Tell Overture instead. He said, "If you win the bidding, I'll make sure you can conduct any piece you want." I was excited and terrified at the same time. If I won, it would be the chance to fulfill my childhood dream. It would also be a chance to make a complete fool of myself in front of eighty professional musicians and thousands of paying ticket holders. The thought of "blowing it" terrified me.

Before I put in my final bid, I asked my friend Robert Henderson (the brilliant associate conductor of the Utah Symphony) if he would help me *before* the rehearsal if I won. When he assured me he would, I gained the confidence to put in my bid. I won! Had Robert not agreed to be a partner and mentor to me prior to the rehearsal and performance, I would have not put in that final bid, and I would have never fulfilled my childhood dream.

As it turned out, I rehearsed the overture once at the symphony's Thursday night rehearsal and then conducted it before a sold-out crowd the following Saturday. The rehearsal and the performance provided the most thrilling six minutes of my forty-eight years. The audience gave us a standing ovation, and as wonderful as that was, it could not compare to the awesome thrill of standing three feet in front that orchestra as it played my favorite piece of music, louder and more spectacularly than I had ever heard it performed through my head-phones. This dream would have never come true had I not identified, recruited, and utilized a "partner" named Robert. Once again, the kinds of partners we need to recruit is dictated by our weaknesses, inabilities, and lack of resources.

Going back to my favorite example of effective partnering, look at the kinds of partners Steven Spielberg has to identify prior to every film he makes. These include a studio to pay for the production, marketing, and distribution of the film; a screenwriter; a casting director, set designers, set builders; a special effects facility; a model-making facility; a cinematographer; a second-unit director; executive producers; production managers; location scouts and location man-agers; stunt coordinators; sound director; a composer; a film editor; and dozens and dozens of other "unofficial" partners.

In the last chapter I focused on a woman whose revised Shooting for the Moon dream became "a marriage where her husband would meet her deepest emotional needs." The kinds of partners she said she would need to recruit to achieve this dream included:

Mentors: 1. A woman who already has a marriage in which her husband meets her deepest emotional needs.
2. An author/counselor who can show her what she needs to do.
3. An author/expert who can help her to communicate her needs and desires in a way that will enable her husband to understand her and want to meet her needs and desires.

Advisers: 1. Friends or relatives who have great marriages.
2. A marriage or family therapist.
3. Husbands of friends or relatives who effectively meet their wives' emotional needs.

Partners: 1. Friends or relatives who have great marriages and have the time to meet with her on a regular basis.

As you can see, she successfully completed the first step of igniting her effective partnering engine.

Step #2: Identifying the Specific Individuals or Companies You Need to Recruit

Once you have identified the kinds of people you need to recruit, the next step is to identify where you go to find them. Steven Spielberg identifies his need for the same kinds of partners on every film. Some of those slots are filled by the same individuals again and again, while others change. For example, he has used John Williams to fill his need for a composer on a number of his biggest films. He shoots for the moon in his selection process, always aiming at the top of the "A" list, and never moving down to the second person on the list until he knows the first choice is truly unavailable.

When I needed to find a director for the contemporary music group I formed in college, I wanted the absolute best choral director in the state of Arizona, Ron Patti. Unfortunately, Ron was already directing five choral groups, employed full-time, raising three children with his wife, Carolyn, and trying to maintain his 4.0 grade point average in his effort to earn his doctorate. Ron didn't even know me, and when I told my group that I wanted him as our director, they told me I was crazy. But he was at the very top of my "A" list, and I didn't even want to try to identify number two until I was turned down by number one. I was a sophomore in college at the time.

Step #3: Recruiting the Individuals You Have Identified as Potential Partners, Mentors, and So On

Now comes what can be the hardest step in the process: recruiting the individuals at the top of your "A" list. Notice that I say it *can* be the hardest step in the process, I don't say that it *is* the hardest. For most people, this is not only the hardest step, it is the impossible step; and it prevents them from ever igniting this most powerful engine in their Saturn V rocket. Yet for most dream-makers, it is not a difficult step at all, and I will show you some very specific techniques to make this step a lot easier a little later in this chapter.

After everyone in my group told me there was no way I could ever recruit Ron Patti, I became very nervous about approaching him. And yet he was the director I wanted. So I created a strategy that started with a phone call. Little did I know that it would become the strategy and technique I would use throughout the rest of my life for recruiting partners and mentors. It has had a phenomenal success rate.

When I placed my call to Ron, he was polite enough to hear me out before telling me of his commitments and of all the demands on his time. He didn't think there was any possible way he could take on another commitment. Then I asked if he could at least meet with us once, give us a few pointers, and rehearse us for just an hour. He obviously felt sorry for us (what could be more pathetic than a contemporary choral group without a director). In a moment of weakness he agreed to give us that one rehearsal. Prior to that, we had been rehearsing two days a week for four weeks. To my amazement, he took us further in the first ten minutes of our rehearsal than we had progressed in the twenty hours we had previously rehearsed. At the end of the first rehearsal, he agreed to meet with us again the following week. To make a long story short, he became our director, and none of our lives has ever been the same. Ron not only became our director, he became one of my mentors and one of my lifelong friends.

SAME OLD HUSBAND . . . BRAND-NEW MARRIAGE

Returning to my friend who wanted a marriage where her deepest needs would be fulfilled, she identified Gary Smalley at the top of her "A" list as the perfect potential mentor for her marriage.

Knowing she couldn't recruit Gary to meet with her personally, she recruited him by reading his books and viewing his tapes. You see, you don't necessarily have to meet with a person for them to be your mentor or partner. Reading Gary's books and viewing his tapes was in some ways even better than meeting with him because she could do them at *her* own pace, taking as much time as she wanted. Through his books and tapes, Gary taught her how to communicate with her husband far more effectively. She learned how to communicate in a way that not only enabled him to understand what she was saying, but more important, actually *feel* what she was feeling.

Sue's husband was so moved by the changes she was making in her efforts to meet his needs that he began viewing Gary's tapes. Today, she rates her marriage as a perfect ten! Her husband not only ceased his constant criticism (which was her original dream), he has learned how to meet her deepest needs and meets them consistently. Her impossible dream came true through the Dream Conversion Process, Shooting for the Moon, and identifying and recruiting the right partners and mentors.

Remember June Morris, my neighbor who started her own airline? I was talking with her son, Rick, and he told me that the single greatest key to his mom's success was her ability to recruit the right partners and key employees. He said she was so generous in her giving of stock options to key people that others thought she was giving away far more than was necessary. But you tell me who was right and who was wrong—her critics, who still have to work for a living, or June, who sold her profitable new airline for $130 million?

THE MULTIMILLION-DOLLAR LUNCH

After Simon & Schuster published *A Millionaire's Notebook* in January 1996, I began receiving letters from people asking me to be their mentor and for my company to become their partner. I received nearly a thousand such letters in less than a year. Although I was truly touched by each letter I received, there was only one that followed the strategy and techniques I gave in the book for recruiting a mentor. Without realizing that he was using my own techniques on me, I found myself instantly wanting to respond to this letter and meet its author.

I called him the same day I received his letter, and we scheduled a lunch. I met with him and his partner and they asked my advice regarding a buyout offer they would soon be receiving from a major bank. I told them how I would respond to the bank's offer no matter how good it appeared to be. They followed my advice, and as a result were offered millions of dollars more in a second offer from the same bank.

I was so impressed with these two young men that months later we set up our own side business that I believe will ultimately generate a significant income for each of us. All of this grew out of their using the strategies and techniques I had listed in my first book; these tips appear at the end of this chapter.

AVOIDING THE WRONG PARTNERS IS AS IMPORTANT AS RECRUITING THE RIGHT ONES

I do a fair amount of public speaking, and I nearly always talk about the importance of effective partnering. At almost every event at least one member of the audience approaches me afterward and tells me a horror story about a partnership in which he or she was involved. Inevitably, they were devastated by the actions or inactions of the partners. One of my closest friends in life nearly lost his securities license because of the illegal acts of his partner. The only thing that saved him was that a board member had tape recorded a board meeting that proved my friend had no knowledge of his partner's activities.

Just as nothing can accelerate your success better and faster than an effective partnership with the right people, nothing can cause a faster and more devastating failure than a partnership with the wrong people. That is why it is critical that you follow the strategies and techniques at the end of this chapter as a guide to identifying and recruiting your partners. As you'll see, one of the seven strategies is to look at the character and integrity of your would-be partner. Even though it's number four on the list, it is definitely the most important. If your partner's ethics and morals aren't extremely high, sooner or later there is a good probability he or she will either betray or mislead you, someone else in your company, or your customer.

This morning I received a call from one of my best friends in grade school and high school. His name is Ron Carter, and we hadn't talked in years. He had picked up my first book and was reading a chapter on partnering and decided to give me a call. He told me a horror story of how his former partner had cheated their business out of $250,000, causing the business to fail and Ron to lose everything. He told me that in spite of that failure, he still agreed with me that partnering was critical to achieving extraordinary success, and that finding the right partner and avoiding the wrong ones were equally critical. He said that if only he had thoroughly checked out his former partner's character and ethics, he would have had a great business today and a lot more money in his bank account.

I asked Ron why he hadn't looked into the man's character before he joined up with him, and he replied that he was so enamored of the man and his abilities that he just never bothered to check out his character. I've heard this story at least a hundred times since I wrote *A Millionaire's Notebook*. When we identify a potential partner who has the strengths, talents, or abilities that we lack, or that we admire or envy, we either fail to notice or choose to ignore any character flaws that may appear. We downplay, or even defend, those flaws because we desperately want to gain the benefits of that person's talents and strengths. Every horror story I've heard about bad partners and partnerships could have been avoided had the person simply investigated a would-be partner's character. But character isn't the only issue that needs to be looked into.

You need to know if the person is a theorist or a doer. The world is full of idea people and armchair generals. They may be good at maintaining the status quo, but they are the last people on earth that I would want to be partners with. It is critical that your would-be partner be a doer and desirous of working his butt off to achieve your vision. And for that to happen, you need to know that he has genuinely caught your vision and is totally committed to it. I have had a lot of entrepreneurs complain to me that they are working sixty or eighty hours a week while their partner comes and goes at his leisure. Once again, I deal with all of these issues at the end of this chapter.

Step #4: Effectively Motivating and Utilizing the Official and Unofficial Partners You Recruit

This is the step that people often pay the least amount of attention to and consequently screw up more than any other step in the process. And when this step isn't performed correctly, it can, by itself, totally invalidate partnering. When used correctly, it can empower a partnering effort like nothing else.

The Fifty-Million-Dollar Race

Imagine that you have been given the opportunity to take part in a boat race. The winner of that race will win $50 million. All of the other contestants have conventional boats with outboard engines ranging from 50 to 80 horsepower. On the other hand, you have been given a racing boat that has an inboard 400-horsepower turbo-charged engine. You have been equipped to not only win the race but to finish three or four times as fast as your nearest competitor. You're already beginning to envision all the things you are going to do with your new fortune.

Now imagine that just before the race starts you notice that there is no key in the ignition. You hear the other boats begin to "rev" their puny engines, and you see the race master wave the starting flag. All of the other boaters put the pedal to the metal, and even though they don't have near the potential power or speed that you have, they leave you behind, dead in the water. You think about that $50 million first prize and you realize that you could win it hands down . . . if you could only start your engine. As you are desperately looking for the key, you may be yelling and cursing, even threatening your boat and any other crew members on board, but you are *still* dead in the water. Finally you realize you are not going to find the key and get the engine started, so you put paddles into the hands of all your crew and you all start paddling as fast as you can.

Now as ridiculous as this story is, it illustrates reality for many adults and countless corporations. Many successfully identify and recruit the right partners, key employees, and so on. But they never learn how to effectively utilize and motivate their partners. They never find the key. So all the potential power that could be generated remains dormant and untapped. How tragic and what a waste! You could literally assemble the strongest, most talented group of people in America, make them your partners, and still have total failure.

On the other hand, if you can find the key to effectively utilizing and motivating those with whom you partner, you can accomplish things that will dwarf the achievements of those who have far more talent and infinitely greater ability. The effective utilization of talent, commitment, and motivation is 99 percent of the battle. If you find this hard to believe, how do you think the rag-tag rebels of Afghanistan were able to frustrate and defeat the vastly superior Russian army and air force? How could Henry Ford begin a company in his garage that would soon out-produce multimillion-dollar companies that had been in business for decades? How could our little company (American Telecast) defeat in the marketplace companies a hundred times our size when we didn't have a single MBA, and virtually no significant experience among six of the seven original partners? And yet, for several years, we were more productive (by Forbes's definition of productivity) than any public corporation in America. The answer to all these questions is found in three words: utilization, commitment, and motivation.

GREAT PARTNERS + INEFFECTIVE UTILIZATION = UNREALIZED POTENTIAL AND ULTIMATE FAILURE

A friend of mine has a reasonably successful business. She has several incredibly talented partners and key employees. And yet she is paddling her racing boat toward the finish line rather than using its 400-horsepower engine. Her problem is that she is so fearful of failing that she feels she must control or be a part of every aspect and every decision in every department of her company, no matter how big or small that decision may be, and regardless of the talents and abilities of the people who run those departments. This is not only a waste of her time and energy, it discourages her partners. If she would learn to let go and truly delegate and utilize each of their strengths, she would not only begin to enjoy her life a lot more, her company would begin to perform like never before. It would mean the difference between paddling the boat from start to finish versus igniting the 400-horsepower engine and putting the pedal to the metal.

Another friend of mine owns a huge company with thousands of employees. He is a man who is incredibly loving, and has motivated his employees and management with love ever since he started his company in his home years ago. This has not only been a critical key in his company's phenomenal success, it has resulted in his employees' willingness to do almost anything to show their love and commitment to him. Unfortunately, there is one man who is in a critical position in this company who uses fear to control and motivate his subordinates rather than love. Consequently, dozens of the company's most important employees have become demoralized and it's starting to show in their performance.

In my first eight jobs, I achieved almost no significant success . . . and made no significant contribution to the success of the companies for which I worked. On my ninth job, my mentor and I created a marketing campaign that doubled the company's annual sales—from

$30 to $60 million. On my tenth job, I was able to create campaigns that generated over $1 billion in sales and produced more than $100 million in profits for my six partners and me. What was the difference between the first eight jobs and the ninth and tenth? In job number nine I found a mentor, and for the first time in my life my business talents were effectively utilized.

In job number ten, my strengths and talents were even more effectively utilized, and my mentor and boss motivated me and my partners with a degree of love that I had never before received in a business environment. Bob Marsh, that mentor and boss, was better at motivating and effectively utilizing the talents and abilities of others than anyone I have ever known.

THE ABSOLUTE BEST WAY TO MOTIVATE AND UTILIZE THE PARTNERS YOU RECRUIT

The single greatest motivating force in life is love. Whether you are the one who is giving it or the one who is receiving it, when love is present, it raises your level of performance unlike any other force or factor in life. And yet, when it comes to partnering, whether in one's professional or personal life, we rarely use love as a means of motivating those we are partnering. Man's natural tendency is to use manipulative tactics or, more often than not, fear. "If you can't do it the way I want it done, I'll find someone who can" and "You better do this or *else*" are typical statements that reflect tactics of fear. Though fear is an incredibly powerful motivating force, it is also a highly demoralizing and destructive one. It can be used to get people to do what you want them to do *now*, but in the long term, they will never give you a fraction of the creativity or performance of which they are capable. When a person is motivated by fear, they only work from their will, *never* from their heart! And it is only performance from the heart that rises above all expectations and makes unimaginable breakthroughs and contributions.

Think about it. Think about the times a boss, a teacher, or a parent threatened you. If they said or implied that you better do this or else you would face the consequences, what would you do? You probably did what they demanded and nothing more. You obeyed and performed to the letter but *not* in the spirit. Think back to your teenage years. If your parent said, "Clean up your room, or else you're grounded," you probably cleaned your room just well enough to avoid being grounded. I doubt that you would respond to such a threat by thoroughly cleaning your room, your sister's room, doing the dishes, and mowing the lawn.

Now imagine you are at home and you get a call from your girl-friend. You are head over heels in love. This person is all you can think about. Imagine if she called you and said, "Sweetie, I want to surprise my mom and dad and have the house spotless, the dishes done, and the lawn mowed by the time they get home tonight, and there's no way I can get it done by myself. Could you come over and help me?"

You would probably drop everything, rush over to her house, and become the White Tornado. You would not only get everything done, you would perform every task with enthusiasm and a level of excellence your own parents had never seen.

And yet, as true as all of this is, most parents, husbands and wives, teachers, employers, supervisors, managers, vice presidents, and CEOs continue to use fear as the primary motivator. Their people do what they are asked to do and little more, and oftentimes, they will do it poorly.

American Telecast became one of America's most productive companies because Bob Marsh loved his partners and employees and treated them with tremendous honor and respect. I have seen other entrepreneurs who have used love in this same way, and their success, like ours, has been near miraculous.

How Can You Use Love to Motivate People?

There is probably more confusion and misunderstanding about love than there is about any other subject ever discussed or written about. The first two books I wrote I coauthored with Dr. Gary Smalley back in 1979. In my opinion, Gary is America's number-one expert in the area of love, relationships, and marriage. And though I am far from an expert on the subject, after writing those books with Gary and producing his eighteen-tape video series, "Hidden Keys to Loving Relationships," I am, at the very least, one of his greatest admirers and a well-versed student.

When people think about love they usually think of romance or the romantic feelings that go with falling or being "in love." Thousands of books and millions of pages have been written about that facet of love, but this is *not* the facet I'm talking about now. I'm talking about what Gary calls genuine or committed love. This kind of love is based upon a decision to honor and value people, their feelings, their opinions, their time, their concerns, and their commitments. In fact, Gary's original seminar was entitled "Love Is a Decision." Gary and I share the same belief that the first rule of love, the very foundation upon which genuine love is built, is the concept of honor.

One of the best ways to illustrate what I call the first rule of love is an event that took place when we first filmed Gary's seminar back in 1988. For those of you who read *A Millionaire's Notebook,* I apologize for repeating this story, but it is the best way I can think of to accurately illustrate what I want to say.

We filmed Gary's first video in front of a live audience of about eight hundred men and women in Phoenix, Arizona. A few minutes into the first session, Gary walked over to a table and picked up an old, beaten-up violin. Its bridge was broken and dangling by its strings. Holding up the violin for all to see, Gary asked the audience how much they thought it was worth, and everyone laughed. Like everyone else in the audience, I figured $10 or $20 at the most. Gary then said, let me read you something that's written just inside it. As he read the inscription, everyone in the audience gasped. He read: "1723, Antonin Stradivarius." As Gary passed it around to the people in the first row, they handled it gently, with respect.

Now here is the amazing thing. Before Gary read the inscription, eight hundred people laughed at what looked like a worthless piece of junk. That's how they saw it and that's how they reacted to it. And yet only moments later, that same audience viewed that broken violin as an object of tremendous value. Had anything changed? Not at all. It was still the same old broken violin. Before Gary read the inscription, I'm sure no one in the audience would have given $50 for it. But afterward, there were probably some in that crowd who would have gladly—and wisely—traded their entire bank account to own that violin. Same piece of wood, same condition, but eight hundred people made a *decision* to honor and value it. They no longer looked at it as a piece of junk, rather they chose to honor it as a rare treasure.

You can choose to honor and admire anyone or anything you want. Regardless of outward appearances, when you look closely enough, you can find attributes in nearly anyone that are worthy of praise and honor. The only catch is that you have to *choose* to honor that person. Deciding to honor and value someone, who they are and what they do, is the foundation of genuine love. *This* is the kind of love I am referring to when I talk about using love to motivate others.

MICHAEL LANDON PROVED THAT LOVE IS THE GREATEST MOTIVATOR, EVEN IN HOLLYWOOD

One of the reasons I had such a deep admiration for Michael Landon was the way he treated his cast and crew. Like my mentor Bob Marsh, Mike used love to motivate all who worked for him. For three decades, he was one of the biggest names in Hollywood and certainly one of the most successful television stars in the history of television. And yet he treated everyone with whom he worked as if they were just as important as he was. Yes, he was their boss, but he was also their mentor, their silent partner, their counselor, and their true friend. He treated them as if they were valued members of his family. He valued them as individuals and he honored their contributions to his show. The result? His crews were among the most productive in television history. *Highway to Heaven* was the only one-hour dramatic series on television where each weekly episode was actually produced for *less* money than the network allocated for its production.

Coming in under budget every week produced a sizable profit by the end of the year for Mike's production company. He could have justifiably taken all of that money home—after all, it was his company and his show. He not only starred in it, he created the stories and often wrote the scripts and directed the episodes. But taking all of the profit for himself wasn't Mike's style. Instead, right before the crew wrapped their last show before the Christmas break, two eighteen-wheelers rolled up to the set, filled with twenty-six-inch Sony television sets that he had purchased for the entire crew—all 150 of them. In addition to the sets, he paid out almost all of the remaining profits for the year as bonuses to his employees.

How hard do you think Mike's people worked for him? How

motivated and committed do you think they were to him, and to all of his goals for the show? I can tell you from experience, people who worked with Michael Landon gladly gave 110 percent!

Using "love" as a motivating force in the lives of our partners, family, and others means treating them the way we want to be treated. It means taking time to listen to their ideas, learning what their dreams and goals are, and helping them to convert their dreams into reality. In the businessplace, it means sharing a significant part of your profits with those who make significant contributions. It means giving them a chance to come up to the plate and swing at the ball, giving them the freedom to strikeout without criticism or recriminations. It means becoming a coach and a fan. It means *deciding* to do all of these things even when you don't feel like it. When you learn to motivate others with love, honoring and valuing them, you will see the levels of performance and achievement skyrocket beyond anything you would have ever seen accomplished using any other kind of motivation.

"SHOW ME THE MONEY": NOTHING MOTIVATES IN BUSINESS LIKE A PIECE OF THE PIE

No one who saw the movie *Jerry Maguire* can ever forget the line "Show me the money." I once worked for a man who was quick to pat everyone in the company on the back and tell them how much he loved them. And yet he kept every dime of profit to himself. In fact, he was known for underpaying his employees. I went to work for him in March 1975 (my seventh job) for a starting salary that was below what I wanted on the promise that he would give me a raise July 1. Between March and July, I created a catalog and a mailing for his company that significantly raised his sales volume. On July 1, I walked into his office and reminded him about the raise. He got a blank look on his face, having completely forgotten about the promise he had made. "I really can't get into that right now, let's talk about it tomorrow," he said. The next day came, and he fired me. His company went out of business just a few years later.

On the other hand, when Bob Marsh asked me to join his company and start a direct-response subsidiary, he not only offered me a higher salary than I was currently making, he offered me a huge piece of the new company. Like my former boss, Bob also would put his arm around me and tell me how much he appreciated me, but unlike any other boss I had ever worked for, he proved it—and he proved it with money. Yes, love is the single most powerful motivating force in any arena, personal or business. But when it comes to business, *money,* or the potential to make it, is a very close second. And when money is combined with love, the motivation is remarkable. June Morris, Bob Marsh, Michael Landon, and Steven Spielberg and their respective stories are proof that love and money are the most effective motivating forces a businessman can use.

EVERYONE NEEDS A MENTOR—EVERYONE!

For me to discuss the power of effective partnering without focusing on the awesome power of mentors would be a gross neglect of truth and duty. I've always believed that failures are the second greatest teachers in life; mentors are the first! Every person I've ever met, known, or read about who achieved his or her dreams in any area of life had at least one mentor in that particular area. George Lucas had Francis Ford Coppola; Steven Spielberg had Sid Shineberg; and I have Bob Marsh as my mentor in business and Gary Smalley as my mentor in relationships and marriage. Lee Iacocca told me that he attributed his success to two mentors he had when he was first starting out as an engineer at Ford. Even Henry Ford credited one of his mentors for his success, his former boss, Thomas Edison.

IN WHICH AREAS OF YOUR LIFE DO YOU NEED A MENTOR?

As I stated in Chapter 9, you need a mentor in *any* area in which you want to achieve your dreams—especially those where you are shooting for the moon. Mentors will not only enable you to reach the moon when you shoot for it, they will help you reach it far more quickly than you would ever be able to on your own.

HOW TO FIND THE RIGHT MENTORS AND AVOID THE WRONG ONES

Unfortunately, you can't drive to your nearest shopping center and find a store called "Mentors Are Us." Finding the right mentor for any given dream or project takes a little time and effort. It can be as simple as going to your nearest bookstore or library and finding a book written by an expert who has already achieved success in the area in which you are seeking help. Or, finding a mentor can be as involved as identifying and recruiting someone with whom you can interact on a regular basis. You may choose to start your search in your own company or among people you currently know, but you don't have to limit your search to them.

For example, if you sell computers for IBM, your search for a mentor might begin by looking for the most successful salesman currently working at IBM. If you don't find what you're looking for, you would be wise to seek out the most successful IBM salesmen who have retired. You can just as easily look outside IBM to other successful computer salesmen or retired computer salesmen. Or you can choose someone who's been incredibly successful selling something other than computers. And then there are sales experts who now write and teach seminars for a living. You can study their books or attend their seminars. Even though I am only able to talk with Zig Ziglar occasionally, I consider him a great mentor. His books and tapes have significantly changed the way I look at life and the way I relate to others.

Now I should warn you that it is just as easy to recruit the wrong mentor as it is to recruit the right one.

A few years after my company began marketing Gary Smalley's video series on relationships, the airwaves became full of so-called relationship experts touting their books and videos. My friend Sue could have easily decided to recruit one of these people to be her mentor by simply ordering their books or tapes. Had she done this and followed their advice, there's a pretty good chance her marriage might have gone in a completely different direction. You see, two of these so-called experts received their degrees from a nonaccredited "diploma mill." One from which you could buy a Ph.D. for a few thousand dollars. One expert was currently in her fifth marriage—one of her failed marriages had even been with one of the other experts who was selling his books and tapes. In fact, his book on relationships has become an all-time best-seller. I don't know about you, but the last person I want to mentor me in my relational skills is someone who hasn't been able to succeed in his or her own relationships. These people tend to teach what they *think* will work rather than what they have personally experienced and proven to work.

All of this is to say, that when you are seeking a mentor or an adviser of any kind, find the answers to the following four questions.

1. *What degree of success have they* personally *achieved in their area of expertise?* I would never recruit a mentor for my marriage who had failed in a marriage, and I would never recruit a mentor in business who has never succeeded in business.
2. *How legitimate are their credentials?* People can buy degrees today in just about any field they want. I would rather be mentored by a person with no credentials than one with bogus credentials. My mentor in business didn't have an MBA. In fact, he never attended college. But he was a marketing and entrepreneurial genius.
3. *Are they a man or woman of integrity?* This may be a little harder to check out, but it's worth it if you can. Discover all you can about their reputation. Do they practice what they preach?
4. *Does their personal experience reflect the degree of success you are dreaming of achieving?* Only recruit mentors who are living examples of what you want to achieve.

On pages 159–160 are my Strategies and Tips for Identifying and Recruiting Mentors. If you follow these, you will find it much easier to recruit mentors who will make an incredible difference in your ability to achieve your dreams. On the next page you will find my Strategies and Tips for Identifying and Recruiting the Right Partners.

Steven Spielberg Partnering is the most powerful rocket engine you possess, and igniting this engine will enable you to achieve more of your dreams than any other engine. While effective partnering will give you the power to reach the moon, the *next* engine we're going to look at will make every mile of your "ride" a lot more fun and fulfilling.

STRATEGIES AND TIPS: IDENTIFYING AND RECRUITING THE RIGHT PARTNERS

1. Assess your own strengths and weaknesses. What you *don't* need is a partner who is a carbon copy of yourself.
2. Identify the talents, abilities, and strengths that you need in a partner to compensate for the areas of your weaknesses, inabilities, and lack of interest.
3. Look for a person who has the same vision as you for your business venture or personal dream. Your partner not only needs to see it, he needs to be overwhelmed by it.
4. Look at the character and integrity of your would-be partner. This is a lot harder to evaluate than his talents, but it's far more important. If his ethics and morals aren't extremely high, sooner or later there's a pretty good chance he'll betray you, someone else in your company, or your customer.
5. Look for a partner who is willing to be totally committed to your vision to achieve success. If you are totally committed and he isn't, I can promise you that the partnership won't last long. Look at how he has performed in other situations where he has been committed. Are his commitments short-lived or faithful until the end.
6. Is your would-be partner a positive or negative person? Negative people tend to be very poor partners. A partner doesn't have to be as positive or as optimistic as you, but if he is quick to tear down others or find the negative in situations, he's likely to jump ship when the going gets tough or, worse, steer the ship in the wrong direction.
7. Look at your would-be partner's natural drive and gifts rather than his résumé. Is he a theorist or a doer? How do you know? It's simple: Look at what he has personally done, not what he has had other people do.

STRATEGIES AND TIPS: IDENTIFYING AND RECRUITING MENTORS

1. *Determine the specific dream or area of your life for which you want a mentor.* Do you need a mentor to help you in relationships, to help you in your profession in general, or to help you in a particular area of your job, career, or profession, such as managerial skills or marketing skills and so forth. (I've had two important mentors in the areas of relationships, and one key mentor in business.)

2. *Create a list of potential mentors for each dream or area you've decided on.* Using your prioritized list of dreams, and starting with your most important dream, make a list of the people you respect most who might be able to give you insight, wisdom, and advice for each dream. List the names in order of preference. In other words, the person at the top of each list should be the person you would choose if you could pick anyone in the whole world. Even if you don't think there's a prayer of this person giving you a minute of his time, he should be at the top of your list.

3. *Starting with the mentors at the top of your list and, working down, note the status of your current relationship with each one* (boss, friend, acquaintance, friend of a friend, total stranger, etc.).

4. *Write down everything you know about that person through either your personal experience, or through second- or thirdhand knowledge.*

5. *Research everything you can about your potential mentors.* What are their likes, dislikes, passions? How do they spend their time on and off the job, what motivates them, and so forth.

6. *If they're mere acquaintances or strangers to you, do you know anyone they know?* If you do, begin to find out all you can from that person and consider using him or her as a reference when you make your initial contact with a potential mentor.

7. *Prepare to contact a potential mentor on the phone or in writing with a brief proposal or request.* Whether you plan to make your contact in person, on the phone, or in a letter, you need to prepare your proposal or request well before you do anything else. If you

are contacting someone who knows your reference but doesn't know you, your reference should be stated in your opening sentence. Your next sentence should touch on the quality or qualities that you so admire about this person. You should then briefly explain why those qualities are so important to you and how you want to gain this person's insight and wisdom in making those qualities a part of your life. Finally, ask if the person could spare a brief amount of time each week or month (a lunch, a breakfast, a coffee break, a round of golf) in which you could ask questions that might help you grow in this particular area.

8. *Make the contact.* Nothing beats a personal appointment. Depending upon your potential mentor, this strategy may not be practical. If you can't make an appointment to see him or her, the next best thing is a phone call. Only use a letter when you have failed to set up a meeting or make the contact by phone. Regardless of how you make your contact, make it brief and to the point. Any mentor worth his salt (unless he's retired) already has a very busy schedule, and if he thinks future contacts with you are going to take too much of his time, he will either turn your proposal down outright, or simply avoid you like the plague.

9. *Follow up.* After you've made your first contact, follow up with a brief note of appreciation, commenting on something specific that he or she said or did.

10. *Go to the next person on the list.* If your first choice turns you down, be sure to find out why. Then go through this same procedure with the next person on your list.

POWER SECRET #9:
Recruiting the Partners and Mentors of Your Dreams

1. FOR EACH OF the dreams that you have defined in your Dream Conversion Journal, identify the specific "kinds" of partners or mentors you should try to recruit that would enable you to more quickly and effectively achieve the dream and reach the moon. Begin with your most important dreams. (Before beginning, review Strategies and Tips: Identifying and Recruiting the Right Partners and Strategies and Tips: Identifying and Recruiting Mentors. Review the strengths and weaknesses that you listed in your notebook at the end of Chapter 4. Also review the four personality types in Chapter 8.)

2. For each kind of partner or mentor that you have identified, on each Dream Page, make a list of specific individuals who fit your qualifications for each kind of partner or mentor you want to recruit.

3. In your notebook, using the methods outlined in Strategies and Tips: Identifying and Recruiting the Right Partners and Strategies and Tips: Identifying and Recruiting Mentors, lay out your plan for recruiting the partners and mentors you need.

4. How do you currently motivate your peers, your loved ones, and those under your authority? Do you usually motivate with fear or with love? In your notebook, write down some of the people you want to motivate, and write down any ideas you can think of on how you can begin to motivate those people with love.

CHAPTER 13

Engine #4: "Helen Keller Positiveness"

SPEEDING UP YOUR HAPPINESS AND SUCCESS!

**TAKE CONTROL OF THE FACTOR THAT DETERMINES YOUR HAP-
PINESS AND IMPACTS THE LIVES OF EVERYONE YOU MEET.**

*"They took away what should have been my eyes, but I remem-
bered Milton's Paradise. They took away what should have been
my ears, Beethoven came and wiped away my tears. They took
away what should have been my tongue, but I had talked to God
when I was young. He would not let them take away my soul—
possessing that, I still possess the whole."*

—HELEN KELLER

I CAN'T THINK of too many circumstances that would be worse than
being a young child who couldn't see, hear, or communicate. I can't
imagine growing up without being able to see the faces of my mother
and father or hear their "I love you's" each night before I went to bed. I
can't imagine wanting to express how I was feeling and yet not being
able to get any words out. And yet that was the world in which seven-
year-old Helen Keller grew up. It was only through the incredible love,
commitment, and persistence of Anne Sullivan that Helen's dark,
silent world was gradually brought into the "light." Though she never
regained her sight or hearing she did learn to communicate, and
through her spoken and written words, she has inspired millions.
Living in a world surrounded by people who could see all the beauty

she could never gaze upon, who could hear all the wonderous sounds she could never listen to, she had every right and reason to become bitter and resentful. And yet, as demonstrated in the quote at this chapter's opening, she harbored no bitterness or resentment. To the contrary, she was perhaps one of the most fulfilled and positive people in the twentieth century.

Although you will not find the word "positiveness" in a dictionary, it is the word that best describes this fourth giant engine so critical to successfully completing your journey to your dreams. While you may be able to reach your dreams without this engine, if you fail to ignite it there will be little joy and fulfillment along the way.

Positiveness, has two component parts: (1) positive attitudes and (2) fulfilling relationships. Now, the great news is that you can take charge to improve and maximize both of these areas. Yet the converse is also true. You can abdicate your responsibility in these areas by letting other people and circumstances control your attitude and relationships. You can do just enough to get by in any endeavor or situation, and you can wait for others to take the initiative to make your relationships better. Unfortunately, it is always easier to be reactive than proactive.

Picture yourself walking along a level trail on the side of a mountain. You come to a place where there is a sheer wall of rock directly in front of you. The trail, however, forks, enabling you to go around the wall. The path to your left goes uphill at a steep incline, all the way to the top of the mountain. The path to your right goes downhill at a very easy incline all the way to the bottom of the mountain. Taking the uphill path requires a lot more time, effort, and commitment, while taking the downhill path requires very little time and almost no effort. Still, the uphill path takes you to the top of the mountain and whatever lies beyond. And you've been told that the other side of the mountain contains a lush paradise full of beautiful lakes and rich green meadows. So, there you are, standing at the fork in the road thinking about the effort required, not knowing if you'll have the endurance to reach the top, and having never experienced the other side of the mountain, you really don't know the fulfillment and joy that await you. Taking responsibility for your attitudes, initiating better relationships, and striving for excellence is an uphill climb, while abdicating responsibility is taking the downhill path.

There's really no in-between. You either take charge and be proactive in your attitudes and relationships or you don't. Unfortunately, your natural inclination will always attract you to the easy, downhill path. Your natural tendency will be to do as little as possible to achieve a minimally acceptable outcome or level of comfort. Today, most people fail to rise above their natural inclinations. They only do what comes naturally. Those people may be dreamers, but unless they change their habits and become proactive, they will never be dream-achievers.

So, the bad news is that your natural inclination is to take the downhill path and just get by. But the good news is that you don't *have* to be controlled and directed by the gravitylike pull of your natural inclinations. You can *choose* to take the uphill path. You can *choose* to take responsibility and become proactive in all the areas that make up this positiveness engine. And no matter how bad your circumstances may be right now, it's never too late to make that choice.

"Go Ahead, Make Your Day!"

Taking Control of Your Attitudes

Perhaps the most memorable line ever delivered by Clint Eastwood came in one of his Dirty Harry movies. With his gun aimed at a criminal who was holding a hostage at gunpoint, Clint delivered his line as only he could: "Go ahead, make my day!" Well, I hope one of the most memorable lines in this book will be a slight revision of Clint's famous line: "Go ahead, make *your* day!" This statement embodies a powerful truth that can radically change your life. It says the ultimate outcome of your day is not dependent upon anyone or anything else. You don't have to let your circumstances, your environment, or other people ruin your day or even a portion of it.

Mother Teresa spent her days in the most depressing circumstances imaginable. Day in and day out, minute by minute, hour by hour, she lived among the impoverished dying. The sights and smells of disease and death filled her senses every waking moment. Though she ministered comfort to the dying, she forever faced her own insufficiencies, since she didn't have the ability to relieve them from their physical pain and agony or deliver them from the grip of death. And yet her life was filled with neither depression nor despair. You see, she knew that her mental and emotional attitudes did not have to be determined or controlled by circumstances around her or by what happened to her.

DO YOU RESPOND OR REACT?

The Critical Choice

Zig Ziglar draws the insightful distinction between responding and reacting to circumstances. He points out that when a doctor puts you on a new medication and you come back to his office a few days later, the doctor makes one of two pronouncements. After he checks you out, he either smiles and says, "Good news, you're body is *responding* to the medication," or he frowns and says, "This is not good, your body is *reacting* to the medication." You can react to negative circumstances, or you can respond to them. Reacting means relinquishing control of your attitude and emotions to the circumstances, while responding means taking responsibility to take control of your attitude and corresponding behavior. When you react, nearly all of the outcomes to you and others are negative. When you respond, the outcomes are far more positive.

A few weeks ago I was scheduled to catch an 8:30 A.M. flight from Salt Lake City, Utah, to Atlanta, Georgia. I was scheduled to direct a film crew in Atlanta in the early evening and then to fly on to Orlando, Florida, to direct another filming later that night. I boarded the plane a few minutes past 8:00 A.M. We were delayed thirty minutes because the plane needed to be deiced. I didn't react to the delay because I was grateful that the captain was taking no risks with my life. We then taxied onto the runway. As the captain revved up his engines he noticed one engine wasn't acting quite right. He announced that he was going to taxi to the maintenance hangar and have it checked out. That added a delay of about an hour and a half. I looked at my watch and realized that I could still make the Atlanta filming, but it was going to be close. I *chose* not to get upset and focused on the captain's caution, and once again felt grateful rather than resentful. Maintenance checked it out, and said everything was okay and we could proceed.

We taxied back out to the runway, and the captain revved his engines once more as he prepared to take off. Once again, he felt a drop in power and didn't like it. This time, we taxied back to the gate to get a second opinion from maintenance. At the gate, we remained on the plane for another hour. This time, maintenance discovered a real problem. They weren't sure how long it would take to repair it, so once again they asked us to remain on the plane. Was I starting to get angry? I was going to miss the filming in Atlanta altogether, but how could I be angry? Once again, I focused my attention on the captain's caution. "I'll take a delay over a crash any day," I thought. I asked if I could turn on my laptop computer and was given permission. I was able to write an entire chapter for this book in the time we remained on the plane. Finally, at 11:30, we were told the flight was going to be delayed until three o'clock. A lot of passengers got very upset. Not only had their morning been "ruined," now their "reacting" was going to ruin the rest of their day.

Once again, I faced a choice. Do I react or do I respond. I went to the ticket counter, changed my ticket to fly direct to Orlando at 2:30. I then found a chair, pulled out my laptop, and got another three hours of writing in before the flight. It turned out to be a great day for me. It was also a good day for my producer, who directed the filming in Atlanta. Had I not heard Zig talk about responding to circumstances instead of reacting to them, I would have been angry and my anger would have blocked my ability to think and to write. My great day would have turned into a bad one.

I relate this story to show how the power to take control of our attitude can come from simply changing our focus. Had I allowed my focus to remain fixed on how the flight delay was going to affect my filming, I would have wasted hours being angry and worrying about circumstances that I could not change. But by shifting my focus to the more important priorities (namely survival), I felt grateful to the captain rather than resentful toward the airline. And by shifting my focus from my "missed-opportunity to direct" to my "current opportunity to write," I was able to be a lot more productive and stay on schedule for the completion of this book. This was one time when I controlled my attitude by refocusing my attention. There have been many other times when I was not as successful.

For example, when my computer crashed the other day, I reacted for more than an hour before I finally realized what I was doing. I then began to "respond" to the circumstances and changed my focus from lamenting over the problem to taking specific actions to positively resolve the problem. I then refocused my attention to other priorities I was facing that day. As a result, the remaining hours of my day were very productive ones.

The choice between "responding" and "reacting" obviously isn't a "once-in-a-lifetime" decision, and from that point on we become positive people. It's not even a once-a-week decision. It's a choice you make several times a day. In the case of my computer crashing, I faced that choice twice in a single hour. But the good news is that each time you choose to respond to a circumstance rather than react, it becomes that much easier to *respond* to the next circumstance you face.

By the way, taking control of your attitudes and responding rather than reacting doesn't mean becoming artificial. It doesn't mean you don't cry when you're hurting or that you put on a happy face when you're dying inside. My wife would tell you that I wear my emotions on my sleeve. A single thought about my dear father who passed away in 1995 will bring an instant lump to my throat and, often, tears to my eyes. I have always been more emotional then most men I know. When I talk about taking control of your attitudes, I am simply talking about taking responsibility for how you view and respond to life in general and your circumstances in particular—taking the initiative rather than being complacent, and responding to circumstances rather than reacting to them.

ARE YOU A POSITIVE PERSON OR A NEGATIVE PERSON?

Whether you are a negative or positive person depends on two things. One is the frequency with which you respond to circumstances or react to them. The other is where you choose to focus your attention. Do you focus on all the benefits and blessings that fill your life and on the opportunities you have to help others, or do you focus on your deficiencies, inabilities, and hardships?

My wife is one of the most positive people I've ever known. Before we met, the person who was setting up our blind date described her in detail. The very first thing she said about her was, "Shannon is such a positive person who, if she were given a glass of water that was three-fourths empty, instead of complaining about how empty it was, she would be happy and grateful for the water that remained." Boy, was she right. Anyone who knows Shannon will tell you that when she walks into a room the whole room lights up. For my readers that are old enough to remember Doris Day, Shannon is more "Doris Day" than Doris Day ever was.

Now that I've had seven years to watch her at close range, I can understand why she is so positive. It's for the same two reasons we've just discussed. She responds more often than she reacts, and even in the hardest situations, she refocuses her attention on the positives of that situation rather than the negatives.

THE SINGLE GREATEST SPRINGBOARD TO BECOMING A POSITIVE PERSON

There is one attitude that is without a doubt the single greatest springboard that can turn a negative person into a positive person. If you are a positive person, this attitude is alive and well within your heart. In fact, the more dominant this attitude, the more positive you are. The converse is also true. The less dominant this attitude is, the less positive you are. If you are a negative person, this attitude is most likely nonexistent in your heart. Fortunately, if this attitude is missing in your life, you can plant its seed and, if nurtured daily, it will take root and grow. If you already have this attitude, you can continue to nurture it, and it will grow ever more dominant. The more dominant it becomes, the more positive you will become.

The attitude about which I am speaking is gratitude, which is the realization that everything of worth that you possess has been given to you by God. The Bible reveals this truth in the form of a question. It asks, "For what do you have, that you didn't receive? And if you received it, why do you boast as if you didn't receive it?"

My former pastor once told me of an encounter he had with a proud and very negative self-proclaimed "*self-made* millionaire." The millionaire told my pastor, "I started out with nothing. My parents were broke and couldn't give me a thing. I put myself through school, and from the time I was a kid until now, nobody's ever given me anything. *I* did it all! I've worked my butt off, but it's paid off because today I've got a booming business and homes all over the world."

"And you did it all by yourself?" my pastor asked.

"That's right," came the man's reply, "every bit of it!"

"And nobody ever gave you a thing?"

"Not a thing," replied the millionaire.

"Well let me ask you this," said my pastor. "Who gave you life? Who decided you would be born in a hospital in America instead of the alleys of Calcutta? Who gave you your marvelous brain, your talents, and your natural abilities? Who changed your diapers and put food on your table as a child? Who taught you how to read and write? Who spent hours, weeks, and years educating you? Who gave you your first job, who mentored you in business? Who lent you money to start your own business? Who raised a little girl and nurtured her into a woman who could give you herself, her love, and your children? Who buys your products? Who takes care of your customers and manages your offices? Who gave you your health and continues to care for it? Who cleans your home, your office buildings and toilets? If you can still look me in the eye and tell me that you've done it all by yourself and that nobody has ever given you anything, then my last question is, who has blinded your eyes and given you such a foolish, arrogant, and ungrateful heart?"

My pastor told me the man was silent and his eyes filled with tears. The light went on and the man replied in a quiet and broken whisper, "My God, what do I have that I *haven't* been given?"

For years this man had been an angry, bitter person. He resented his parents for not being wealthy enough to give him anything. He resented others who had been given anything to everything. He was so negative that no one who knew him liked being around him. After years of being consumed by anger and bitterness, thinking it was him against the world and thinking he deserved all the credit for everything he had acquired in life, there wasn't a grateful bone in his body, nor a positive one. And yet, within a matter of minutes, a transformation had taken place. For the first time in his life he had to honestly open his eyes to all the incredible gifts that he had been given by God, his parents, and so many others.

The result was amazing. He began a letter-writing campaign to everyone he could think of, from past teachers and professors to his office workers and janitors, thanking them for the contributions they had made to his life. He became an incredibly positive person. He became more successful than ever, but more important, he became a loving, giving man who shared his love, success, and fortunes with countless others.

"But he's a millionaire. . . . if you knew my circumstances, there's no way you could be grateful!"

"But you don't know my circumstances" might be your comment. You're right, I don't know your circumstances. But I have sat with parents who have suffered one of the most agonizing events a human can experience: the death of a child and grandchild. I've known others who have lost the use of their arms and legs in accidents. I've known women who were sexually molested as children by their fathers. A friend of mine lost both his wife and firstborn child during childbirth. Another friend found his seven-year-old daughter raped and murdered, and then he lost his wife during childbirth. And as terrible as all these circumstances have been, I have seen these same people transformed as they shifted their focus from the pain they've suffered to the permanent treasures they've gained.

Gary Smalley leads people through a process he calls "treasure hunting," in which they search for and find unbelievable treasures that have been permanently deposited into their lives as a result of the hurts they have suffered. As men and women discover these treasures and learn how to share them with others, their anger and bitterness are transformed into gratefulness and happiness. He has created a wonderful video on this in his series "Hidden Keys to Loving Relationships," and also leads readers through this process in his book *Making Love Last Forever.* If your negative circumstances and hurts have robbed you of joy and happiness, I would urge you to go through this process. You can actually begin your treasure hunt right now. Here are some of the treasures that Gary says men and women often discover when they "treasure hunt" their greatest hurts. Stop right now and think about one or more of the greatest hurts you have experienced. As you think about them, see if any of the following treasures have been deposited into your heart.

- Do you have a greater ability to empathize with the painful experiences of others?

- Do you have a more acute sensitivity to the needs and trials of others?
- Are you less judgmental and more tolerant of others?
- Are you more protective of children or others who may face the same kind of hurts that you have faced?
- Do you have a much greater capacity to be patient?
- Are you more thoughtful, kind, tender, and caring?
- Are you more serious about life and spiritually sensitive?

These are all incredible qualities that many people can go their whole lives without gaining. If you have gained any of these, they are treasures you can begin to use to bring love, comfort, help, and encouragement to those who are hurting, who can only be helped by those who have suffered similar experiences.

In college, I became friends with a blind student named Dan Duffy. He had a disease of the skull that had blinded him in his early childhood and he could not remember what anything looked like. One day, when we were walking down the mall, I was looking at him and feeling sorry for him. My momentary silence must have tipped him off that something wasn't right because he asked me what was wrong. "Danny," I said, "sometimes I just feel so bad that you can't see. I wish there was something I could do, and yet I'm helpless." This conversation took place thirty years ago, and yet his answer was so unbelievable I've never forgotten it. "Steve," he said, "*never* feel sorry for me about my blindness. . . . Don't you realize that the very first thing I'll ever see will be the face of my Savior! My sight is being saved for the most beautiful sight in all of the universe. And when my gaze finally turns from His loving eyes, the next thing I'll see are the streets of heaven and all of its angels."

Danny had been deprived of the precious treasure of sight for nineteen years, and would continue to be deprived of that treasure for the rest of his life on earth. And yet, rather than focusing his attention on his tragedy and hardship, he focused it on an unimaginable blessing that awaited him in the future. But that wasn't all he focused on. Danny was one of the most positive students I knew in college. He focused his attention on all the other blessings that filled his daily life. His ability to think, to attend college, to have wonderful friends, his ability to hear and speak and sing. And he loved playing his guitar. But most amazing of all, he had learned that the greatest treasures are often found in the deepest and darkest mines.

Another friend of mine was terribly crippled from severe rheumatoid arthritis. He was in pain twenty-four hours a day. The only two parts of his body that didn't hurt were his neck and his head. He was confined to a wheelchair and anytime a shoulder, hand, arm, leg, or foot moved, you could hear the bones creak and see his face grimace. And yet, Elmer Lappen was not only one of the most positive and fulfilled people I've met in my lifetime, he had an incredible impact on the lives of more than ten thousand college students during the twenty years he served in a campus organization at Arizona State University. I was just one of those ten thousand students. His mouth contained the only joints he could move without pain, and he was an awesome public speaker with a voice that could be heard a block away without a microphone. I never heard Elmer complain—not once! And yet I saw as many smiles on his face as I saw grimaces of pain.

You are not a robot controlled by other people or circumstances. You alone control the eyes of your mind and attitudes and you can focus them wherever you choose. When adversity first strikes you, of course it captures your attention. But when the initial sting subsides, you can choose to refocus on the wonderful benefits and blessings that have filled your lives. Martin Luther once said, "You can't stop a bird from landing on your head, but you can stop him from building a nest." If you choose to focus your eyes upon the blessings and opportunities that surround you, you, too, will become a more positive person and reap the benefits that are reserved for positive people only.

Positive people also focus their attention on the needs of people and upon fulfilling those needs. Zig Ziglar is known for saying that your happiness and success are directly proportional to the number of people you make happy and successful. Certainly, one reason Mother Teresa could remain positive in such negative surroundings and circumstances is that she kept her attention focused on what she could do to ease the terrible plight of those she was serving. Michael Landon was another good example of this. When an actor he was directing seriously blew a scene, rather than get angry and focus on the lost time and money that the actor's mistake cost, Mike focused on the actor's need for help and direction, and with an encouraging smile he quickly reached out and met that need.

TAKING THE INITIATIVE TO BUILD BETTER RELATIONSHIPS

The second part of our positiveness engine is taking the initiative to build better relationships. Is it possible to develop this positiveness engine without building better relationships? Absolutely. However, the engine won't run as efficiently and won't develop as much power without this component as it would with it. I've known a number of very positive and successful dream-achievers who have been terrible in the area of building relationships. In fact, some not only fail at it, they are great at destroying them. And yet they are still positive and successful. But just think how much more positive and successful they could be if they had learned how to take the initiative to build strong and fulfilling relationships.

The questions for you are how successful do you want to be in pursuing your dreams, how fast do you want to achieve them, and how happy do you want to be along the way? Taking the initiative to build better relationships will raise your level of success, accelerate your rate of achievement, and bring a lot more happiness your way.

Thousands of books have been written on the subject of relationships, and I will hardly do the subject justice in the next few pages. Gary Smalley and I wrote two books on relationships back in 1979, and Gary has since written another eleven. He has created eighteen videos on the subject as well. So what can I possibly hope to accomplish in the next few pages? My hope is to give you Seven Keys to building better relationships. These keys are little things you can do that can make a big difference in the relationships you want to strengthen. Remember, small rudders turn giant ships.

SEVEN KEYS TO BUILDING BETTER RELATIONSHIPS

Key #1: It All Begins with Honor

As I pointed out in the last chapter, honor is the foundation upon which any fulfilling relationship must be built. And as you learned in the last chapter, the great thing about this is that honor is something you can choose to give, whether you feel like it or not. Honoring or valuing someone is not dependent upon them, but rather it's dependent upon you. (Remember the junk violin that people first laughed at and then chose to honor? Same violin, same condition, different choice.)

You can choose to honor or value anyone, anytime you want. All it takes is a little time and attention. Everyone wants to be noticed, appreciated, and treated with respect rather than simply viewed as someone who performs a service. One of the most effective ways you can honor anyone is to listen and pay attention to their thoughts and ideas. When you are with them, force yourself to stop thinking and focus instead on what they are saying to you.

Key #2: We All Need Encouragement

Life isn't easy for anyone. And yet you are often so focused on your own daily needs and battles that you fail to notice the hurts and needs of others. Every day you are surrounded by men and women, boys and girls who need a daily dose of encouragement. That doesn't mean you have to spend hours giving it. Sometimes just a pat on the back and a smile are all that are needed. A few words of encouragement or a willingness to just listen can make all the difference in the world in how a person will face the rest of his or her day.

Look for ways to be thoughtful, show appreciation or give encouragement when it's not expected. A card, a note, or a bouquet of flowers can make someone's day, week, and month. And people remember those little moments and acts of encouragement for years.

When my fiancée broke up with me in college, and later called me and told me that she was going to marry my best friend, I was devastated. My world had come crashing down. I was lying facedown on my bed weeping, when I felt a hand patting me on the back. It was my roommate, Doug Broils. He was supposed to be going out on a date with his fiancée, who was waiting in the living room of our apartment. As he patted my back, he quietly whispered, "I know there's nothing I can say, but I've decided not to go out. If you want to talk, or go out and do anything, I'm here for you. I'll be in the living room." That was thirty years ago, and I can still remember it like it was yesterday. His words, his tone of voice, and how important and valuable he made me feel are as fresh in my mind right now as they were back then. Never underestimate the power or the worth of your encouraging words and actions.

By the way, whenever people are hurting, especially over a failure of any kind (from a bad report card to being passed over for a promotion), the last thing they need is a lecture, an analysis, or advice and a solution. When people are hurting, the best way you can encourage them is with a gentle embrace and a listening ear. To do anything else can only deenergize them and make them want to withdraw. The time to help them resolve a crisis or solve a problem is later, when the pain isn't so fresh. That may be in a few hours or a few days. The worst thing you can do is try to "force-feed" solutions during their initial pain.

Key #3: Infuse Security and Safety into Each Relationship

One of the greatest needs of any man, woman, boy, or girl is to feel safe and secure in a relationship. And yet, in today's society, almost no one feels that way. I'm not talking about *physical* safety and security but rather *emotional* safety and security. Children don't even feel secure in their families much less with their peers. Whether at home or in the workplace, men and women alike often feel as if they are unappreciated and expendable. Therefore, anything you can do to increase the feeling of safety and security will strengthen your relationship with them. And the more safe and secure a person feels, the more they are able to joyfully give of themselves, their efforts, and their abilities. The less safe and secure they feel, the more they will withdraw, and the less they will offer.

So, how can you infuse safety and security into a relationship? First, by letting the person know on a regular basis that you are truly committed to them for the long term. There are lots of ways to do this, from simply telling them—verbally or in writing—to actively helping them to learn and utilize the Dream Conversion Process in their own personal and professional lives. By helping them to define and achieve their dreams, you are showing your long-term commitment to them.

Another powerful way to infuse safety and security into a relationship is to give people the day-to-day freedom to share their thoughts, opinions, feelings, and needs without fearing interruption, criticism, or ridicule. A friend of mine could hardly say a thing without her husband interrupting or criticizing her. His interruptions told her that whatever she had to say was totally unimportant to him, and his criticisms told her she wasn't safe to share how she really felt about anything. By giving others the freedom to express themselves without worrying about being attacked builds tremendous safety and security into the relationship.

Key #4: Communicate Respect and Admiration

Gary Smalley maintains that the greatest single need of a man is to feel admired. I believe he is absolutely right. I also believe that even though it may not be the greatest need of a woman, it is certainly high on the list. One reason so many men end up having affairs with women at the office is because they no longer feel admired at home. But the women at the office not only admire them, they are quick to express their admiration.

By the way, when you try to communicate admiration, you should be careful to distinguish between flattery and true praise. Flattery typically focuses on superficial things while praise focuses upon specific actions and attitudes that reflect character qualities or specific or attempted performance. Everyone needs a little flattery, but not an abundance of it. Genuine praise, on the other hand, should be given whenever there is a true opportunity to give it. The more specific the praise, the more appreciated it will be, and the greater impact it will have. For example, instead of just saying "You did a nice job" or "I liked your report," state *specifically* what you liked. Once again, nonverbal communication is as important as verbal communication. Tone of voice, eye contact, smiles, handshakes, or pats on the back can underscore any praise communicated verbally.

Key #5: Develop Effective Communication Skills and Begin to Use Them

One of the greatest roadblocks to building strong relationships is the inability to effectively communicate. First, people don't usually set aside the amount of time needed to effectively communicate, and second, they don't know *how* to effectively communicate. As you'll see in the next chapter, effective and persuasive communication is one of the most powerful rocket engines you possess, and it's one that most people never learn how to ignite.

Because I cover communication in detail in that chapter, the only thing I'll say at this point is that communication is like a vital oil pipeline. To be effective, you must have three things: a supply of oil, an adequate pipeline to deliver the oil, and time to move the oil through the pipeline to its intended recipient. The content you want to communicate is like the supply of oil. The pipeline is the method of communication that allows the most effective and efficient movement of the content; and finally, you need to set aside time to effectively move the content to its recipient. And these will be covered in the next chapter. Effective communication can strengthen a relationship like no other ingredient.

Key #6: Quickly Resolve Conflicts, the Right Way

Gary Smalley taught me that conflicts can be the doorway to divorce or the gateway to intimacy. It's a choice. Unfortunately, most people don't even know the gateway exists, so rather than conflicts drawing them together, they simply drive them apart. According to Gary, there are five levels of communication, and the deeper you go into each level, the greater the intimacy you will experience. Most relationships rarely go into to the two deepest levels of communication. But when used correctly, conflicts can quickly move us into these deepest levels and bring about greater intimacy.

LEVELS OF COMMUNICATION

Level 1 Clichés (How's it going? How are you doing? I'm okay.)

Level 2 Facts (Who won the game? It's cold outside. What do you want for dinner?)

Level 3 Opinions (I think it would be better if you would do it that way.) Sharing opinions is usually the level where conflict begins.

Level 4 Feelings (I feel like I don't matter to you; I felt hurt by what you said.) Feelings are easier to avoid than to discuss, especially if they are usually denied or met with disdain or criticism.

Level 5 Needs (I need more help at home. I need you to listen to me more often. I need you to be more verbal. I need time alone with you.) If you or your partner have communicated your needs before, only to have the other person criticize, debate, or ignore those needs, you or the other person may be extremely fearful of even approaching this level. Neither of you feels safe and either may fear the hurt that's been felt before when needs have been stated but gone unmet.

The tragedy is that it is these last two levels that bring the greatest amount of joy and fulfillment to any relationship, and yet they are often avoided like the plague. Conflict can be used to open the gate to these deeper levels of communication when it is conducted in a positive way.

When I first heard this, I thought Gary was crazy. I have always feared and hated conflicts. And yet, like it or not, even though you can reduce the number of conflicts you engage in, you can't eliminate them altogether. They will still occur—occasionally or frequently or somewhere in between. So since some amount of conflict is unavoidable, I decided to give Gary's "do's and don'ts" the acid test. The results have been far less hurt, and much greater intimacy, in my marriage, my relationships with my children, and my relationships with others. Learning the right way to resolve conflict is essential to building strong, fulfilling relationships. Here are just a few do's and don'ts that can mean the difference between a conflict being destructive or constructive.

RULES FOR CONSTRUCTIVE CONFLICT: CONFLICT "DON'TS"

1. Don't bury the problem or the hurt it's causing you.
2. Don't deny or run away from the problem or the confrontation required to address it.
3. Don't let your addressing the problem degenerate into an attack on the person or his character. (If his character is the issue, address, don't attack, the specific character failing . . . not the character in general.)
4. Don't use inflammatory remarks, sarcasm, or name calling.

5. Don't enter a conflict in the spirit of a self-righteous, "better-than-thou know-it-all."
6. Don't let the conflict broaden to issues other than the one or ones you are trying to address.
7. Don't use generalizations, exaggerations, or such superlatives as "you always" or "you never."
8. Don't use ultimatums or threats.
9. Don't use body language or nonverbal communication that shows disbelief or lack of respect, such as rolling your eyes or shaking your head.
10. Don't interrupt.
11. Don't raise your voice.
12. Don't withdraw, walk away, or hang up the telephone in the middle of a confrontation.

"Well what the heck am I supposed to do in a confrontation?" I'll give you the answer in a moment, but first, remember that the goal of your confrontation is to resolve the problem or issue in a way that will have the most meaningful immediate and long-term results. I'll admit it's pretty hard to get through a confrontation without doing at least one or two of the "don'ts." But the fewer you do, the more effective and positive the end result will be. Here is a list of "do's" that if followed will not only minimize the damage inflicted by a conflict, but more important, they will actually lead you through the gateway to greater intimacy.

Conflict "Do's"

1. Take a "time-out" to gain control, calm down, and reduce your anger before you engage in the confrontation.
2. Prepare for the confrontation before you engage in it.
   • Determine your specific goal for the confrontation. For example, do you simply want to resolve a current problem or stop a behavior pattern? Or do you want to replace a destructive behavior pattern with a constructive one. Do you want to correct, encourage, or punish?

- Determine what specifically you want to say and how you want to say it. Write it down if time permits so you can make sure you avoid all of the "don'ts" in your message.
- Determine how to begin the confrontation in the least inflammatory way. Include your positive "goal" for the confrontation. (For example, "I really want to be the best friend I can be to you" or "Because our relationship is so important to me, I wanted to share something that could make it better for both of us.")

3. Approach the confrontation in the spirit of a learner, as one who also makes mistakes and has weaknesses.

4. If criticism is to be given, use the sandwich method discussed in the next few pages.

5. Use as many encouraging and positive statements as you can in the context surrounding the central issue you are trying to address or resolve.

6. Be willing to offer and accept a "progressive" resolution of the problem or issue. In other words, be willing to come up with a solution that involves a period of time. Don't demand that a solution be agreed upon, enacted, or achieved by the end of the confrontation.

7. Ask for advice on what you can do to help resolve the problem on your end, or to reduce your contribution to the problem.

8. If the person attacks you, don't defend yourself or retaliate. Assure him or her that you also have weaknesses that you need to work on.

9. Keep the confrontation "on track." Don't be diverted to side issues or opportunities to deal with problems other than those you have planned to address. If the other person won't proceed unless these other issues are addressed, you can always agree that the concern is legitimate and ask if you can set aside time later to deal with that issue.

10. Control your words, tone of voice, and nonverbal communication. Respect and honor the person, even in the midst of conflict. Remember the wisdom of the Proverb of Solomon, "A soft answer turneth away wrath, but grievous words stir up anger." In other words, giving a soft answer defuses and prevents anger,

while destructive, divisive, or inflammatory words or answers, turn up the heat and cause the other person's anger to boil over.

11. Reassure the person of your ongoing care and commitment to them and to your relationship.

Key #7: Only Give Criticism When Necessary, and Only Give It the Right Way!

In Chapter 6 I focused on the right way to receive and respond to criticism, how to turn it from your enemy into your ally. But how about *giving* criticism. Is giving criticism ever right? Absolutely yes. Criticism, when given correctly, can have extremely positive benefits. There would be a lot more dead pilots had they not received criticism from their instructors. There would be a lot more dead patients had interns not received criticism from their medical professors. And all of us would be more poorly prepared for just about everything in life had we not received criticism along the way.

That's the good news about criticism. The bad news is that almost nothing can be more devastating and destructive to a person or to a relationship than criticism. So criticism can either have very beneficial results or devastating consequences, depending upon *how* it is given. In my forty-eight years of life, I have discovered that there are hundreds of wrong ways to give criticism, and only *one* right way. Once again, I have to give Gary Smalley the credit for teaching me this. I learned this from him nineteen years ago when we were writing our first book together. Subsequently, I've had thousands of opportunities to put it to the test and I can tell you that it's been proven to work every time!

When given correctly, criticism not only results in an awareness of a problem, it stimulates a long-term desire to resolve that problem. There are two factors in giving criticism the right way: the spirit in which it is given, and the method in which it is delivered. You should never criticize when you are angry. Even if you have to go off alone for a few minutes, do whatever it takes to offer the criticism with a gentle spirit. When it is offered in anger, a person instantly becomes defensive and responds with retaliatory statements. As in the case of constructive conflicts, offer criticism in the spirit of one who also has weaknesses and makes mistakes.

THE "SANDWICH METHOD" OF CRITICISM

Simply stated, the sandwich method of criticizing places one slice of criticism in between two slices of praise. You begin by pointing out a very positive quality about the individual or his or her performance and offering specific praise for it. As in: "Ryan, you were so sweet and thoughtful to pick those beautiful flowers just for Mommy. That makes her feel so loved and special. I love all of the special things you do that show Mommy how much you love her!"

Next, comes the criticism, addressing a wrong activity or choice, not the person's character: "Ryan, as much as Mommy and Daddy love that you picked these beautiful flowers, the Smiths next door worked real hard to plant and grow them. Taking flowers from someone else's garden isn't right. In fact, it's never right to take anything that belongs to someone else. Do you understand what Daddy is saying?"

Finally, after the criticism has been delivered and understood, it's time to put the last slice of bread on the sandwich: "Ryan, remember that Mommy and Daddy love it when you do kind and thoughtful things to make other people happy. You are the most considerate little four-year-old I've ever known. Can you think of some other nice things you could do that would make Mommy feel special?"

While this example may oversimplify the process, I wanted to use one that clearly illustrated what I mean. Also, it actually happened, and is one of the few personal criticisms I've delivered that I feel the liberty to share.

Warning: Proceed with Extreme Caution

Even when given correctly, criticism should only be offered *sparingly,* when there is no other effective way to deal with a problem. It should always be a last resort and *never* a first resort. Even the sandwich method is less effective when used too frequently.

GREAT RELATIONSHIPS CAN BE THE MOST ENJOYABLE COMPONENT OF THE POSITIVENESS ENGINE

While your positiveness engine can run without building great relationships, you are the real loser when you neglect this part of the engine. I have met men and women who have ignited this engine without building strong relationships, and whatever success they have achieved has been hollow. The sad thing is that had they focused upon this one vital part of their engine, they could have not only increased their success, they could have *enjoyed* it infinitely more. As I said at the beginning of this section, there is no way that I can give you everything you need to build great relationships in just a few pages. I would strongly encourage you to view what I believe is the most entertaining and enlightening material on relationships ever recorded. The title of this series is "Hidden Keys to Loving Relationships" and it can be ordered by calling 1-800-246-1771.

SUCH A LONG CHAPTER DESERVES A SHORT CLOSE

Positiveness is critical for everyone who wants to dream big and achieve their dreams. And though it can be an inborn trait, it isn't for most people. Yet it can be acquired, and must be by anyone who wants to be a dream-maker.

Developing positiveness puts you in control. For all of recorded history, in every imaginable field and endeavor, positiveness has driven mankind to the heights of human accomplishment. It is a trait common to all who achieve their dreams. Whether or not you ignite this engine is totally up to you. If you do, you'll enjoy the ride of a lifetime. If you don't, you'll never know what you could have achieved.

POWER SECRET #10:
Igniting the Engine of Positiveness

Taking Charge of Your Attitudes

1. Write down recent situations or circumstances in which you "reacted" rather than responded. Describe your reactions and any negative consequences they produced with you or someone else.
2. Looking at the situations you've just described, write down how you could have *responded* to each so that you would have produced more positive outcomes.
3. For the next two weeks, take a few minutes each night to write out any situations that occurred during the day that you reacted to and the negative consequences of those reactions. Then, for each situation, write out how you could have better responded.
4. For the next two weeks, take a few minutes each night to write out any situations that occurred during the day that you responded to and the positive outcomes you experienced because you responded rather than reacted.
5. Ask people at work and at home if you are generally a negative person or a positive person. If they answer positive, have them rate you on a scale from 1 to 10 (1 being a little more positive than negative, 5 being fairly positive, and 10 being very positive). Ask those same people to name things you do that reflect negative attitudes and things you do that reflect positive attitudes. Finally, ask these people how you could be even more positive. Be sure to take notes!
6. What are the greatest hurts you have suffered that may still affect your attitudes (abuse, divorce, job firings, hurtful actions or words of friends, physical disabilities, etc.)?
7. Go "treasure hunting" through your hurts. For each "hurt" you've listed, write down the spiritual insights or character qualities you have gained as a result of these hurts (see example on page 171).

Building More Enjoyable Relationships

1. How can you begin to show more honor and greater value to those you relate to, both professionally and personally?
2. What are some of the specific things you can begin to say or do that will encourage people to whom you regularly relate?
3. How safe and secure do those you relate to feel in their relationship with you, and what can you do that will infuse more safety and security into each relationship? (If you struggle with this question, ask those you relate to what you could begin to say or do, or not do, that would make them feel more secure in the relationship.)
4. What can you do that will encourage others to feel a freedom to express their opinions, thoughts, and feelings?
5. Look back at some of your recent conflicts and compare how you handled them to the Rules for Constructive Conflict on pages 178– 181.
6. Think back to the last few times you've criticized someone. Write down how you could have done it using the sandwich method.

CHAPTER 14

Engine #5: "Earthquake Persuasiveness"

A LEARNABLE ART ANYONE CAN MASTER

THE SINGLE KEY THAT UNLOCKS MORE DOORS TO YOUR DREAMS THAN ANY OTHER.

MY FACE-TO-FACE ENCOUNTER WITH PERSUASION OF THE GREATEST MAGNITUDE

I walked into my hotel room about midnight and couldn't wait to feel my head hit the pillow. I had been shooting commercials in Malibu since six A.M., and was due back on the set the next morning at seven. My room was on the top floor of a nineteen-story West L.A. hotel. As I turned out the lamp on the nightstand I noticed the time was just after midnight. I thought, "Well, I'll get a good six hours before the wake-up call comes," and with that I fell asleep. It seemed as if I had only been asleep for a few minutes when all of a sudden it felt like somebody was trying to wake me by forcefully shaking my bed. When I opened my eyes I could see that the room was violently swaying back and forth. The clock read 2:22.

I tried to jump out of bed but was instantly thrown back onto it. I tried getting up two more times, and each time the swaying was so intense I fell back onto the bed. It honestly looked and felt like the same amount of sway you feel when you're on a swing set. I instantly thought, "This is it . . . this is the big one, and I'm going to be buried in nineteen stories of rubble." It was the only time in my life that I truly believed I was going to die. The building continued to sway for another two minutes.

Finally the swaying stopped and, to my amazement, the building hadn't collapsed. I instantly leapt to my feet, jumped into a pair of jeans faster than I had ever dressed in my life, and ran to the door. As I opened my door, every other door on the nineteenth floor opened at the same time. It was if we were all extras on a Hollywood set and had just received our cues to open our doors. We all ran down the hall to the elevators. As soon as the elevator door opened, everyone crammed into it and down we went to the lobby, where we found about two hundred other people. The hotel manager told us that the building was on a set of Teflon bearings and could have safely swayed for another five minutes. I don't know if the manager was telling the truth or if he was just trying to calm us down. It was truly the most terrifying two minutes of my life.

As I was thinking about this chapter, I tried to think of the one individual the majority of Americans would view as the most persuasive person. Then I realized that no one is as persuasive as an earthquake. As I thought about that particular earthquake, and the other half-dozen I have experienced since that night, I realized that an earthquake is not only more persuasive than any speaker I've ever heard, it truly illustrates all the key elements in the art of persuasion.

IF YOU HAVE A HUSBAND OR A WIFE, A BOSS OR A CUSTOMER, FRIENDS OR CHILDREN, YOU NEED TO LEARN THE ART OF PERSUASION.

Whenever I speak to groups about our seven giant booster engines and get to this one, I get a lot of questioning looks. Everyone seems to be asking, why is this important to me? Well, if you have a husband or a boyfriend, how often have you thought "He just doesn't understand me," or "Why can't he get it?," or "If only he could feel what I feel." Becoming an effective and persuasive communicator can solve the "understanding" and "feeling" problem every time. If you are a husband who wants to be understood and responded to (without being mistaken for an insensitive and unfeeling dictator), you also need to learn the art of persuasion.

If you are the mother of a teenage daughter and you want her to do the "right thing" without being ordered, forced, or manipulated, persuasion can become your greatest ally. If you have an eight-year-old son who would rather play Nintendo 64 than do his homework, for *his* sake you need to learn the art of persuasion. If you want to accomplish more at work and raise your pay and career achievements, you need to become persuasive. If you want your boss, your peers, or your employees to honor, respect, and respond to your opinions, suggestions, or directions, persuasion is the key you've been looking for. In fact, once you learn the true meaning of persuasion, you'll discover that this is an art you can utilize to accomplish more in one day than you would ever think possible.

WHAT'S THE DIFFERENCE BETWEEN PERSUASION AND MANIPULATION?

When most people hear the word "persuasion" they think of it as simply another word for manipulation. There is, however, a *huge* difference. In fact, I loathe manipulation. Although Webster might not agree with me, here is how I would differentiate between the two: *Manipulation is using any means necessary to motivate or force a person to do something that fulfills your desire or need, whether or not it is in his or her best interest.* The focus of manipulation, then, is the desire or benefit of the manipulator, *not* the benefit of the person being manipulated.

Persuasion is the art of guiding one's mind through a field of ignorance, misinformation, or misunderstanding to a destination where there is enough information and understanding to make a logical choice to do that which is in the best interest of the person being persuaded.

In essence, true persuasion enables another person to understand what you are saying, feel what you are feeling, and consequently become motivated to do what you truly believe is in his or her best interest to do.

If I were a real estate agent and I tried to convince a young couple to buy a home they couldn't afford, I would be manipulating them. If, on the other hand, I found a home that had everything they wanted at a price they could easily afford, and I knew it was the best deal in town, and that they could look for a year and never find a deal like it, *and then* I presented the right information in the right way, helping them to understand what a great deal it is and why it is in their best interest to take it, I would be engaging in the art of persuasion. True persuasion isn't a dirty word, it is an art that can enable you to accomplish wonderful things with and for other people.

You often fail to persuade others not because you don't have a good idea but because you are simply not skilled in the art of persuasion. You can have the best idea or product in the world, but if you can't adequately convey this, you won't even get to first base, much less score a run.

Clara Barton, Thomas Edison, Orville Wright, and Dr. Jonas Salk were not salesmen, and yet, had they not learned the art of persuasion, their dreams would have never been realized—and the whole world would be a lot different place to live. Had Barton not persuaded her superiors, in 1862, that she should be allowed to go to the front lines to nurse the wounded soldiers on both sides, not only would millions of men and women have died on battlefields since then, but we would also have no Red Cross. Had Edison not been able to persuade his investors and his fellow engineers that electric light was possible, and been able to repersuade them throughout his quest, you would all be reading by the light of kerosene lamps. If Wright had not convinced government officials that powered flying machines were more than just a novelty, you would still be riding trains, buses, and boats for days or weeks whenever you took a trip. And if Salk had not learned the incredible art of persuasion, you would still be watching millions of boys and girls, men and women suffer and die because of polio, the "incurable" disease for which he found a cure.

THE SINGLE KEY THAT CAN UNLOCK MORE DOORS THAN ANY OTHER!

Thank God men and women like these have learned the art of persuasion. Most of the things you take for granted today would never have existed if risk takers hadn't persuaded employers, peers, bankers, investors, and governments to take a chance on their ideas. At the same time, imagine all the wonderful things that individuals and families, not to mention governments and societies, have *missed* because others were *not* persuasive. How many marriages could have been saved if one partner could only have persuade the other to seek counseling? How many students have dropped out of high school or college because no one could persuade them that education was in their best interest? How many struggling businesses have failed because bankers or investors couldn't be persuaded to invest another dime? How many diseases remain "incurable" because scientists and doctors can't convince their superiors to test a new approach or a new drug? Yes, the benefits of persuasion are all around you. What you don't see are the millions of opportunities that have been lost because most adults are ineffective persuaders.

Is learning the art of persuasion important? It's absolutely *critical* for anyone who wants to achieve a dream and help others to achieve theirs. It is the key that unlocks the doors to the minds and hearts of others, and enables you to make a lasting positive impact upon their lives.

HAVE YOU EVER BARGED INTO A STRANGER'S HOME AND SOLD HIM SOMETHING IN UNDER TWO MINUTES?

Before I get into the principles and techniques of persuasion I should tell you why mastering this art became so critical to my success. When I was invited to start a television marketing company with my partner, I had already lost nine jobs in my first six years after college. I was twenty-eight years old and broke. I had moved my wife and two children three thousand miles away from home as I tried to achieve success one more time. I honestly believed that if I failed at this one, I was going to be doomed to a life of financial failure. My partner, who was funding our little venture, had allocated $5,000 to launch our business. I would be given only one chance to come up to the plate and swing the bat. That's all he could afford. If we swung and missed, it would mean going out of business as fast as we had gone into business. We found the product we wanted to launch and we signed our commercial spokesperson. Now came the tricky part.

Our product was not going to be available to consumers at any store in the United States. The only way it could be purchased was to watch our two-minute television commercial, memorize the phone number in the last twenty seconds, call the number, and order the product. Sound easy? Look at it this way: You are in your living room watching a television show you really like. The show fades to black and up comes a commercial. Do you immediately tell everyone in the room to quiet down so you can listen to the commercial? Of course not. You start hitting the buttons on the remote control to either mute or lower the volume or change the channel, or you get up and go do whatever you need to do, knowing that you've got two minutes before the show comes back on the air. This is how most people react to commercial breaks.

Yet my entire future depended upon barging into your living room and instantly convincing you to stay put and listen to what I have to say. I have to introduce you to my product, show you all of its benefits, tell you why it's better or different from anything you could get in the store, answer all of your objections to the product, persuade you that owning this product was in your best interest, and then convince you to memorize an 800 number, go to your telephone, fight the busy signals, and order the product. And I have to do all of this in only two minutes!

Sound difficult? It is. Yet I figured out a way to do it, and more than a million people ordered our first product, generating about $20 million in sales. From that point on, I had to find new products and create new winning commercials every three months for the next twelve years. In all, I wrote and produced about eight hundred two-minute commercials that generated about twenty million phone calls. Then, eight years ago we began using thirty-minute infomercials to sell our products. After spending twelve years trying to persuade people in two minutes, having thirty seemed like an eternity. To date, we've sold well over a billion dollars' worth of products using the persuasion techniques I have learned or developed.

What has been so gratifying, however, has been to watch these same persuasion techniques work in every other area of my life. I have six children: a daughter age twenty-five, and five sons ages twenty-one, sixteen, nine, four, and two. I have found that these techniques have worked in dealing with all my kids; from my toddlers to my teenagers, to my adult children. They work with my wife, and she uses them with me as well. Because these techniques aren't manipulative, it's not the least bit offensive when other people use them on me. They have worked with my banker, my friends, my employees, my partners, Hollywood agents, celebrities, business managers, and even attorneys. In addition to our television campaigns, I've also used these techniques in magazine ads, newspaper ads, and catalogs. I have even seen them work wonders with irate customers.

All of this is to say that if these techniques can persuade over twenty million consumers to respond in only two minutes of communication, if they can work with two-year-olds and teenagers, wives, bankers and attorneys . . . then they can work for you.

YOU CAN'T BUILD A SECURE HOUSE WITHOUT LAYING THE RIGHT FOUNDATION!

The First Principle of Persuasion: Honor and Respect

In a few minutes, you are going to learn some incredibly effective techniques that, when used correctly, will make you far more persuasive than you have ever been. However, they will only be effective once or twice with any one individual if they are used without first laying the right foundation. Once this is done, these techniques will be effective over and over again, as often as they are used. The foundation for persuasion begins with honoring and respecting the person you hope to persuade.

Honor and respect are communicated in a number of ways. First, you respect people's time. Instead of demanding an opportunity to talk with someone immediately, you request it at their convenience, or you at least become sensitive to the timing of your communication. If your spouse is under pressure to focus on something that is important to him, demanding that he talk with you *right now* is saying that he and his activity is not as important as you and your desire. You tend to be more honoring and respectful of the time and attention of those in authority over you than you are of those who are not. You tend to be the least respectful and honoring of the members of your family, because you think that you can barge right in on anything they are doing and expect them to instantly set everything aside and focus on what you want to talk about. Because that is both disrespectful and dishonoring, you lay the foundation for argument and resentment rather than for effective and persuasive communication. If you are asked to wait for a better time, prove that you honor and respect them and their opinions, activities, and needs by being willing to bend to *their* schedule—unless it's truly urgent. That sends a wonderful message that you consider their time to be as important as yours.

In addition to not honoring or respecting a person's time and activity, you also tend to dishonor them with the words you choose and your nonverbal communication such as your tone of voice, facial expressions, and body language.

I can spend ten minutes with a couple and tell you how good their relationship is just by watching the nonverbal communication between them. More often than not, couples communicate disrespect and dishonor to one another. The rolling of eyes, the shaking of a head, looking away, inattentiveness, looking at the watch, or interrupting the other are among the many ways you tell a person, "You and what you are saying are not important to me." When people believe that they and their opinions, feelings, and needs are unimportant to you, there is no foundation for persuasion. You also send the same message of disrespect by using sarcasm, a condescending word or tone of voice, or just by telling them to do something instead of asking them to do it. Without laying the foundation of honor and respect, you may be able to manipulate a husband or wife, child or employee to do what you want them to do, but they will perform out of their will, and not from their heart or mind. And they will perform only to the letter of your request rather than to its spirit.

On the other hand, there are specific things you can do that communicate honor and respect to the person with whom you're communicating—for example: look them in the eyes, pay attention, ask questions, and repeat what you think you heard them say. If you truly honor and respect those with whom you wish to effectively communicate, they will begin to trust you and your opinions, and you will have begun to lay a great foundation that will last for the life of that relationship.

The Second Principle of Persuasion: Understanding the Other Person's Frame of Reference

Countless times each week, American women ask themselves, "Why can't he 'get it'?" They don't understand why the men in their lives can't understand what they are saying or how they are feeling; or why these men simply can't do what they are being asked. One reason is that men *truly* don't understand what women are saying or feeling, partly because both men and women are usually such ineffective communicators. I'll look at that problem in a minute. But the primary reason men can't "get it" is the same reason why women don't understand why men can't get it. Namely, neither one has an inborn natural understanding of the other person's frame of reference. And this problem is not just a problem between the sexes. It's also a problem among the four major personality types.

For example, a Lion enters a meeting with one goal: make the meeting as productive as possible and end it as soon as possible. An Otter enters a meeting looking forward to socializing with the attendees who are the most fun to joke around and talk with. A Golden Retriever enters a meeting hoping there won't be any conflicts or hurt feelings, and a Beaver enters the meeting with pad and pencil in hand to make sure that he or she takes accurate notes and gets everything right. What happens? The Lion quickly takes charge and begins to move the meeting from point to point as fast as he or she can. The Otters get offended because they can't get all of their opinions voiced. The Golden Retrievers feel sorry for the offended Otters and think the Lion is an insensitive jerk. And the Beaver wants everybody to be quiet and slow down because he missed a point that was made while he was writing down another point. The Lion is upset because he can't understand why every Otter thinks they have to put their "two cents" in on every point that's made. So who's wrong and who's right? Whoever you say is right is probably your same personality type, because you understand and agree with their point of view and because you don't understand the frames of reference of the other personality types.

But the frame of reference problem isn't just a matter of gender differences or personality types. Just as everyone has his or her own unique set of fingerprints, everyone also has unique personality prints. For even though you may fall into one or two of the broad personality categories, within that category you are the only person on the face of the earth that feels and thinks and speaks exactly like you do.

So how important is it that you understand the frame of reference of the person with whom you are communicating? It is *critical* to both effective and persuasive communication.

"Wait," you say, "how can I ever understand other people's frame of reference if I'm not them?" You can do two things that will take you 80 percent of the way, and a third that will take you another 15 percent. You'll never understand their frame of reference 100 percent, but even reaching 80 percent is a tremendous help. First, you can learn about some of the basic emotional and psychological differences between men and women. Why does a man have to drive four hundred miles at a time without stopping, even though his wife and children are starving? How can a woman go shopping for a blouse in a store where there are thousands of blouses and not find one that she likes? The best book I've read on this subject is Gary Smalley's *Making Love Last Forever*.

The second thing you can do is to learn all you can about the four basic personality types. (Gary has another wonderful book, entitled *The Two Sides of Love*, that also covers this.) Learning the differences between men and women and how to recognize the four personality types will take you 80 percent of the way to understanding another person's frame of reference. The next 15 percent can only be learned one way. You need to ask questions. Let people guide you into an understanding about their frame of reference on the subject you are going to discuss with them. Ask how they feel about the issue and why they feel that way.

It is absolutely critical that you not interrupt their answers, that you do not attack, criticize, or belittle their thoughts and feelings either verbally or nonverbally. If you do, they will mentally and emotionally withdraw from the conversation and build a defensive wall that you will not be able to get beyond. Remember, when you are trying to gain an understanding of someone's frame of reference, your goal is not to change their mind or argue a point. It's not even to enlighten them. That may come later in the process, but first, you must simply gain as much of an understanding of their frame of reference and point of view as possible.

I once sat behind a newlywed couple on a flight to Florida. As the plane began to taxi toward the runway, the woman began to cry quietly. I heard her new husband say, "Come on, honey, why are you so afraid of flying?" She started her answer with "I'm just so afraid . . . if we crash, I knew we . . ." She didn't even get to complete her sentence. Her husband interrupted with, "Oh come on . . . don't be ridiculous! There's no way we're going to crash. We're a lot safer here than we were on the freeway an hour ago. You don't have a thing to worry about."

I instantly saw her body pull away from him. She continued to cry, and as the plane began rolling down the runway, she began weeping out of control. Her husband had not only failed to persuade her, he had dishonored her by interrupting her. By belittling and criticizing her feelings, he had caused her to withdraw from any attempt to lead him into an understanding of her frame of reference. The next time he asked her to share her thoughts about something, I am confident she would hesitate out of fear of the same type of reaction on his part. They were headed for their honeymoon, and he was already establishing a pattern of communication that could ultimately bring down their marriage.

On the other hand, if her husband had let her express her fears about flying without interruption, criticism, or ridicule, she would have felt more understanding and honor on his part, and instead of pulling away from him, she probably would have snuggled a little closer. More important, the next time he wanted to gain an understanding of her frame of reference on something else, she would have felt more secure and safe in sharing her true thoughts and feelings.

One of the greatest problems in families is the lack of effective communication between parents and children of any age. Children learn very early that if they say something stupid or something their parents disagree with, they will be belittled, criticized, or even ridiculed. They discover that it's a lot safer to simply say what the parents want to hear, whether it's true or not. Or they simply don't say anything at all. You will never be able to teach your children how to make wise judgments if you can't honor their opinions and feelings and gain an understanding of their frame of reference. Even when their opinions and feelings are totally wrong, they have to be known and understood before they can be changed through effective persuasion. So learn to bite your tongue and not roll your eyes or shake your head when someone begins to tell you how they think or what they feel.

"ALL THE RIGHT WORDS" DOESN'T MEAN "ALL THE RIGHT MESSAGES"!

The Third Principle of Persuasion: You've Got to Be an Effective Communicator Before You Can Be a Persuasive One!

Gary Smalley was having dinner with a retired minister and his wife who were both in their eighties. He told Gary that when he was a new minister, he and his wife came out of church one Sunday and his Ford Model T wouldn't start. He asked his wife to borrow her father's car to give him a push. Knowing his wife had never given anyone a "push" before, he began to tell her what to do. "It's very important that you get your speed up to thirty-five miles per hour, or my battery won't turn over when I pop the clutch," he said. "Thirty-five miles an hour?" she asked. "Thirty-five," he replied emphatically.

As she walked back to her father's car, the minister dropped some change underneath the seat. He looked down and began to feel around for the coins. A few moments later he looked up into his rearview mirror and, to his horror, saw his wife in her father's car far away at the other end of the parking lot. She was aiming her car directly at his and putting the pedal to the metal. When she hit his car at nearly thirty miles an hour, it knocked him onto the church lawn. She jumped out of the car and came running up to him. "What *on earth* were you doing?" he shouted. "I didn't think it sounded right," she replied. In a panic she continued, "It didn't even feel right, but you said get my speed up to thirty-five, and even when I questioned you, you *insisted* . . . thirty-five miles per hour . . . and that's *exactly* what I tried to do!"

As funny as this story is, it makes a very important point: Effective communication involves a lot more than just saying or writing the right words. Think about the times when someone did something that surprised you, and when you asked why they did it, their reply was "But you said. . . ." Or how many times have you told someone who didn't do something the way you asked them to do it, "But I told you to do it *this* way!" In both of those cases, and countless others, you probably said the right words, yet the person didn't understand what you truly intended to communicate. Does it mean they weren't listening or that they were lazy or disrespectful? Not at all. They simply did not understand. There was nothing malicious or disrespectful at all. And yet such miscommunication is often the source of frustration, and can escalate into disagreement and even bitter conflict. In business meetings, I've even watched men yell back and forth at each other with statements like, "You *told* me to do it," "You're crazy . . . why would I ever say anything like that. . . . I *never* said it," and so on.

And if you think there's verbal miscommunication, multiply it by ten when it comes to writing. When you communicate verbally, some miscommunication is avoided because nonverbal communication— facial expressions, gestures, tone of voice—helps the other person correctly interpret what you are saying. In writing, your words receive no such help.

THE HEART OF EFFECTIVE AND PERSUASIVE COMMUNICATION

Most people are terribly ineffective communicators some of the time, and somewhat ineffective communicators most of the time. That's because effective communication involves two factors: understanding and feeling. You have effectively communicated with someone only when they: (1) *understand* what you are saying; and (2) *feel* what you are feeling. It is this second factor where most communication breaks down or fails. In a meeting with my partners today, I told them of something that had happened seven years ago that had "hurt" my feelings. When another partner entered the room and sat down, my partner John, who had been involved in the conversation, said, "Steve was just telling us about something that happened a few years ago that he resented."

I was shocked when John used the word "resented." I had said that I had felt "hurt." I had said nothing of resentment. I quickly corrected my miscommunication and reassured John and my other partners that I felt no resentment whatsoever. Even though I had used the right word (hurt) John had completely misread what I said I was feeling. Was it his fault? Not at all! All he did was misunderstand what *I* said, and repeat what he understood to be true.

When you are misunderstood, or not understood at all, it's *your* fault and no one else's. It is up to you and you alone to effectively communicate what you want to say and how you feel. People cannot get inside your heart and mind on their own. You have to take them by the hand and lead them there. The problem is that no one teaches you *how* to do this. Effective and persuasive communication is an easily learnable skill, but it is *not* taught in high school or college.

THE SUBSTANCE OF PERSUASION: COMMUNICATING UNDERSTANDING, FEELING, AND THE MOTIVATION TO ACT

Whenever you communicate, whether verbally or in writing, you are trying to reach three dimensions of a person. These are the person's mind or understanding, their heart or emotions, and their will. Most communication enters at one level, but doesn't penetrate to the other two very often. When this happens, the communication is only superficially effective.

One-Dimensional Communication

One-dimensional communication can focus on any one of the three dimensions. When you ask or tell someone to do something and he doesn't understand *why* he should do it, you are communicating to his will. If he asks for an explanation, it's a sign that he wants to go to the next level, "understanding." If you answer, "Because I said so, that's why," then you are choosing to ignore his other two dimensions and simply focusing on his will. This is the *least* effective means of communication. It may result in action or obedience for this particular moment and event, but it will do nothing positive to motivate that person in the future, and may even produce significant negative consequences. It's a missed opportunity to convey understanding and feeling, and it can result in lower self-esteem and greater resentment for not considering that person important enough to be given the time, consideration, and explanation he deserves.

Aiming your communication at a person's mind or understanding is certainly more effective than just focusing on his will. In this case, you attempt to give him a logical understanding of what you are communicating. If he understands what you are saying, he feels a higher degree of honor and self-respect. However, if this is the only dimension of the person your communication reaches, he still may not have enough input to respond or perform the way he should, and may well lack the motivation to put forth a great amount of effort.

For example, most teenagers understand that cigarette smoking is dangerous to their health—they've heard it all their lives. They also understand that by driving too fast they could injure or kill themselves or others. And yet, in spite of their *understanding* of these dangers, many teens continue to smoke and to drive recklessly. So communicating to one's mind or understanding may be more effective than just communicating to the will, but it is still somewhat impotent in terms of the long-term results it can produce.

The third dimension of a person that you are able to communicate with is the heart or emotions. When you focus on this dimension alone, you may truly affect the person emotionally. Yet without reaching her understanding or will, the longevity of this communication's impact is also short term. In fact, the results can be as inconsistent as a person's mood swings. A woman's tears communicate to a man's emotional level, and can often stop him dead in his tracks and instantly soften his heart. But if there is no communication with his understanding or will, whatever he did that caused those tears will most likely be repeated in the hours, days, weeks, or months ahead.

For communication to be truly effective, it must reach both the understanding *and* the emotional levels. For communication to be truly persuasive, it must reach these two levels *and* the will. Let's look at good working definitions of effective communication and persuasive communication.

> EFFECTIVE COMMUNICATION: Communication that enables a person to *understand* what I am saying, and *feel* what I am feeling.
> PERSUASIVE COMMUNICATION: Communication that enables a person to *understand* what I am saying, *feel* what I am feeling, and *motivates* him or her to take the course of action that I believe is in his or her best interest.

Notice that to be effective, communication must reach one's mind and heart; to be persuasive, it must reach the mind, heart, and will. In light of these definitions, let's revisit the earthquake.

As soon as I woke up, I totally understood with my mind what the earthquake was communicating: I understood that it was shaking the building so violently that my life was in danger unless I could reach a safe place. It also reached my heart: I felt a true fear of being injured or killed and felt a longing to see my family. And it communicated with my will: It motivated me to take immediate action. I tried three times to get out of the bed, and when the shaking stopped, I dressed faster than I had ever dressed before. Its communication was 100 percent effective and 100 percent persuasive. I offered no rebuttal, no debate, no argument, no rationalization, no resistance or delay whatsoever! I understood . . . I felt . . . I acted! *That* is persuasion in its purest and most powerful form. That is "Earthquake Persuasion."

THE THREE MOST EFFECTIVE COMMUNICATION AND PERSUASION TECHNIQUES I HAVE EVER USED

Techniques That Enable Us to Achieve "Earthquake Persuasion"

How would you like to be able to capture anyone's undivided attention and hold it until you have said everything you wanted to say? How would you like to be so captivating that your listeners not only hang on every word, they actually become more anxious to hear what you are going to say next? Or how would you like to be such a great communicator that your listeners not only understand what you are saying, they actually feel what you are feeling? You can achieve all of these scenarios when you use the right techniques.

The first problem you face anytime you want to communicate with people, whether in writing or face-to-face, is gaining their undivided attention. When the communication first begins, even if you think you have their undivided attention, you probably don't. They are most likely thinking about something else—something someone said, or something that happened a few minutes or a few hours earlier, or something that's going to happen later. They might be thinking about lunch, dinner, or their weekend plans. They may even be focused on your appearance. But the mind is *not* on what you are going to say. So, to effectively and persuasively communicate, the first thing you must do is grab their undivided attention—grab it and turn it away from wherever it is focused, and bring it face-to-face with what you are about to say.

Did the earthquake successfully grab my undivided attention? Absolutely! It not only grabbed mine, it grabbed everyone else's in that hotel and in the entire city of Los Angeles. So, how can you grab someone's undivided attention? The best way I've found to do this is to use what I call a "hook"—the technique I first learned from Bob Marsh.

Nothing Grabs a Person's Undivided Attention Like a Good Hook

For a moment, imagine you are a small fish swimming down a stream with your friends to your favorite group of rocks. You notice an attractive little fly floating just off to your right. It looks real tasty, so you quickly turn your head and grab it. To your dismay, there's a hook in it, and that hook is instantly embedded in your mouth. Where is your attention going to be focused now? Will you be looking at your friends still swimming downstream? Will you be thinking about all the fun they're going to have when they get there? Or will you be focusing 100 percent on that stupid hook in your mouth and what to do about it? The answer is obvious. You will be focusing on the hook, and you will be looking and swimming directly toward the fisherman. They now have your undivided attention.

When it comes to effective and persuasive communication, I have found that there are three types of very effective hooks. The most effective, which is not always available, is a strong personal reference. It uses the name and credibility of someone that the person with whom you are communicating knows and respects. For example, I recently flew from Salt Lake to New York City with Utah's former U.S. senator Jake Garn. Jake was not only a distinguished senator, he had the privilege of flying on one of the Space Shuttle missions. Jake is on the board of directors of a company that is headed by a mutual friend of ours. A few days later, I called that friend at his home to arrange a meeting. I could tell my friend was busy and so I "hooked" his undivided attention when I said, "I flew to New York with Jake Garn the other day, and boy did he have some nice things to say about you!" Now, whatever my friend was thinking about before I made that statement, the moment I said it, I had his undivided attention.

Anytime you are communicating with someone and have a legitimate "personal reference" you can open with, it will bring that person's undivided attention to what you are going to say next. As I mentioned in an earlier chapter, after *A Millionaire's Notebook* was published in 1996, I received hundreds of letters from people asking me to be their mentor. The person that I ended up taking on as a protégé, started his letter by referring to a mutual friend of ours and telling me how that friend had given him my book and insisted that he read it. This hook really worked. He grabbed my undivided attention.

As you can see, this hook can be just as effectively used in written communication as it can be when used face-to-face. It's also just as effective when addressing a group. I recently spoke at a meeting of about three thousand people, and each time I made a statement about the leader of that group, I could see an instant rise in their attention and interaction. I've even used this hook in my television campaigns, where I've got at most two seconds to gain the undivided attention of viewers before they pick up the remote control.

I do this by hiring celebrities known to millions of Americans and using them as spokespeople. For example, we used Charlton Heston, Tom Selleck, and Ronald Reagan on a political product; Chuck Norris, Jane Fonda, and Christie Brinkley on fitness products; Cher on a beauty product; Michael Landon on health and educational products, and Richard Simmons on weight-loss products. In each of those cases, having those celebrities speaking on camera, directly to the viewer, created an irresistible hook to those viewers who were in the market for each particular product.

The second type of hook that I use is a question. To be effective, the question must be very specific, requiring the listener to think carefully. It can't be a question like "How is your day going?" or "How are you?" because general questions like that can be answered with clichés—"Okay" or "Fine." On the other hand, if you ask "What are your thoughts about the new product our competitor is introducing next month?" the listener must turn her mind and attention away from whatever he or she is doing to think of a response. Even a simple question like "Would you rather have cereal or eggs for breakfast?" requires them to focus their attention on your conversation for at least a few moments, and that is all a hook needs to accomplish. The purpose of a hook, then, is not necessarily to hold a person's attention for a long time but simply to capture it away from wherever it is and bring it in to the communication. Holding one's attention for the duration of the communication is the job of the second technique, which we will look at in a minute.

The third type of hook that can be extremely effective is a strong statement. The commercial that launched our company back in 1976 opened with a hook that was directed at the potential users of our product and their parents. It would be meaningless to anyone else, but in this commercial, the only ones we were interested in "hooking" were the potential buyers. The product was for acne, and the spokespersons were Pat Boone and his daughter Debby. Pat began the commercial with the statement, "Acne is painful . . . both physically and emotionally! I don't care if you're a teenager or an adult, acne causes embarrassment and anxiety!" How did I know that this statement would hook our potential buyers (people with acne and their parents)? As a teenager I had a terrible case of acne that lasted for years. I was not only deeply embarrassed each time a new pimple appeared, I hated my weekly trips to the dermatologist, who would painfully lance each new cyst.

As good as each of the three types of hooks are, they are even better when used in combination with each other. For example, I opened one fitness commercial with Jane Fonda asking, "Are you one of the fifty million Americans who have tried to lose weight . . . or one of the millions more who have given up?" I then followed that question with Jane making a strong statement: "Diets simply don't work!" So in the space of a few seconds, I had three strong hooks: a credible personal reference (Jane Fonda), a specific question, and a strong statement. I guarantee you that any overweight person in America who tuned in for those first twenty seconds was "hooked" into focusing their undivided attention on what Jane was going to say next. I also combined three hooks by having Cher open a commercial with the question "Have you ever looked at your hair in the mirror and wanted to cry? Well, that's what happened to me!" With Cher, that question, and that statement we hooked every female viewer who ever had a bad hair day.

Now That You've "Hooked" Their Undivided Attention, How Do You Hold It?

Unfortunately, our attention level begins to wane or decline within ten to twenty seconds. So the next roadblock to effective and persuasive communication is a person's declining attention span as thoughts begin to drift away to more pressing issues. So if you are to effectively and persuasively communicate, you need a way to keep raising the level of a person's attention whenever it begins to decline. This holds true whether you are speaking to a two-year-old, a teenager, or the CEO of a Fortune 500 company.

Twenty-five years ago, two of the best communicators I have ever known taught me a method for raising a listener's level of attention anytime it started to drift away. Gary Smalley's mentor was the first person I heard who taught this method, but it was Gary himself who really taught me how to use it. I've seen him use this method in one-on-one conversations as well as when he speaks before audiences as big as seventy to eighty thousand. Like Gary, I have used it in nearly every one-on-one conversation or written correspondence that I've had in the last twenty-five years. I've used it in my television scripts, in my books, and in my public speaking. It is the single most effective means I have ever found of raising a person's attention level, and in fact, I am using it with you right now! This method is so powerful, I've seen it hold my four-year-old's and eight-year-old's attention even when there has been a group of kids waiting for them to come out and play. Now *that's* powerful!

You Can Lead a Horse to Water, but You Can't Make Him Drink. You Want to Bet?

Gary calls this method or technique "salting," and he took the name from the old adage "You can lead a horse to water, but you can't make him drink." Gary, who owns a small farm, says this saying is absolutely untrue. He can make any horse drink every single time he leads him to the water. All he has to do is salt the horse's oats before he takes him to the water. The salt makes the horse so thirsty that he's got to take a drink. Salt has the same effect on me. There's absolutely no way that I could eat a sack of popcorn at the movies without wanting a soda at the same time.

Believe it or not, there is a way you can salt your communication that will make the other person terribly thirsty for what you are going to say or write next. The more you want to raise the attention level, the more "salt" you sprinkle into your words. This "salt" is a statement, a group of statements, or a question that creates curiosity. When used correctly, it makes the person you are talking with or writing to want to hear what we are about to say even more than you want to say it.

Three paragraphs ago I began telling you all about this powerful communication technique before I ever revealed what it was called or explained how it worked. I was "salting" you, creating curiosity about this technique before I revealed it. Knowing what you know now, if you went back and reread this book, you would see that I have used the salting technique over and over again in every chapter.

During my first book tour, I was interviewed by a news anchorwoman for a local NBC affiliate. Early in the interview, she asked me for an example of my communication techniques. I decided to show her the power of salting without telling her what I was doing. I told her that one of the most powerful techniques I teach is a technique called salting. When she asked me to explain it, I told her that I would give her an example of how it is used. Here's what I said:

"You know, as I've been interviewing around the country, I've discovered that there are three things the best interviewers always do. In fact, I first noticed it when Maria Shriver interviewed me, and then after that I noticed that interviewers who did all three of these things not only ended up with a lot better interview, but the ones who did them on their radio call-in shows got ten times as many calls as the ones who didn't. And I've noticed you do two of them, but if you did all three, you'd be the best interviewer in the city because you already do two of them so well."

She couldn't stand waiting any longer. She reached across the desk, grabbed my arm, and said, "Quick, tell me what they are."

I said, "We really don't have time right now; I'll tell you after the interview. But I have just given you a great example of this salting technique. I've made you very 'thirsty' to hear about these three interviewing techniques *before* I've revealed what they are." The anchorwoman then interviewed me for another forty minutes. The moment the interview was over, even before she could take the microphone off her lapel, she reached across the table, grabbed my arm once again and said, "Now . . . will you please tell me what those three things are that the best interviewers always do." Even though she had been conducting the interview for forty minutes, she could not get her mind off the information that I had salted her for. *That* is the power of the salting technique when it is correctly used.

A friend of mine wanted his teenage daughter to read a biography about a woman of tremendous integrity. He had read this biography himself and was so impressed with this woman he really wanted his daughter to discover the principles that had guided her life. Here's what he said to "salt" her about the book:

"Carey, I've just finished reading this book about this woman and I was really impressed."

"Why?" his daughter asked.

"For a lot of reasons. One thing was that she was very resourceful. She fell in love with a guy who wouldn't even give her the time of day . . . in fact, he hardly even knew she existed."

"I know what that's like," his daughter said.

"But guess what happened?"

"What?" Carey asked.

"She did something that worked like magic on this guy. He not only began to notice her, he fell head over heels in love with her faster than she had fallen in love with him. In fact, he chased her so hard, it was only a matter of days before he was begging her to marry him!"

"Wow . . . What did she do?" Carey asked excitedly.

"It's too hard for me to explain, but it's in the book." Carey grabbed the book out of my friend's hand and asked, "What page is it on?"

"I can't remember," said my friend.

"Can you remember the chapter?"

"No, but you'll find it. It's pretty fast reading."

With that, Carey took the book, went to her room, and finished it within two hours.

The Right Way vs. the Wrong Way to Use Salt

Too much salt or salting the wrong things can have negative consequences. You may want salt on popcorn and steak, but you probably wouldn't enjoy it on a graham cracker or a piece of chocolate cake. And even if you like salt sprinkled on your steak, you probably wouldn't want it poured on. The same holds true with communication. You sprinkle salt into your communication when it's needed to raise a person's attention level, or when you want to make a person very thirsty for an important point that you want to make. If you pour too much salt into the conversation the person will think to himself,

"Enough already, get to the point." And if you use salt for every point, the important ones won't stand out. So always use it to prepare your listener or reader for the most important points you want to make, and use it anytime you see someone starting to drift off or lose interest in what you are saying.

Finally, don't be afraid to experiment. The more you use it, the more proficient you will become and the more effective and persuasive your communication will become.

THE MOST POWERFUL COMMUNICATION TECHNIQUE I HAVE EVER USED!

The first technique we looked at was the hook, which is used to capture or recapture someone's undivided attention. The second technique was salting, which is used to make people thirsty for important points or information we want them to pay special attention to. The third technique is the most powerful and effective communication technique I have ever learned or used, and it is one that has been relied upon by the world's greatest communicators. Ronald Reagan, Teddy Roosevelt, Winston Churchill, Mark Twain, Abraham Lincoln, Ben Franklin, and even the biblical writers and prophets used this technique regularly and skillfully to move their listeners and readers to the heights of human understanding and emotion.

It is the one form of communication that can simultaneously communicate to a person's mind and heart, to convey understanding and emotional feelings. Gary Smalley calls this communication technique "emotional word pictures."

Your understanding or analytical abilities come from the left side of the brain, while your emotions or feelings come from the right. Emotional word pictures, or EWPs, not only bring added clarity and understanding to the left side of the brain, they can also stimulate feelings and emotions on the right. Consequently, they become the single most important tool you can use to produce effective and persuasive communication. When you use a good emotional word picture in your communication, it instantly enables the other person to understand what you are saying and feel what you are feeling. And remember, understanding and feeling are the two elements in effective communication, and two of the three elements in persuasive communication.

So What *Is* an Emotional Word Picture?

An emotional word picture is a word, statement, or story that immediately creates a picture in the listener's or reader's mind that clarifies what you're trying to say and communicates a feeling that you want the listener to experience. An EWP can be as simple as a word or statement or as complex as an analogy or short story.

In Chapter 3, I created and used an emotional word picture that I have continued to use throughout this book. I told you about the Saturn V rocket that took American astronauts to the moon. I described its thirty-six-story height, its five massive rocket engines, and the power it generates when it blasts off. I told you that you were just like this Saturn V rocket, except you have seven giant booster engines instead of five. I told you that most people live and die on their launching pads, never having ignited their massive engines. I said that you were anchored to your launching pad by six chains, and that if you wanted to achieve your dreams, you needed to cut these chains and ignite your seven rocket engines.

This is the emotional word picture that I used to communicate an understanding and feeling about what I wanted to share with you in this book. I could have chosen not to use this emotional word picture, and instead simply said: "There are six forces that work against the achieving of your dreams and seven potential forces that can empower you to reach them." You tell me which one you think is more effective, that best clarifies the mission of this book and best motivates you to read it.

Jim and Suzette had been married for ten years. They loved each other and adored their three children. And yet their relationship was going downhill faster than a speeding bullet. Jim was a high school principal and football coach whose time was dominated by his school responsibilities. Suzette had tried to tell Jim that she really needed more of his time, attention, and help, but nothing she said seemed to make any difference. After attending a Gary Smalley seminar and learning about emotional word pictures, Suzette decided to give it a try. She created one that she hoped would help Jim to finally understand what she was saying and feel what she was feeling. Here is a very abbreviated account of what she said.

"Jim, every day you leave me and the kids early in the morning and go off to work. You start your day with a breakfast with your friends and associates and take all the time you need to talk about anything and everything you want. At the end of the meal, you take a few leftovers from your conversation, maybe a teaspoon of eggs and a corner of your buttered toast and drop them into a doggie bag. Then you go do a lot of interesting and fulfilling things throughout the morning and throw a few of those leftovers into the same doggie bag. You go to lunch and once again you have interesting conversation and times with those you care about. At the end of your lunch you throw a few more leftovers into the doggie bag, maybe a little asparagus with hollandaise sauce.

"Your afternoon is filled with more conversation and activities and then you go out to a nice dinner with your friends. You have a mental and emotional feast. At the end of the meal, you throw a piece of cold steak and the corner of a hard roll into your doggie bag.

"When you finally come home, I'm really excited. The kids and I haven't eaten all day. We can't wait to feast on our time and conversation with you, to hear all about the interesting things you did during the day, to hear about your conversations and activities and to tell you about the things we did. But when the door opens and you walk in, you simply hand us the soggy bag of leftovers, and walk into the TV room and watch television until you go to bed. Jim, the kids and I are tired of doggie bags every night. We want to feast on you and have quality time and conversation with you."

Jim was deeply moved by her word picture, and then gave her one that clarified how he often felt when he came home.

"Sue, remember your grandfather's little puppy?" Suzette's happiest childhood memories were of her times with her grandfather and his dogs. "When I go off to work, it's kind of like Grandpa's puppy digging out of the yard and going off into a scary world. I go out and I get chased by big bad dogs. These dogs catch me and bite me and scare the crud out of me. Later, I run into some great big humans, and they throw rocks at me. One hits me in the head and really hurts. Another hits me in the tailbone and I don't think I'll ever be able to sit up for

Grandpa again no matter what kind of bone he offers me. I then run into a big tomcat. He scratches my back and leg, and opens up a cut right above my eye. I pick up all kinds of briars and thorns on the way home, and all I can think about is getting back to my nice comfortable home and seeing Grandpa. I think about the food he'll give me, how he'll get all the thorns out and put me in my nice comfortable doggie bed. I finally see Grandpa's house. I'm so happy I want to run, but I'm too exhausted and hurting too much. I crawl back under his fence and go up to the doorstep. He opens the door and I get all excited. I bark out 'Grandpa.' But as soon as he sees me, he grabs a broom and starts yelling at me and hitting me. 'You ungrateful mutt, how dare you dig a hole under my fence and run off.' Whack, whack. 'Get back up here, I'm not finished talking to you,' and he hits me again. Whack, Whack. Sue, that's how you make me feel when I come home from a hard day at work, and you instantly greet me at the door and start complaining about all the things I haven't done."

Now the unique thing about any emotional word picture is that it can often be very meaningful to the people who are communicating and totally irrelevant to anyone outside of the situation. While these word pictures may not have been effective with you or me, they were incredibly powerful and effective with Jim and Suzette. After he finished his word picture, Suzette cried for more than an hour and then asked his forgiveness. He was so moved by her word picture, he resigned from his job and took one that would not only give him a lot more time with Sue and the kids but would not leave him as emotionally and physically drained, so that when he came home, he would have the emotional and physical energy he needed to give his family the attention he felt they deserved.

While emotional word pictures can be stories such as these, they can also be in the form of a much simpler analogy. One couple I know uses the analogy of a savings account. If Joe does something that offends Patty or hurts her feelings, she'll tell him, "You just made a withdrawal." Joe then asks, "A big one or a little one?" If Patty says just a few bucks, Joe knows it was only a minor offense. If she says, "A giant one . . . bigger than our entire house payment," then he knows it's serious. I've even heard Joe say in response, "What could I do right now that would be a deposit bigger than the withdrawal I just made?" As you can see, they can be very simple yet extremely effective.

Five Important Reasons to Begin Using Emotional Word Pictures

1. They grab and direct a person's attention.
2. They have the power to change a person's thinking, beliefs, and life.
3. They make communication "alive." By stimulating both the left and right side of the listener's brain, the person begins "picturing" or envisioning what he or she is hearing.
4. They lock words into a person's memory. (For example, for the rest of your life, I'll be able to instantly communicate with you by simply asking if you have "cut your anchor chains and ignited your engines.")
5. They provide the gateway to deeper relationships.
6. When used correctly, they can enable you to reprove someone's behavior in a way that can be more easily received without negative consequences.

Six Steps to Creating and Using Emotional Word Pictures in Important Situations

1. Set aside specific time to create an effective word picture. As you become skilled at creating and using them, you'll be able to create some in a few seconds, and others in a few minutes. In the beginning, however, it could take you ten to twenty minutes to create a word picture that will effectively communicate what you consider to be very important.
2. Learn about the other person's interests. Get to know her hobbies; her likes and dislikes; how she spends her spare time; who her favorite singer, actor, or athlete is; her most treasured memories; what makes good days good and bad days bad; and so on. This knowledge will provide the background material you need to create a word picture that truly evokes the right feeling in the other person. Jim knew that Suzette loved her times with her grandfather and she loved playing with his puppies. As soon as he began that word picture, she was instantly drawn into the wonderful feelings she had experienced as a child.

3. Create your word picture from one of five inexhaustible sources.
   • The passions, hobbies, or interests of the person with whom you are communicating.
   • Memorable events from a person's past or the present events he is involved in.
   • Everyday objects that the person is familiar with.
   • Images from nature (oceans, lakes, storms, animals, space, etc.).
   • Imaginary stories that picture the points you want to make.
4. Practice using the word picture you've created, first by yourself, and then (if appropriate) on someone other than the person you are planning to use it with.
5. Pick a convenient time with minimal distractions to communicate your word picture.
6. Without overusing them, be persistent in using word pictures.

By using emotional word pictures you are enabling the other person to clearly understand what you are saying and, more important, feel what you are feeling. When the other person can do this, he has come 99 percent as far as he needed to come to be persuaded. All that remains is that last one percent, which involves motivating him to act. In fact, many times an emotional word picture will take him all the way. When my wife or partners use an emotional word picture that helps me to understand their thinking and feel what they're feeling, nine times out of ten I will do whatever they need or want me to do. However, when their emotional word picture doesn't persuade me to act, they need to add the "motivation to act" to the communication.

MOTIVATING A PERSON TO ACT—THE FINAL ELEMENT OF PERSUASION

Going back to my first major earthquake, you'll remember that it successfully grabbed my undivided attention. Like a good emotional word picture, it clearly communicated understanding and feeling. But it didn't stop there. If it had, it still would have been a totally effective communication, because those are the only two elements in effective communication. Yet it needed one more element to be 100 percent persuasive. It needed to motivate me to act. And as you'll recall, it did exactly that. I tried three times to get out of bed, and when I finally did, I dressed faster than I had ever dressed and I moved to my door, down the hall, and to the elevator as quickly as I could without running over anyone. Why was that earthquake so persuasive? The answer is that it appealed to the two greatest internal motivating factors in my life—in fact, in *anyone's* life.

The Two Greatest Internal Motivating Factors in Anyone's Life

The *desire for gain,* which includes any kind of gain (love, security, acceptance, success, material goods and wealth, physical appearance, health, spirituality, intimacy with God or a person, and so forth) and the *fear of loss,* which includes any kind of loss (love, person, security, acceptance, success, material goods and wealth, physical appearance, health, spirituality and intimacy with God or another person) are the two greatest internal motivating factors in anyone's life. Of course, one of the greatest fears is that of losing one's life or the life of loved ones.

So, if we are to gain the third element of persuasion—the motivation to act—we must always appeal to either the person's desire for gain or the person's fear of loss. In the case of the earthquake, it appealed to both. It appealed to my fear of loss (if the building collapsed I would have lost my family, my health, and most likely my life) while at the same time it appealed for my desire for gain (personal safety and security). Therefore, the earthquake successfully persuaded me to act.

Whenever you are creating a verbal or written communication in which you wish to persuade someone to do something, you need to examine your argument and identify which desires and fears you are appealing to. Is the appeal clear or is it foggy? Is it the *greatest* desire for gain or fear of loss that you *can* appeal to, or are there others that are greater?

When my friend salted his teenage daughter to read the biography, he appealed to her desire for gaining more success in her relationships with boys. While this was very persuasive, had he appealed to her desire for health, his appeal would probably have fallen flat.

Every person has a different set of values and priorities. In business, people desire gain in their careers, as well as with their customers and projects and so on. They, of course, also fear losing their careers and customers. A man who values his time with his family above all things may have very few fears or desires in the area of material wealth. So, appealing to the areas of greatest individual concern will increase the persuasiveness of your appeal.

AN HONORING, LOGICAL PRESENTATION—THE STRUCTURE OF A PERSUASIVE PRESENTATION

You can have a great foundation and all the right materials you need to build a wonderful house, but if you fail to design a sound structure, the house may still collapse. When you are trying to persuade someone on a minor issue, all you may need is the foundation of honor and the three techniques of effective communication. However, when the issue is greater, correctly structuring your presentation can be the difference between success and failure. On such occasions, I have found that a particular structure has brought me success far more often than it has failed me. So, a persuasive presentation must begin with preparation.

PREPARING FOR A PERSUASIVE PRESENTATION

1. Make sure everything you write or say in your presentation treats your listener with honor and respect and avoids condescension.
2. Be sure to focus on the person's two greatest internal motivating factors, appealing to the greatest desires for gain and the greatest fears of loss that your idea or product affects.
3. Create a written worksheet that includes:
   - A list that identifies all the benefits your idea or product offers.
   - A description of your listeners and the desires or needs your idea or product will fulfill. Identify their desires for gain and fears of loss that your idea or product will address.
   - State why your idea or product fulfills these needs or desires better than any other idea or product available to the listener.
4. List and prioritize every possible objection and excuse your listener could use for not accepting your idea or proposal.
5. List and prioritize how your idea or product overcomes each objection or excuse.

6. Write a presentation that follows the structure given below:
   - Create an opening that will immediately grab the listener's or viewer's attention with as strong a hook as you can create. (Use an emotional word picture if appropriate.)
   - Describe the problems your idea or product is going to solve.
   - Salt the presentation with curiosity-building statements or questions as often as you need to keep the individual's undivided attention.
   - Use emotional word pictures to make your most important points crystal clear and unforgettable. Use your idea or product benefit list and your answers to objections and excuses to form the body of your presentation.
   - Use the testimonials of those who have benefited from similar ideas or from your product. If this is a sales presentation, use the testimonials of satisfied customers, industry experts, or other credible sources to increase the credibility of your product and your claims.
   - Use comparisons to other ideas, products, or prices to build a perceived value of the idea or product that far exceeds what you are proposing, or the selling price of your product.
   - Close the presentation with a quick summary (when time allows) of the benefits of your idea or product. Give a risk/reward comparison, a clear-cut reason for action, and finally, a call to action.

You may think that this kind of presentation requires a great deal of time to put together. It doesn't. But whatever time you invest in it will be well worth it. I've written over eight hundred two-minute commercials that followed this structure. Commercials that persuaded more than twenty million consumers to go to the phones and order our products. So I know it works!

In summary, persuasive communication is like a magnificent building. It has a solid foundation, the finest building materials, and an attractive and sound structural design. The foundation is honoring and respecting the people you are communicating with; honoring and respecting them with your attitude, the words you choose, and the manner in which you present those words. The building materials are effective hooks, salt, emotional word pictures, and an appeal to their greatest internal motivating factors—desire for gain and fear of loss.

The structure itself is a logical presentation that honors the time and needs of your listeners.

Persuasive communication is the single key that opens more doors to people's minds and hearts than any other. It is a learnable art that you *can* master. In the beginning, it may take a little time and effort. But like any art, the more you practice, the more it will become second nature.

POWER SECRET #11:
Effectively and Persuasively Communicating

Complete the following exercises in your notebook.

Laying the Foundation of Persuasion

1. Think back on any situation, either personal or professional, in which you either attempted or desired to attempt to persuade someone to do something that was important to you, and then answer the following questions.
   - What could you have said or done that would have shown a greater degree of honor or value to the person you desired to persuade?
   - What was their frame of reference (personality type, opinions, past experiences, concerns, etc.) as it related to you and the situation or issue?
   - What could you have done to have more clearly understood their frame of reference?
   - Were you a good listener?
2. If there is any situation in the immediate future in which you are going to attempt to effectively communicate an important issue or wish to persuade someone, complete the following exercise before you do so.
   - What specifically can you do or say that will show a greater degree of honor or value to the person you are desiring to persuade?
   - What is their frame of reference (personality type, opinions, past experiences, concerns, etc.) as it relates to you and the situation or issue?
   - What can you do ahead of time to gain a better understanding of their frame of reference?
   - What specific questions can you ask that will help you to understand their frame of reference, and help the person to know that you value his or her opinions and concerns?

- Is your motive to inform him, to persuade him to do what is in his best interest, or to do what is in your best interest?

BECOMING A MORE EFFECTIVE AND PERSUASIVE COMMUNICATOR

1. Think back on any situation, either personal or professional, in which you either attempted or desired to persuade someone to do something that was important to you, and then do the following:
   - Write out several different hooks that could have grabbed the person's undivided attention.
   - Write out salting statements or questions that could have kept his curiosity high throughout your conversation or presentation.
   - Write out one or more emotional word pictures that could have enabled your listener or reader to better understand what you were saying and feel what you were feeling.
   - How could you have appealed to his greatest motivating factors?
2. Before your next attempt to effectively communicate an important issue or wish to persuade someone, complete the following exercise:
   - Write out several different hooks that can grab their undivided attention.
   - Write out statements or questions that can salt their curiosity.
   - Write out one or more emotional word pictures that can enable your listener or reader to better understand what you were saying and feel what you were feeling.
   - Write out the ways in which you appeal to the greatest motivating factors.
3. Using the outline on pages 215–216, create a persuasive presentation for the situation you've outlined in #2 above.

CHAPTER 15

Engine #6: "Pit Bull Persistence"

AN EASY DISCIPLINE ANYONE CAN LEARN

THE SECRET OF WINNING 90 PERCENT OF THE TIME

Before American Telecast was created, my partner John Marsh had made his living as a dog trainer. I once asked him why a pit bull was such a ferocious dog. He told me that pit bulls are usually friendly and mild-mannered dogs unless they are threatened or attacked. When a pit bull is attacked, he said, you can pity the poor dog that attacked it—even if the dog is three times its size. John went on to tell me that pit bulls were originally bred in the 1800s in England to fight other dogs in an arena or "pit." Even though they were a small dog (eighteen to twenty-one inches high and forty to fifty pounds), they rarely lost fights against much larger and more ferocious breeds. John explained: "First, they are so tenacious that the only time they lose a fight is when they are killed. They would never give up and run away. Second, they usually win by finding a vital area on their opponent and then, when their teeth find their target, they would lock their jaws in place and not let go until the fight was over." They have, far and away, more muscle strength per pound than any other breed of dog. Now, if you think about it, that is an incredible picture of persistence.

A professor of entrepreneurship at UCLA was asked by a reporter,

"What do successful entrepreneurs have in common?" Her answer was, "Tremendous tenacity . . . they just don't give up!" If I had been asked, "What do people who achieve their dreams have in common?" I would have had to give the same answer as the professor. Dream-achievers all have learned and mastered the discipline of persistence. This is true for people who achieve their professional dreams as well as for those who achieve their personal dreams. Couples who have the happiest marriages and strongest families have achieved their success by working at it day in and day out, year in and year out. It is the same for dream-achievers in business, sports, and entertainment. And even though this trait is universally common and dominant among dream-achievers, in the general population it is rare.

We live in an age of instant gratification. Adults want their dreams fulfilled right now! And when they aren't, the dreams are quickly scaled down, postponed, or abandoned altogether. We are known as the disposable society. Marriages are often the most tragic examples of this. Couples routinely give up their hopes and dreams for a fulfilling relationship within weeks of the honeymoon's end. A high percentage of divorces take place within the first year of marriage and countless more take place by the end of the fifth. And even those couples who remain married often quickly give up on their dreams, accepting mediocrity in place of fulfillment. They stay together out of convenience or fear of the consequences of separation rather than passionately pursuing their dreams for their marriage. They take the institution that was meant to be a lifetime source of security, joy, and fulfillment and allow it to become no more than a convenient place to "crash" after a busy day.

You don't need persistence to go downhill, but you can't go uphill without it!

In your personal as well as your professional life, dreams are never found lying on the floor of a valley; they are never reached by coasting downhill. Dreams are always perched in the rocks at the top of the highest mountains. The pathways are often steep and treacherous, filled with boulders and other obstacles. They simply cannot be reached without persistence. If you hope to achieve any of your dreams, you must learn how to ignite this sixth powerful engine, and keep it burning until you successfully reach each dream.

PERSISTENCE CAN BE ACQUIRED!

If persistence were simply a behavioral trait that you were either born with or born without, we would all be in trouble. Persistence is an inborn trait in only a very tiny percentage of the population. In fact, the vast majority of people who exhibit this trait have acquired it over a period of time. It is literally a discipline that anyone can develop. But while developing it is not hard, it does require learning a few basic skills and then putting those skills into practice. It's a little like tennis. Once you learn a few basics like the right way to hold the racket, how to address the ball, how to return a serve, and how to make a forehand and a backhand shot, you can begin to play effectively and enjoy the game. Once you learn the basics of persistence and begin to practice them, you will begin to enjoy increased levels of achievement, almost overnight.

I LOVE THOMAS EDISON!

If ever there was one American whose life was the personification of persistence, it was Thomas Edison. By the time Edison died, he had not only invented the phonograph, the electric light, and the motion picture projector, he had been awarded 1,094 patents, more than any man or group of men in history. Two of his more famous quotes were: "When the going gets tough, the tough get going," and "Genius is one percent inspiration and ninety-nine percent perspiration!" Edison, who had only been considered a genius after inventing the electric light, had rightly determined that true genius was a lot more about persistence than about IQ.

During his three-year pursuit of the electric light, Edison was reportedly asked, "Why do you keep trying to create an electric light when you've already failed ten thousand times?" He is said to have answered, I have not *failed* ten thousand times; rather, I have successfully discovered ten thousand alternatives that don't work, and with each one of those discoveries, I am that much closer to finding the one discovery that will work. He is said to have tested five hundred filaments before finding one that worked. Had he given up after testing number four hundred, we might still be reading by candlelight or kerosene lamps. But fortunately for us, Edison had developed and mastered the discipline of persistence long before he began his quest for an electric light. And by the time he was in his early twenties, he had also mastered the entire art of Dream Conversion. By age twenty-four, he had cut all six anchor chains and had ignited all seven of his Dream Conversion rocket engines.

For example, when Edison got an idea for some device that did not exist, he wrote it down with as much detail as he could muster. (Step one of the Dream Conversion Process: gain a clear vision of your dream and then define it in writing.) Then, before he even considered what it would take to create such an invention, he began to imagine all of the potential long-term and global ramifications that could result from it. In fact, he would devise vast concepts and schemes of what could be accomplished from such an invention and all of its potential derivatives. In other words, he would raise his sights to the moon and beyond. And he would do all of this visualizing and shooting for the moon before he would even try to figure out if such an invention was even possible.

Edison's Secret

And here is one of the greatest secrets of Edison's phenomenal success. Whenever he would begin to get discouraged by all of the minutiae and failures that precede the birth of a working invention, he would return to his broad vision, with all of its long-term and global ramifications. And without fail, his broad vision would reenergize his emotions and his commitment to persist. It was his broad vision that would ignite and then continually fuel Edison's passion and "pit bull persistence" in his pursuit of his invention.

So, now that you've seen persistence accurately pictured in the fighting nature of a pit bull and personified in the person of Thomas Edison, it might be helpful to give what I believe is a good working definition of persistence. I have found that many people have the wrong concept of persistence, one that can result in tragic failures and discouragement.

WHAT PERSISTENCE IS NOT: True persistence is *not* hitting a brick wall, getting up off the ground, dusting yourself off, and then hitting it again and again and again. That's stupidity!

WHAT PERSISTENCE IS: True persistence is hitting the brick wall, getting up, dusting yourself off, and realizing that you're not going to get through it; so you have to figure out a way to get over it, under it, around it, or to blow it up.

HOW YOU CAN ACQUIRE THE DISCIPLINE OF PERSISTENCE

Step #1: Gaining a Vision and Utilizing the Dream Conversion Process

As we saw with Thomas Edison, persistence begins with a vision. The incredible wisdom of Solomon attested to this when he wrote in Proverbs 29:18, "Without a vision the people perish." Solomon wasn't speaking of physical death but rather the death of the soul. Without vision, people lose their joy and passion for life and slip into the quagmire of mediocrity, simply existing or just getting by, rather than truly living. Without a vision there is no passion, and without passion there is no fuel for persistence.

It should be obvious by now that utilizing the Dream Conversion Process is both foundational and critical to igniting and fueling all seven engines in the art of Dream Conversion. And gaining a clear and precise vision of your dreams and then putting that vision into writing is the first and most important step.

However, the remaining steps in the Dream Conversion Process are equally important to developing persistence. When you convert your dream into tangible goals and then convert those goals into steps and those steps into tasks, you are not only gaining a road map to achieving your dream, you are gaining a new vision of how you are going to achieve your dream. And this, in turn, creates a well-founded hope that fuels your passion and persistence.

Remember Dick Clark's offer of a dream vacation for two? All you had to do was drive from New York to his home in California in seven days without having his address or using a map or asking directions. You would never even start out on such a hopeless journey. But once you were told you would be given his precise address and clear directions to his door, everything changed. Such a map not only gave you what you physically needed to accomplish the trip and of doing it with time to spare, it also provided all the hope you needed to persist all the way to the end. Just as the Dream Conversion Process ignited and fueled your persistence in this hypothetical dream, so it will ignite and fuel your persistence in the pursuit of your actual dreams.

Before 1849, there were many pioneers who decided to "go west" to seek out a better life for themselves and their families, but very few made it all the way to California. Their somewhat "general" dream did not provide enough "fuel" to persist in such a long and difficult journey. Then, in 1849, gold was discovered, and all of a sudden thousands of families not only started out for California, they persisted through all kinds of terrible conditions, trials, and tribulations until they finally reached the gold fields. You see, unlike the earlier settlers, they weren't simply "going west" to fulfill a general dream of a "better life." Rather, they had a very specific vision that fueled their persistence. They were going to search for gold, find it, and become rich—or they were going to get rich by supplying goods and services to all the other people who were going for the gold. But they had very specific dreams, and they converted those dreams into goals, and then converted their goals into steps, and the steps into tasks. And the result was they ignited and continually fueled their persistence engine. They had all the persistence they needed to overcome mountains and deserts, outlaws and Indians, disease and pestilence.

So the first step to acquiring or developing persistence is gaining a clear vision of a dream and utilizing the Dream Conversion Process.

Step #2: Shoot for the Moon and Broaden Your Vision

The next step once again follows Thomas Edison's example: ignite the second engine in the art of Dream Conversion and shoot for the moon. This means looking at all of the greatest potential benefits and possible ramifications of your dream. For example, if your dream is to have a marriage where all your deepest emotional needs are met and where you are able to meet all the deepest needs of your spouse, list all the potential ramifications of achieving that dream. In addition to the greater level of joy and fulfillment that you'll experience, your children will also gain greater security and fulfillment. They will gain a clear picture of what a marriage should be, seeing how a husband and wife can truly meet each other's deepest needs and desires. You visualize how that will help them to work toward their own fulfilling marriages, and likewise be a tremendous blessing to their children. You see generations of strong families resulting from the achieving of your dream. You think of the tremendous contribution you and your children will be able to make to others who want the same kind of fulfilling relationships you have.

As you begin to see all of the potential benefits and ramifications of your dream, your broad vision will give you all the persistence you need to wade through the hardships and overcome the obstacles that stand between you and your fulfilled dream.

Step #3: Spread Your Vision to Others

As soon as Edison gained and made a written record of a vision for an invention, with all of its broadest ramifications, he communicated that vision to his staff and workers. He did everything he could to make sure they caught the entire vision. They then became a team of people, unified and motivated by the same vision. In doing this, Edison ignited the third and most powerful engine in the art of Dream Conversion, Steven Spielberg Partnering. In addition to the other benefits of partnering, its impact on persistence is awesome. When Edison became discouraged and his persistence engine began to burn out, he wanted to abandon his dream for a new invention. However, one or more of his associates were still fired up with persistence, and *their* persistence carried him through until his persistence engine was reignited.

American Telecast has been run by seven partners for twenty-one years. We have nearly gone under and lost everything at least three times. But the reason we were able to persist through the hardest times was because there was never a time when all seven of us gave up or burned out at the same time. When one or more of us no longer had the stamina to persist, there was always at least one or two who did!

Solomon echoed this principal in the fourth chapter of Ecclesiastes. He wrote: "Two are better than one; because they have a good reward for their labor. For if they fall, the one will lift up his fellow: but woe to him that is alone when he falleth; for he hath not another to help him up. Again, if two lie together, then they have heat: but how can one be warm alone? And if one prevail against him, two shall withstand him; and a threefold cord is not quickly broken."

A threefold cord is not easily broken, and when you share your vision with others, your persistence will be fueled and empowered by theirs, and vice versa.

Step #4: Expect Criticism and Strikeouts, and Learn the Right Ways to Deal with Them

No one enjoys criticism or failure, and yet, for dream-achievers, they are as much a part of life as eating and drinking. In Chapters 5 and 6, we looked at the right way to view and deal with failure and criticism. I have met a great many people in my life who have never learned the right way to deal with either criticism or failure. Those people rarely persist at anything worthwhile. The reason is that they are so easily distracted, detoured, or defeated by criticism and by their strikeouts or the strikeouts of others. As I've talked with people who have given up on their dreams too early, I've discovered that they not only lacked persistence, they all shared a common trait. They were always surprised by criticisms and by their strikeouts and the strikeouts of others. And yet these things are part of everyday life.

If you really want to develop persistence, you must first begin to expect criticisms and strikeouts, and be prepared to deal with them in the proper ways. Chapter 6 gave you everything you need in order to deal with criticisms. But what about strikeouts? I have two very close friends who are midway through their lives and they have still not learned the right way to handle strikeouts—theirs or others'. As a result, they have achieved only a tiny fraction of what they are capable of achieving. Even worse, they are unhappy a great deal of the time and nobody likes working with them. When something goes wrong on one of their projects, they typically blow up, attack, blame, criticize, and so forth. Who wants to work with someone like that?

How do you currently deal with your strikeouts and the strikeouts of others? Let's first look at how you handle your strikeouts. Whether it's at home or on the job, when things don't go the way you want them to, or when you make a mistake or fall flat on your face, what do you do? Check the appropriate responses to the following question:

HOW DO YOU REACT WHEN YOU STRIKE OUT?

1. Do you become: _____Defensive _____Angry _____Discouraged _____Depressed
2. Do you: _____Pout _____Withdraw _____Deny _____Make excuses _____Rationalize _____Attack _____Blame others _____Blame circumstances

Or

3. Do you: _____Accept responsibility for the strikeout? _____Analyze, discover, and learn from the strikeout? _____Seek insights from others? _____Become determined and diligent to try again and not make the same mistake that caused the strikeout?

If you are not really sure how you normally handle your strikeouts, show this questionnaire to your spouse or friends and ask them to help you check the right spaces. They are often more aware of how you routinely react than you are.

Although the reactions in the first question are all fairly routine, it is important to once again realize that you can choose to *respond* instead of following your inclination and react the wrong way. After you strike out, you may want to give up rather than face the possibility of striking out again. If you do return to the plate to try again, your inclination may be to hope for a walk or to just try for a bunt or a single. In a sense, this is returning to the safety of mediocrity. Instead, if you want to achieve your dreams, after the initial sting of the strikeout subsides you must analyze why it happened. If you can't figure it out, you must seek the advice and insights of others.

HOW DO YOU HANDLE THE STRIKEOUTS OF OTHERS?

How you handle other people's strikeouts is critical to achieving your dreams, because your most powerful rocket engine is your ability to effectively partner. If you consistently mishandle the strikeouts of others, your partnering engine will lose its power or burn out altogether. Even if you don't lose your partners, you will lose their minds and hearts and render your partnership impotent. Correctly handling other people's strikeouts is also critical to your acquiring persistence. Remember that there will be times when their persistence will keep you going even when yours is nonexistent. If you fail to correctly respond to their strikeouts, you will deflate their sense of motivation, and consequently, it will not be available to help fuel yours. Look at the question below and see if you can recognize how you handle other people's failures.

How do you react when others strike out?

1. Do you become: ____Critical   ____Angry
2. Do you: ____Lecture   ____Advise   ____Criticize   ____Discipline   ____Correct   ____Withdraw   ____Attack
Or
3. Do you: ____Allow recovery time   ____Listen   ____Comfort   ____Encourage   ____Show patience   ____Offer help and partnership

Here again, the natural inclination will be to react with the attitudes and actions described in question one. However, once again you can choose to respond with the attitudes and activities described in question two. When you do, you will strengthen the person, his persistence, and his commitment to you. You will help alleviate his fears of trying again. And ultimately, you will see him begin to succeed.

I would encourage you to ask others how you normally respond to their strikeouts and then ask them how they would like you to respond. Remember, nobody likes a lecture after a strikeout. They are already hurting and have probably begun to analyze the whys and why nots before you ever get to them. What they need is an ear and encouragement. If you choose to respond to their strikeout, you will both be the beneficiaries of your actions.

A Lesson from the Strikeout King and His Teammates

In addition to his home run and slugging records, Babe Ruth also set the record for the most strikeouts in a major league career. Imagine if every time he struck out, he threw his bat down and came storming back to the dugout, swearing and yelling, "I hate striking out. . . . I hate this game. That lousy pitcher . . . he tricked me. And that ump . . . that last strike he called was a mile away from the plate!" Now, imagine that with each strikeout the fans all booed him and when he made it into the dugout, his coach threw his clipboard down and yelled, "What the heck are you doin', Babe. How many times have I told you, don't swing at the high balls." And then imagine if all of his teammates yelled, "Yeah, Babe, what were you thinking about? You left three men on base. Thanks to you, we're going to lose this game."

Now, I can assure you that very little of that kind of activity or dialogue took place. If that had been the way the Babe, his fans, his coaches, and his teammates had reacted to his strikeouts, there would be no Yankee Stadium today, and chances are major league baseball would have died after the 1919 Black Sox scandal. But fortunately, Babe, his fans, his coaches, and his teammates had all learned the right way to respond. They knew that his strikeouts were not only okay, they were a necessary part of his strategy for hitting home runs. He had to swing with all his might, and when you make that choice, you're going to miss the ball more often than you're going to hit it. Everyone knew that, and they were willing to correctly respond to his strikeouts because they knew that a home run was just around the corner. If you can take responsibility to begin to correctly handle your strikeouts and the strikeouts of those around you, you will begin to see more home runs than you would ever imagine possible . . . for you *and* your teammates! Responding the right way will reduce the amount of discouragement and despair you will experience and will greatly enhance your ability to persist.

I had never written or directed a single commercial when we started American Telecast in 1976. I wrote and produced my first commercial that summer. From that point on, I was writing, producing, and directing more than one hundred two-minute commercials per year. In the beginning, my success rate was 25 percent. That meant I was striking out 75 percent of the time. And yet my partners were incredibly patient. They never lectured me after a failure. We would all talk it over after the sting had worn off, and we would try to figure out why it didn't work. The result was that my average eventually rose to an 82 percent success rate in an industry where the average success rate was under one half of one percent. Had my partners and I not learned how to handle my failures, I probably would have quit the business in our first or second year.

When you fail, if the people around you all begin to criticize and second-guess you, don't get defensive and don't look for others to blame. Just ask them to put all their thoughts, analyses, and suggestions into writing so you can thoughtfully analyze what happened after the dust has settled and you can see a little more clearly.

When those around you fail, remember they are hurting. They are already going over everything in their own minds, and the last thing they need from you is criticism of any kind. Give them all the space, listening, and encouragement they need at the moment. And then, when their pain has subsided, hours or days later, approach them in the spirit of a learner rather than in the spirit of a "know-it-all." Ask them for their thoughts on why they struck out. Ask questions and brainstorm together. You'll both learn a great deal and your relationship and the resulting persistence will be greatly strengthened.

Step #5: Expect Obstacles and Roadblocks and Respond to Them with Creative Alternatives

For twenty-one years, American Telecast has been selling its various products direct to consumers through television commercials and infomercials that provide an 800 number for ordering. This industry is referred to as Direct Response TV. There are only five or six companies that have survived in our industry as long as we have. And every year, there are scores of newcomers, and most of these fail within the first year. This is a business that is very specialized and has some treacherous pitfalls that are nearly invisible to the untrained eye. When a company falls into one of them, they don't lose thousands of dollars, they lose millions. As a result, what they thought was going to be a get-rich-quick campaign ends up bankrupting them almost overnight. They are not able to persist through failure because they never expected to run into the massive obstacles and roadblocks that they encountered. And when you don't expect obstacles and roadblocks, you aren't prepared for them.

On the other hand, the handful of veterans in our industry are keenly aware of the pitfalls, as we have all fallen victim to them at one time or another. We not only prepare in advance for the obstacles and roadblocks, we have become skilled at developing creative alternatives on the spot as they arise.

My partners and I have created hundreds of projects in our twenty-one years together, and I can't imagine beginning any worthwhile project, personal or professional, without encountering obstacles and roadblocks. Yet I hear people complain and make excuses every day about the failures they've experienced because of something happening that they didn't expect. If you expect the unexpected to happen, instead of being surprised, you'll be prepared.

Of the hundreds of projects I have completed, I have never completed one that wasn't filled with unforeseen problems. I've had celebrities furious at me, ready to cancel a shoot hours before we were to begin. I've had shoots in progress when critical equipment failed. I've even had my appendix rupture two days before a shoot that supposedly could not be postponed. And yet the key to persisting over the obstacles and around the roadblocks has been our company's ability to develop what I call creative alternatives.

For a moment, let's go back to the working definition of persistence. I said, "True persistence is hitting the brick wall, getting up, dusting yourself off, and realizing that you're not going to get through it; so you have to figure out a way to get over it, under it, around it, or to blow it up."

The higher the wall, the greater the inclination to walk away from it. But the higher it is, the more creative you have to be in devising an alternative. If you are unable to devise a creative alternative that works, you need to seek out partners or advisers who can come up with one that does work. I launched our Richard Simmon's "Deal-a-Meal" campaign in 1986 with a series of two-minute commercials and a print campaign. We ran the campaign for six months and generated $10 million in sales. After that, the commercials no longer generated a response that was adequate to continue the campaign. We shot new commercials, but they, too, failed to produce adequate results. We were about to throw in the towel when one of my partners had an idea for a totally different approach. His creative alternative allowed us to run Deal-a-Meal for another five years, generating an additional $160 million in sales.

Step #6: Maintain a Marathon Pace

One of the greatest enemies of persistence is impatience, the desire to chase your dreams at a sprinter's pace. Unfortunately, worthwhile dreams are never only a hundred yards away; instead, they are usually *miles* away. And yet most people gain a vision or a dream and then run as fast and as hard as they can to catch it. The only problem is they poop out shortly after they begin. Think back to the last time you saw a hundred-meter dash. Whether it was the Olympics or your child's track meet, how did the runners look and act after they crossed the finish line? I'm sure they all gasped for air, some of them leaned on their knees, others sat down or lay down and some just walked around, head down and panting. No matter what shape they were in, they were all out of breath and temporarily exhausted.

Can you imagine what would happen if the moment they crossed the finish line the official told them, "The race isn't over, there are 105 laps around the track to go." Chances are not one of them would start running. And if they did, they would certainly not run very fast. In fact, if they did anything other than walk, they most likely wouldn't make it to the finish line. That's because the only thing a marathon and a hundred-meter dash have in common is that they are both races. They require completely different training methods and strategies as well as different running styles. Now, as foolish as it would be for even the fastest sprinter in the world to compete seriously in a marathon, it's even more foolish for you to expect to catch your dreams at a sprinter's pace.

Edison and his staff worked for nearly three years on his electric light project. They worked long days, often sixteen to twenty hours. They solved problems inventors had been struggling with for over fifty years. What do you think would have happened if Edison had entered his lab every morning with the energy and attitude of a sprinter. Imagine him calling his staff together and saying, "Okay everybody, this is it. I want you all to work faster today than you've ever worked. I don't want to see anyone walking or even jogging anywhere. It's run, run, run. The name of the game around here is speed, speed, speed. Ready, set, go! Hop to it!" At this kind of pace, everyone would have burned out in less than a day. But Edison, the master of persistence, knew that gradual steady progress would not only get the job done, but get it done in record time. For his dream wasn't a hundred yards away, it was a hundred miles away. He and his staff even took naps in the lab. They needed endurance and persistence to finish their long-distance race.

Zig Ziglar tells the story of how he wanted to lose thirty pounds in nine months. It sounded like an enormous task in that he had never successfully lost weight in his life. Then he realized that to lose that much weight within that time frame would mean he would only have to lose one and three-quarter ounces a day. That not only made his goal doable, it made it easy. He lost his weight and never put it back on. Richard Simmons told me that crash diets never work. When people quickly lose ten or twenty pounds, they gain it all back almost as fast. But if they take it off gradually, by adopting doable long-term eating and exercise habits, they'll take it off and keep it off.

Remember my résumé? I lost nine jobs in six years. My favorite example of a man who mastered persistence and went through life at a marathoner's pace is a man whose résumé says it all.

At twenty-one, he saw his first business fail.
At twenty-three, he ran for a state political office and lost.
At twenty-four, he saw his second business fail.
At twenty-seven, he had a nervous breakdown.
At twenty-nine, he ran for Congress and lost.
At thirty-one, he ran for Congress again, and lost again.
At thirty-seven, he ran for Congress and won. (At last!)
At forty-six, he ran for vice president and lost.
At forty-nine, he ran for the Senate and lost.

Now, looking at this man's résumé, wouldn't you think he should just give up his dream of a high political office? And yet he didn't burn out. His résumé not only shows persistence, it shows a great deal of patience. In the end, it paid off—for him and for a lot more for us. In fact, we live in the *United* States of America because, at the age of fifty-one, Abraham Lincoln became the sixteenth president, the one who would have to overcome the greatest obstacle ever faced by an American president, the splitting of our nation!

So, in following through on the Dream Conversion Process, pursue your dreams at a marathoner's pace, no matter how much you are tempted to sprint! Don't try to complete too many tasks in a day or take too many steps in a week. Take your time to correctly complete each task and step. And complete them at a pace that doesn't risk an early burn out.

Keeping the right pace in the Dream Conversion Process not only impacts your acquiring of persistence, it is the final determining factor of whether or not you will actually achieve your dreams in time to enjoy them. The final rocket engine in the art of Dream Conversion is the engine that will truly determine the pacing of the Dream Conversion Process in your life. It is like the accelerator in your car. It becomes your primary tool for determining how efficiently you will achieve each of your dreams. You can drive most of the trip at a cruising speed that will get you to your destination safely and on time. But you'll also be able to slow down when you approach the hazards and detours, and you'll be able to speed up when you need to pass other cars. I call this engine Laser-Accurate Priority Planning. It will enable you to keep on schedule for the highest priority dreams in your life.

POWER SECRET #12:
Acquiring the Discipline of Winning Most of the Time

1. IN YOUR DREAM Conversion Journal, on each of your Dream Pages, write at least one paragraph that outlines your broadest vision and all of the potential ramifications of achieving that particular dream.

2. Share your most important dreams with the people you trust, especially those you might want to recruit as partners or mentors in achieving each dream.

3. Think of the failures you have experienced at home or on the job. In your notebook, write down some of them and state how you reacted. (Use the questions on page 228 to help you recall your reactions.)

4. Think of the failures experienced by those around you at home or on the job. In your notebook, write down some of them and how you reacted. (Use the questions on page 229 to help you recall your reactions.) Ask those closest to you how you normally react to their failures. And then ask them how they would like you to respond. Take notes!

5. In your Dream Conversion Journal, next to each of your Dream Pages, add a page entitled "Obstacles." On each of these pages list as many potential obstacles as you can think of that could keep you from achieving each dream. Once you've made this list, make a list of creative alternatives that you think could help you overcome each obstacle. This is a great place to recruit the ideas of others. You may see one creative alternative for overcoming a roadblock, but someone else might see one that is even more effective or more easily achievable. Also, expect to encounter roadblocks you haven't foreseen. When they stand in your path, instead of panicking, begin brainstorming with others and make a list of possible creative alternatives.

6. In your Dream Conversion Journal, review the deadlines you have set for achieving the necessary tasks, steps, and goals to achieve each of your most important dreams. Ask yourself if you are trying

to achieve those tasks at a sprinter's pace or a marathoner's pace. You may need to move some of your target dates back in order to move into the marathoner's pace. Any important dream is likely to require a long-term commitment, and that means establishing a steady reliable pace for the long haul.

CHAPTER 16

Engine #7: "Laser-Accurate Priority Planning"

A DREAM-ACHIEVING ROUTINE ANYONE CAN ADOPT

WHEN I WAS in first grade, we would play a game on the playground called Crack the Whip. For those readers who have never heard of this game, let me describe it. Fifteen or twenty kids would line up and grasp one another's wrists. Then the person at the front of the line would begin to run, as would everyone else behind him. The person at the front of the line was in total control of which way the group would run. When everyone was running as fast as they could, the front person would start changing directions (doing *S* turns). While this was quite easy for the first five or ten kids to handle, the last four or five (on the "tail of the whip") would be jerked around, totally out of control, and usually thrown off the whip to fall, rolling, onto the ground. As a child I loved Crack the Whip, especially when I got to be on the tail end. It was a wild ride, and it was actually fun being totally out of control, not knowing where you were going or where you would end up.

While that feeling was fun in the game, it's a terrible feeling in life. Feeling out of control causes stress, fear, frustration, and discouragement. It can also cause anger, bitterness, and resentment. And yet, as bad as those feelings are, the terrible realities and devastating consequences of being out of control are much worse.

The Devastating Consequences of Being Out of Control

Unfortunately, nearly everyone I know goes through life at the tail end of the whip, just trying to "hang on." They end every day with the question "Where did the time go?" The minutes and hours of their days are dictated by circumstances and the needs, desires, and demands of other people. This would not be so bad if it only happened one day a week. But for most people it happens nearly every day of the month, every month of the year, and every year of their life. What they get done in their day, what they accomplish in a month, and what they ultimately achieve in their lifetime is not determined by their values and priorities but rather by the values and priorities of others.

And here is the tragedy. By the time most people wake up and realize they've been on the tail of the whip, it's too late to achieve their most important dreams—dreams that truly reflect their personal values and priorities. At the end of their lives they think: "What happened? Where did the time go? What happened to my values, my commitments, my priorities? What happened with my husband/wife? What happened with my children? What happened to my career? What happened with all the things I wanted to do but never did? How could this be?"

Can you think of anything more depressing or tragic than to reach the last years or months of your life and think these thoughts and face these regrets? As tragic as this would be, this is exactly what you will experience if you don't stand up and take control of your life right now! Notice that I said "right now," not tomorrow. And to gain control of your life, you must first *take* control of your time. This involves three simple steps: first, you must realize how time "gets away" from you in the first place; second, you must then learn how to capture or take control of it; and third, once you know how to take control of your time you must act, and actually begin to take control of it.

HOW DOES TIME "GET AWAY" FROM YOU?

1. *You accidentally lose minutes, and purposely throw away hours.*
Time gets away from you in both small and large increments. You
accidentally let go of time by letting your mind drift or wander out of
the present, either sliding back into the past or jumping ahead into the
future. One author quoted a study that showed that people spend as
much as 90 percent of their waking hours mentally dwelling in either
the past or the future. When you let your mind drift this way, you miss
the incredible power of the present. How many times during the day
are you doing something or listening to someone when your mind
begins to think of your next meal, of an upcoming weekend, or an
event that took place earlier in the day or week? Each time that
happens, you miss key opportunities in the present. Opportunities to
think of something significant about a current project. Opportunities
to pick up a key statement of the person you're listening to. Anytime I
notice my mind accidentally thinking about things in the past or
things in the future, I visualize my right hand slapping me in the face to
bring me back into the present, and I simply think to myself, "Focus."
It's a corny little technique, but it works.

Letting time accidentally slip away by letting your mind wander is a
waste of valuable moments and important opportunities. But even
worse are the much larger increments of time you lose on purpose.
Time is your most limited resource. And oftentimes you sacrifice the
best use of it by allocating a block of time to something that is a merely
convenient or good use of that time. As I mentioned in Chapter 9, a
"good" use of your limited resources is often the worst enemy of the
best use of those resources. And that principle especially applies to
your use of time.

I used to come home from work and instantly turn on the television
to CNN while Shannon prepared dinner. One day my eight-year-old
son said, "Daddy, you always watch too much TV when you come
home." Now, in itself, there's nothing wrong with watching CNN. In
fact, it's a good use of my time because it keeps me well informed on
the latest events that affect my life and my business. But as good as it
is, that "good use" of my time was stealing the "best use" of my time
from me, my wife, and my children. My younger sons are only awake

for a couple of hours after I get home from work, and to waste a half hour of that very important time was robbing all of us of quality time together. When it's gone that time can't be recaptured and brought back. The news, on the other hand, can be watched after the kids have gone to bed. Most people don't waste a lot of their time doing bad things. But they do waste hundreds of hours each year choosing to spend their time doing something that is acceptable or good rather than something that is better or best.

Since taking control of your life starts with taking control of your time, starting today, before you sit down to engage in any activity for fifteen minutes or more, ask yourself: Is this merely a good use of my time or is it the best use? Is there something better I could spend this block of time doing? The best use of any block of time can be discovered by viewing it in relation to the highest priorities of your most important dreams. For example, my three most important dreams are: to have a more intimate relationship with God, to be the best husband my wife could possibly have, and to be the best father I can be to my children.

Because a large portion of my day is filled with "nonoptional" commitments of time, primarily during my working hours, I cannot commit those blocks of time to my three most important dreams. However, I have a great many "elective" or optional blocks of time after work. And I can measure the use of those blocks of time against my highest priorities and most important dreams. When measured that way, it was very easy to give up my half hour of CNN and replace it with talk and play time with my kids.

If you followed the assignment at the end of Chapter 7, you have a prioritized list of the most important areas in your life, and have defined your dreams in each of those areas. At the end of Chapter 10, you were asked to convert your Dreams into goals, steps, and tasks. If you have done this, you can begin to measure your "elective" blocks of time against your most important dreams and priorities and the steps and tasks you need to achieve your goals to achieve your dreams. If you will begin to make this simple technique a part of your daily life, you will find yourself with more time than you have ever had for the things that matter most.

2. *You don't plan and prioritize your day before it starts.* The second reason time gets away from you is because you don't plan and priori-

tize your day before it begins. Most people enter each day haphaz-
ardly, figuring they will simply do whatever it takes to handle each
event as it comes their way. While this approach is very easy (it follows
our natural inclinations), it is also very inefficient and extremely less
productive. Think for a minute about the last time you went on a
vacation. When did you decide where you were going to go, how you
were going to get there, what you were going to do once you were
there, and when you were going to return home? All of those important decisions were probably made before you climbed into your car
or went to the airport. You had your schedule all mapped out. You
had thought of most or all of the things you wanted to do and the
people or places you wanted to visit. You knew how you were going to
get there, and when you were going to return.

Think of how ridiculous it would be to show up at the airport the
day you are leaving for your vacation without any of that figured
out. The man behind the ticket counter asks you, "Where are you
going today?" Imagine the look you would get if you said, "Good
question, let's try and figure that out right now." Now imagine the
amount of valuable vacation time you'd waste if you continued
deciding what to do and when to do it as you were confronted by
each choice.

As ridiculous as that scenario is, it is the way more than 95 percent
of all American adults start and face each day. No wonder they feel
out of control. What makes this even more ridiculous is that none of
these people approach their vacation in that manner. All of the major
decisions are determined and planned out in advance. So you make
the most of the seven to fourteen days that you are on vacation but fail
to plan the other 351 far more important days. If you want to gain
control of your life, you must begin to effectively plan and prioritize
your days *before* you start each day. I'll show you how to do that a
little later in this chapter.

Now, a lot of people are afraid to plan their days because they think
that doing so would greatly limit their freedom. They believe that their
days are filled with so many urgencies, there's no way they could plan
around them. They also think they don't have time to plan their day.
Well, it's a lot easier than you think. It only requires a few minutes of
quiet time and the right planning tool. Effective planning gives you
more freedom to effectively handle a day's urgencies, not less!

3. *Your time is stolen by time robbers.* The third way time gets away from you is that it's stolen by what America's leading authority in time management calls "time robbers." These are those activities, events, and circumstances that break into the day and steal time or attention away from doing what is most important. Below is a list of time robbers that are identified in the Franklin Covey time management seminar. Are any of them familiar? Check those that steal time from you.

TIME ROBBERS

_____Unexpected interruptions
_____Unplanned phone calls
_____Requests or demands
      of others
_____Mistakes of others
_____Equipment failures
_____Poor communication
_____Improper planning
_____Inadequate listening
_____Conflicting priorities
_____Lack of self-discipline
_____Meetings

_____Unrealistic time estimates
_____Lengthy phone
      conversations
_____Shifting priorities
_____My mistakes
_____Bureaucratic red tape
_____Indecision
_____Socializing
_____Personality conflicts
_____Unwillingness to say no
_____Involvement with details
_____Failure to delegate

Although time robbers like these may break into the day, there are some very effective ways to prevent them from stealing your time, and we will look at those a little later.

4. *You allow "urgencies" to take precedence over priorities.* The fourth way time gets away from you is by letting "urgencies"—those events that demand your immediate attention and action—take you away from your priorities. They may be totally unimportant, but they still jump out at you and say, "I want your attention and I want it *now!*" Telephone calls are perhaps the best example of this. You can be in the middle of a critical conversation with your spouse, your children, or a business client, and no matter how important that conversation may be, if the phone rings, you stop everything and pick it up. This is literally letting the tail wag the dog. If you are to take control of your time, you must begin to recognize that urgencies are

like people who cut in front of you in a line. They may think they and their needs are more important than yours, but they aren't. You can begin to tell your urgencies to take a number and go to the back of the line.

5. *You procrastinate and put the most important things off until later.* The final way you let time get away from you is by procrastinating. Just as you let urgencies cut in front of the line, you put your priorities in the back of the line. So, urgencies are always dealt with immediately and priorities are nearly always left until later. And unfortunately, for most of your priorities, later never comes. Hyrum Smith, one of the founders of the Franklin Covey Company, says people usually pro-crastinate important activities for one or more of six reasons. First, they sense no urgency for the activity. For example, what kind of urgency do people attach to playing with their kids or having a meaningful conversation with their spouse? And yet, even though they do not sense any urgent need to engage in these activities, they are far more important than many of the other activities they may engage in when they come home. Hand in hand with this reason for procras-tination is Hyrum's second reason, namely that people don't see the value of doing a particular activity at once. "So what if I don't play with the kids tonight, I'll do it tomorrow night. They won't care." Wrong!

The next reason people put off important activities until later is that they are not fun or pleasant, or they are outside the "comfort zone." More people are dying from cancer today than ever. Not because they are unable to effectively treat cancer but because people don't take the time to get regular physical checkups. It's no fun spending half a day once a year taking a thorough physical. And yet, could anything be more important? Hundreds of thousands of people die each year from cancer, heart disease, and strokes because they didn't take time for physicals or didn't quickly see a doctor when they first experienced symptoms. Procrastination is truly a deadly habit. Have you ever put off beginning a healthy diet or a consistent exercise program? Of course you have, and so have I. They are not fun or overly pleasant, and we sacrifice our health because of it.

The last two reasons we put off important activities is our lack of knowledge and our fear of failure. "I'll call that client tomorrow; the last thing I want right now is a rejection." So, you not only put off the call, you postpone a possible success. If you are going to achieve your dreams, you must effectively deal with your natural inclination to procrastinate.

One tip that Hyrum gives for overcoming the tendency to procrastinate is to do those things you are likely to put off, *first*. By scheduling them first, you not only get them out of the way, but you are then free to do those things that are more fulfilling and fun, without the weight of the guilt, dread, or fear that comes with procrastination.

TAKING CONTROL OF YOUR TIME

Taking control of your time is a relatively simple thing to do, and yet less than 5 percent of the population do it. Why? First, they don't recognize the importance of it, and second, they don't know how to do it. I hope I've shown you that taking control of your time is critical to achieving your dreams. Now we will focus on the "how to's." It's not complicated, but it requires learning a few techniques and using a daily planner the proper way.

Seven Steps to Getting the Greatest Return on Your Most Limited Resource

1. *Force yourself to focus on the present.* We talked about this earlier in this chapter. Keeping your mind focused on the present and refocusing it to the present anytime you are aware that it has drifted into the past or wandered into the future is critical to your productivity and attentiveness to others. A technique that has been very helpful to me is having a pen and my daily planner with me at all times. When my mind starts to drift, I can quickly jot down the distracting thought and make a note to come back to it later. That instantly frees my mind to refocus on the present. You can use this and any mental or physical technique that you can think of to help you keep focused and refocus whenever necessary. As I mentioned earlier, I use a mental image of my right hand slapping me in the face and mentally say the word "focus."

2. *Take an inventory of your time.* According to a national study, the average American adult watches between thirty-five and fifty-six

hours of television per week. That is a staggering amount of time, especially in light of the fact that those same adults work an average of forty hours per week. And yet, as staggering as that statistic is, when people are told about that average, nearly everyone instantly says, "Not me." The fact is that time passes so fast, most of us have no idea how we really spend each hour. If you take a simple inventory of how you spend each hour of your day, for seven days, you will be amazed by what you will discover. To do this, simply make two charts on notebook paper or on a yellow pad that are similar to the Time Inventory Form on page 247. On the first chart, take fifteen or twenty minutes and fill in how you think you typically spend each hour in your typical week. Then circle every hour block that is an "elective" block of time—that is, time that you can choose to fill with anything you like.

Take your second chart with you everywhere you go for one week, and once every few hours fill in what you actually did in the preceding hours. At the end of the week you will have an actual log of your average week. Once again circle all the hours that represent "elective" blocks of time. If you find that one-hour blocks are not sufficient, you can break your log into half-hour segments. The final step is to compare your guesstimate in the first chart with the actual log on the second chart. This simple exercise will help you identify blocks of your time that are truly elective blocks.

3. *Replace good uses of elective blocks of time with the best uses of that time.* After you have identified your elective blocks of time, you will have the means to replace good uses of time with best uses. You can fill those blocks with activities that reflect your highest priorities and complete the tasks of your most important dreams.

4. *Delegate every time-consuming activity that can wisely be delegated.* "There just aren't enough hours in the day" is one of the most common complaints ever uttered by man or woman. During the years that I've been in business, I've heard it hundreds, maybe even thousands of times. It's usually offered as an excuse for not finishing something on time. When someone offers this complaint on a regular basis, I'll usually ask to see the "pile" they are under. Without exception, I can find hours of time-consuming details and activities that could easily be delegated to someone else. People often sacrifice the

Time Inventory

	Sun	Mon	Tues	Wed	Thurs	Fri	Sat
6:00							
7:00							
8:00							
9:00							
10:00							
11:00							
Noon							
1:00							
2:00							
3:00							
4:00							
5:00							
6:00							
7:00							
8:00							
9:00							
10:00							
11:00							
Midnight							
1:00							
2:00							
3:00							
4:00							
5:00							

single most limited, irreplaceable resource they have in order to accomplish something that could be delegated for a few dollars an hour. Remember, dollars spent can be replaced, time cannot. Delegating unimportant or noncritical activities is the easiest and most effective way to add a hundred hours to your twenty-four-hour day.

5. *Identify your time robbers and take preemptive measures to protect yourself against them.* On page 243 you identified various time robbers that interrupt your day and impede your productivity. Now that you've done that, you can take preemptive steps to keep you from being a victim of their intrusion. A good number of these intrusions can be thwarted by correctly using a daily planner. For example, you can set aside a specific time to take or make low-priority phone calls. When these calls come in, someone else can tell the caller that you can't talk right now but will be available at a particular time to take the call. You can do the same thing with face-to-face interruptions.

My wife has several friends who will talk to her on the phone for an hour at a time. Shannon is so afraid of hurting their feelings that she will kindly listen no matter how long the conversation. She will then be extremely frustrated because she has let more important matters get pushed back an entire hour or maybe even into the next day. To make matters worse, she has five or six friends that would like to have long conversations, not once a month or once a week, but once a day. None of them have a clue about how hectic Shannon's schedule is. They don't realize all of the urgent and important demands on her time that, as a result, get postponed or set aside. These lengthy calls and the frustration they can create are not their fault; they are Shannon's fault. She really cares about her friends and wants to give them all the time they need. But if she would simply begin the conversation with a phrase like "I've only got ten minutes right now, so if we can cover everything in ten minutes I can talk now; otherwise we should talk later," then nine times out of ten her girlfriends would be more succinct. Shannon would then capture fifty minutes back of what would otherwise be an hour phone call.

One of the great benefits of a Franklin Covey time management seminar is that it shows specific ways to deal with each of your time robbers. And you can deal with urgencies in the same manner. You can allocate a specific period of time in your day to deal with all unimportant urgencies. Surprisingly, most urgencies are less important than the tasks they divert you from.

6. *Plan and prioritize your day before it starts.* Here again an effective day planner and the knowledge of how to correctly use it is critical. I have tried all kinds of day planners and organizers, and as far as I'm concerned, the Franklin Day Planner is by far the most effective of its kind.

Planning and prioritizing your day begins either the night before or in the morning before your day begins. This usually only takes me five to fifteen minutes. I start by making a list of all the tasks I would like to accomplish during the day. I list every one I can think of without prioritizing them. Franklin's daily pages have a column for that list. Next, I put every item on the task list into a "value category" placing an "A" representing high value, "B" medium value, or "C" low value by each item. I then put a number by each task in the "A" category according to priority, beginning with "1" for the highest priority and working down. I do the same for my "B" tasks and my "C" tasks.

By doing this simple exercise, a "C" task (no matter how squeaky its wheel may be) will never cut in line ahead of an "A" task. I will not be sidetracked to complete "B-4" before I complete "A-1." Once you begin this system, you will be amazed by the number of high-priority tasks you'll complete each day. You'll also be amazed by how this system insulates you from time robbers and unimportant urgencies.

If there is any way you can attend one of the Franklin Covey Company's time management seminars—called "Time Quest Seminars"—it will be one of the most important turning points in your life.

7. *Execute your day according to your priorities.* Once you have planned your day, simply carry out each task according to its lettered and numbered priority. As unimportant urgencies invade your day, politely force them into a time set aside for urgencies, either that day or sometime later in the week. You can determine their level of importance by comparing them to your prioritized task list and seeing where they would fit in line. If someone in authority requests or demands that you attend to an urgency that shouldn't replace a higher priority task, explain the task you will be forced to put aside and show the full weight of what is being asked of you. When you do this, your supervisor will often agree with your priorities and either give the task to someone else or move its completion date back to fit in with your prioritized schedule.

KEEPING ON TRACK, ONE MINUTE AT A TIME

If you have a wristwatch or a clock in front of you, take a moment and look at the angle or space between the minute marks on the dial. That tiny little angle is three degrees. When the Apollo spacecrafts were launched from Cape Canaveral, if their course was off by that same tiny angle (one minute or three degrees) they would have missed the center of the moon, not by that same tiny fraction of an inch but rather by a distance of thirteen thousand miles. In other words, if you stacked five more moons on top of our moon, the rocket would have missed the entire stack. The same is true in the pursuit of dreams. If you get off course even a tiny little bit, you can miss your dream by miles. Effective priority planning not only empowers you toward your dreams, it keeps you on course and on schedule, hour by hour, day by day.

In Chapter 10, I gave a working definition of your personal productivity—"The degree and quantity of the significant accomplishments you are able to achieve in a limited amount of time that reflect your true values, dreams, and goals." If you had an unlimited amount of time to achieve your dreams, priority planning would be unnecessary. But time is the most irrevocably limited resource you possess. Your time is like an escalator or a moving sidewalk. It only moves in one direction, and that is toward its end; when you reach its end, there is no going back.

If you hope to achieve your most important dreams, you must be aware of this most limited and precious resource. You must be ever conscious that you spend twenty-four hours of time every day; and once spent they can never be replaced. Whether we are awake or asleep, working or playing, doing important things or foolish things, time just keeps moving us closer and closer to our ultimate end. How tragic that such a limited resource, more valuable than all the gold in the world, is so often wasted. My hope is that you will begin to recognize the incredible value of your time, and make the absolute most of every waking hour, that you take responsibility and control of your time. You *can* achieve your most important dreams, but to do so you must ignite this seventh and critically important engine.

POWER SECRET #13:
Taking Control of Your Life,
One Minute at a Time

COMPLETE THE FOLLOWING exercises in your notebook.

1. Following the sample form on page 247, fill in how you think you spend each hour in a typical week. Then circle every hour that is an "elective" block of time.
2. Using a second copy of this form, every couple of hours, record what you did in the preceding hours. Take it with you everywhere you go for a week. Once again, circle every hour that is an "elective" block of time. At the end of the week, compare this actual log of your time with your guesstimate log.
3. Begin to consider how you can replace *good* uses of your elective blocks of time with uses that reflect your greatest values, highest priorities, and most important dreams.
4. Make a list of any activities that you think you could delegate now or in the future. Than write out a plan on how you can begin to delegate each activity with a deadline for accomplishing that plan.
5. If you haven't already done it, use the list on page 243 to identify the time robbers that interrupt your day and keep you from achieving your higher priority tasks. Determine a routine for beginning to deal with them in a nonurgent manner.
6. If you don't already have a day planner that enables you to effectively plan and prioritize your days, purchase what I believe is the best day planner and planning system on the market today, the Franklin Day Planner. I would also recommend that you sign up for our Dream Conversion Seminars or order our Dream Conversion Tape Series and Manual by calling 1-800-246-1771.

7. Spend a few minutes each night planning and prioritizing your daily tasks and activities for the next day, following the system outlined on page 249.
8. Begin to execute your day according to your priorities, rather than your urgencies.

PART IV

BLASTING OFF!
DESTINATION—YOUR IMPOSSIBLE
DREAM

CHAPTER 17

The Fuel for All Seven Engines: "Oprah Winfrey Passion"

A LIFE-CHANGING CHOICE ANYONE CAN MAKE

PASSION FUELS ALL SEVEN ENGINES.

HOW OPRAH WON MY HEART WITH A SINGLE STATEMENT

The first time I saw Oprah Winfrey was when she appeared in her first interview with Barbara Walters. It was shortly after she had made her acting debut in *The Color Purple*. Her daily talk show was just starting to be syndicated nationally, and I had not yet seen it or the film. As Barbara interviewed her, I was impressed with both her demeanor and her answers. I was already starting to like her when Barbara asked her a question that set up what I believe was the defining moment of the interview. Oprah's answer made me want to reach into the television set and give her the kind of hug I give my kids when they say or do something that makes my heart soar with pride.

Barbara's question went something like this: "Oprah, what was it like growing up as a little girl in the Deep South? It must have been terrible feeling the devastating pangs of discrimination."

With her one-sentence answer, Oprah not only stunned and baffled Barbara Walters, she won my respect and admiration for life. "Barbara, I discovered very early in life that there is no discrimination against excellence!" *Wow!* I jumped to my feet and applauded. Barbara seemed so surprised, she didn't know what to say next. I'm sure she had prepared a line of follow-up questions, but Oprah's answer gave her no place to go.

I have to believe that Oprah did experience discrimination and the hurt that goes along with it both in her childhood and at other times in her life. And if I'm right, it makes her answer all the more powerful and revealing about her and her character. It tells me that she has taken full responsibility for who she is, her attitude, and how she has responded to life. It says that she refuses to assign blame to those who have hurt her. It says that she has wisely and lovingly responded to the negative actions of others, so that any hurts inflicted upon her have produced compassion rather than bitterness.

There are two other ways to interpret her answer. If she truly never felt the pangs of any discrimination, it means that she was so focused on her pursuit of excellence that she was virtually impervious to any such darts that had been hurled at her. Or, if you take her statement at face value, and no darts were in fact hurled, it says that her pursuit and achievement of excellence were so encouraging and inspiring that it totally disarmed her would-be detractors. So no matter how I interpret her answer, Oprah deserves my respect and admiration.

Because Oprah captured my respect in that first interview and has so reinforced it in the years that have followed, I have paid special attention to her personal and professional success. Several of my close friends, including Gary Smalley, have been guests on her show, and I have always been impressed at how quickly and passionately she catches their vision and communicates it in a way that enables millions of her viewers to understand and embrace it. And my friends have told me that she is a very caring and gracious host. But the quality that has impressed me the most and I'm convinced is the engine that has driven her phenomenal success, is her passion: her passion for life, her passion for her work, her passion for others, and her passion for excellence.

PASSION IS THE ROCKET FUEL THAT KEEPS ALL SEVEN ENGINES RUNNING!

What passion has done for Oprah, it has done for every other dream-maker I have known. In fact, I have never known or read about any dream-achiever who hasn't been driven by a passion for his or her dreams. I now realize that passion is the powerful fuel that keeps all seven rocket engines burning. Without passion, your engines will stop burning long before you reach the moon. It is the drive that keeps you going, even when you are physically exhausted and emotionally drained. It is truly a secret power that is shared by everyone who shoots for the moon and hits it.

WHY DO AMERICA'S RICHEST PEOPLE KEEP WORKING?

Bill Gates's net worth is approximately $36 billion. If he and his wife spent $100 million a year, it would take them 360 years just to spend the principal. At that rate, the interest would last him hundreds of years more. With this in mind, the logical question is, "Why does he still show up for work every day?" Steven Spielberg's net worth has been estimated to be a billion dollars. Not as much as Bill but enough to live comfortably for his remaining years of life. Why does he still work nonstop from one film to the next? Bill Cosby's worth is at least $300 million, and he still goes to work five days a week. And then there's Oprah, Lee Iacocca, Ted Turner, Rupert Murdoch, and so on. Not only do they go to work every day, but if you followed them around you would be exhausted by how hard and how long they work. Why do they do it?

There's only one answer: *passion!* They love what they're doing so much that even when they could put their life on cruise control, they never take their foot off the accelerator.

IS PASSION AN INBORN TRAIT OR SOMETHING YOU ACQUIRE?

Even though passion is a universal characteristic you'll find in every dream-maker, it is far from universal among the general population. In fact, it's extremely rare. I'm not talking about moments of passion, which are occasionally experienced by everyone. I'm talking about the kind of passion that drives a person to the heights of extraordinary achievement. It's as rare as diamonds among the population in general and as common as air among dream-makers. Why? Is it just something you are either born with or not? Or is passion something you can acquire? The answer is *both*. Some people seem to be born with it. They seem to be driven by passion almost from infancy. But most of the dream-makers I have known were not born with it; they acquired it along the way.

The people who seem to be born with it, seem to have a natural passion for life in general, and just about everything else they choose to do personally or professionally. My partner Jim Shaughnessy is a good case in point. From the time he was a child, he did everything with all his heart and energy. It got him into a lot of trouble when it was channeled in the wrong directions, but it made him an All-American running back, a successful schoolteacher, and a prosperous businessman when it was channeled in the right directions. Believe it or not, he even grocery shops with passion. But people who are born with passion are as rare as plutonium. Most people who become passionate acquire it. And that's great news for those of us who *weren't* born with it!

HOW ON EARTH CAN YOU ACQUIRE PASSION?

For those of you who weren't born passionate, there are two ways you can acquire passion. One way is to "catch it" much as you might catch a cold; the other way is to "develop it," taking specific steps to bring it into a particular area of your life where you want to achieve your dreams.

Catching passion is the easiest way of gaining it. I have to confess, my passion for writing was "caught" rather than developed. You just stay around something that you begin to fall in love with, and the more you are around it, the more you want to be around it. That is what happened to one of my partners. He was nineteen when he joined our company, and didn't have a clue as to which area of the company he wanted to be involved with. He went from department to department, and was like a duck out of water in each job he undertook. Then one day I took him to Hollywood to assist me in shooting a series of commercials. He saw every step of the process—the directing, the working with the talent and the crew, and editing the finished product. He saw what I did for a living, got a taste of it, and quickly caught the passion. He was twenty at the time, and now he's thirty-nine. He has written and directed dozens of commercials and shows, and made millions of dollars doing it. Some day you'll be seeing his work on the big screen, and I wouldn't be surprised if we see him accepting an Oscar for best director. He really is that good.

But while catching a passion can be easy, waiting around to catch one is risky. You might go through your entire life without catching one, or worse, you may catch one that is more destructive than beneficial. If you gain a passion for golf but can't afford the time or money to play, instead of bringing joy to your life your passion will either bring frustration (if you don't play enough) or poverty (if you do play enough).

Or you may catch a passion in an area that steals your time and attention away from the priorities in your life. It may control you instead of you controlling it. This is often what happens with work-aholics. They love their wives, they love their children, but they sacrifice them all for the job. By the time they wake up to the trade they've made, their kids are grown and their marriage has ended.

So even though catching a passion requires a lot less effort, it's a lot less reliable. You may never catch one, or you may catch a bad one.

DEVELOPING A PASSION IS LIKE HARNESSING NUCLEAR POWER!

Acquiring a passion is like starting an atomic chain reaction. If it's harnessed and controlled, it gives you tremendous power and endurance to achieve your most important dreams. On the other hand, if it's not properly controlled, it can be terribly destructive. Unlike catching a passion, developing one puts you in control, enabling you to harness all its power to achieve your dreams in the most important areas of your life. Although developing a passion requires a lot more effort than catching one, it isn't as hard as you might think when you understand it and learn the specific steps you need to take.

PASSION: LIFE'S HIGHEST OCTANE FUEL

The fuel of passion is a mixture of three ingredients: vision, hope, and satisfaction. It starts with gaining a vision for a desired outcome. Each time I start a new project, whether it's a script for a television show or a marketing campaign for a new product, I have a vision or dream in mind that I want to convert into reality. Passion the fuel always begins with a vision. That's why the first step of the Dream Conversion Process—clearly and precisely defining your dream in writing—is so important. You may not realize it at the time, but when you clearly define your dream in writing, you are depositing the first ingredient of passion for that dream into your heart and mind.

The second ingredient that makes up passion is hope. Hope is not simply a "wish." It is not a wishy-washy ooey-gooey feeling. Hope is the sincere expectation that a particular envisioned outcome is possible. The more confident the expectation or the more probable the envisioned outcome, the greater the hope. This is why the next three steps of the Dream Conversion Process are so important. Converting your stated dream into specific goals, those goals into steps, and those steps into tasks raises your confidence in your ability to reach your envisioned outcome. This process infuses hope for that vision or dream into your mind and heart. And it is hope that is the "explosive" ingredient that adds the real power to a person's passion.

The final ingredient in passion is the satisfaction or joy you experience as you complete the tasks to achieving your goals and convert your dreams into reality. As you experience this joy and satisfaction, it further increases your passion for even more achievement. It has the snowballing effect of more achievement producing more joy, more joy producing more passion, more passion producing more achievement, which produces more joy, and so on. So although your passion, joy, and achievement may start out as a small snowball, by the time it reaches the bottom of the mountain it will be gigantic. So, the Dream Conversion Process is not only a means of converting your dreams into reality, it is a "processing plant" that infuses your heart and mind with the three essential ingredients of passion: vision, hope, and joy.

Bringing passion into the pursuit of your dreams is critical if you are to dream big and achieve those dreams. It is the fuel that, once ignited, will keep your seven engines brightly burning for the duration of your flight. For all of recorded history, passion has driven the world's greatest achievers to the heights of human accomplishment in every imaginable field and endeavor. It can do the same for you.

POWER SECRET #14:
Acquiring the Fuel of Passion

1. ON EACH OF your Dream Pages, describe in writing the passion you currently feel in that area. How often do you think about that dream? How important is it to you to achieve that dream? Rate your passion level for that dream on a 0 to 10 scale with 0 equaling no passion and 10 equaling borderline obsession (you go to bed thinking about it, you wake up thinking about it, in fact you have a hard time staying focused on other things because your mind constantly keeps drifting back to this particular dream).

2. For those "important dreams" where you sense that your level of passion is lacking, answer the following questions.

   • Do you really have a clear and precise vision of that dream?

   • Have you "converted" that dream into written goals, steps, and tasks? If you haven't, your "hope" will be based on a "wish" rather than on a step-by-step plan. And without well-founded hope, there will be little sustaining passion.

   • Are you letting criticism subvert your enthusiasm and passion? (If so, do the "bucket of water" exercise described in Chapter 6.)

   • Do you have a subtle or even a high fear of failure? If so, put that fear into perspective with the exercises from Chapter 5.

   • Are you discouraged by your lack of know-how or your lack of the resources needed to perform the tasks, take the steps, achieve the goals, and accomplish the dream? If so, realize that recruiting the right partners, mentors, and outside resources is critical to fueling your passion.

CHAPTER 18

Igniting Your Engines

ALL THE POWER OF YOUR SEVEN BOOSTER ENGINES IS MEAN-INGLESS IF YOU DON'T IGNITE THEM.

A SINGLE SWITCH HIDDEN IN YOUR HEART CAN INSTANTLY IGNITE EACH ENGINE!

WE HAVE NOW identified the seven massive rocket engines that you have possessed since birth. These same seven engines have enabled the world's dream-makers to achieve their phenomenal dreams during their limited time here on earth. You stand on the launching pad, as awesome and as powerful as the majestic thirty-six-story Saturn V rocket. In the early chapters I revealed the six chains that keep you anchored to your launching pad, and I explained how you can cut them. If you followed those instructions, you are now ready to launch your rocket. The only thing standing between you and your dreams are two questions that only you can answer: Will you choose to ignite your seven engines? And if you do, will you keep the fuel freely flowing to each engine until you've reached your dreams?

The fuel is passion, and in the last chapter we discussed how to acquire that fuel and keep it flowing to each engine. So the remaining question is, "How can you ignite these seven massive engines?" The good news is that you already possess the ignition switch. It's right in front of you and you can flip it on whenever you're ready to launch. The switch can be described in a single word, but since it is such a misunderstood word, I believe the best way to illustrate it is with a good emotional word picture.

In 1859, a French tightrope walker named Charles Blondin ran a small ad in the *New York Times*. He stated that on a particular day he was going to cross Niagara Falls on a tightrope. Now, in case you've never visited Niagara Falls, it may be hard to appreciate the enormity of Blondin's claim. The falls are 1,100 feet across. That's nearly four football fields in length. The falls are 167 feet high, with more than 42 million gallons of water rushing over the falls every minute! When you walk up to the railing adjacent to the falls, you are overcome with awe at the force of the water moving over the edge and falling into the river below.

Nearly five thousand people turned out that day to watch Blondin attempt his crossing. Most of them probably thought they were turning out to watch a suicide. Before he began his crossing he asked the crowd, "How many believe I can successfully cross the falls?" The crowd responded with reluctant cheers and applause. He then climbed onto the rope, and to everyone's amazement he crossed the falls. The crowd now cheered with enthusiasm.

He then asked the crowd, "How many believe I can cross pushing a wheelbarrow?" Well, that sounded a little far-fetched, but the crowd still responded with polite cheers and applause. To their delight, he crossed the falls pushing a wheelbarrow. He then asked, "How many believe I can cross on stilts?" Once again the crowd politely responded. To their total amazement, he quickly crossed the 1,100-foot span on stilts.

He then asked, "How many believe I can cross the falls blindfolded?" Well, this was just a little too much for the crowd to believe, so they applauded but with reservation. And then he did it. He actually crossed Niagara Falls on a tightrope *blindfolded!* The crowd went crazy.

When the cheering and applause ceased, he asked, "How many believe I can cross the falls carrying someone on my back?" The crowd responded with cheers and applause so loud they could be heard above the roar of the falls. Of course they all believed. After all, they had just watched him cross the falls four times, performing feats that seemed far greater than the one he had just announced. And while they were still yelling and cheering, Charles Blondin silenced the entire crowd with his next question. "Who," he asked, "will volunteer?"

The crowd was awkwardly and embarrassingly silent. You see, out of the five thousand people who had been yelling and cheering, professing their belief in his ability to cross the falls with someone on his back, not one person, not a single man, woman, or child *truly* believed he could safely cross the falls with someone on his back. Oh, they all sincerely thought they believed, but when it came right down to it, their "belief" was thinner than air. In fact, it was nonexistent.

"Wait a minute," you say. "Don't be so hard on them. What responsible man or woman would ever do something so risky as get on the back of a tightrope walker to cross Niagara Falls?"

The answer is *any* responsible man or woman who truly *believed* they would safely arrive on the other side. You see, by definition, true belief always acts accordingly. If you truly believed that in thirty minutes an 8.5 earthquake was going to take place where you are now sitting, would you be sitting there twenty-nine minutes from now? Of course you wouldn't. At the same time, when you get into your car and drive down a freeway, do you believe that you are going to safely arrive at your destination? I can tell you that you truly do believe it or you wouldn't get into the car. True belief or faith always has a corresponding action. You sit in a chair because you believe it is strong enough to support your weight.

As it turned out, there was one man in the crowd who did believe that Charles Blondin could safely cross the falls with someone on his back. He was Blondin's best friend. He jumped onto Blondin's back and became the only man in history who crossed Niagara Falls on the back of a tightrope walker.

I have identified all seven engines and given you strategies and techniques that will enable you to successfully pursue your dreams. If completed, the exercises at the end of each chapter will transmit the spark from the ignition switch to the start each engine. But *you* have to flip the switch. That switch is *faith*—the true belief that if you do what each chapter and exercise asks you to do, the engines will truly be ignited. If you truly believe that these strategies and techniques will empower you to your loftiest dreams, you will take the appropriate action. You will complete the exercises and begin to use the strategies and techniques revealed in each chapter. If you exercise that faith, and utilize the strategies and techniques, your engines will ignite and you will begin to achieve your dreams.

The Bible teaches that "Faith is the substance of things hoped for, the Evidence of things unseen." Faith is not some abstract ethereal feeling. It is not hope. It is substantive. It is tangible. True faith always produces an appropriate action that gives evidence of its existence. Most of the people who read this book will agree with the strategies and techniques it contains. After all, they are not just theory but actual strategies and techniques that have worked for me and for thousands of other dream-achievers. And yet even though most readers will agree, very few will truly believe. They will continue to sit on their launching pad, all chained up with their engines cold and dormant. They will finish their lives on that launching pad, never having known the thrill of the launch, and the joy and fulfillment of reaching their dreams.

But what about you? Will you be like so many others and simply live on your launching pad? The choice is yours. People who have lower IQs and far worse situations and circumstances than you will ignite their engines and achieve dreams they never even dared to dream before. What about you? You need not rush through the Power Secret exercises and begin to apply every strategy and technique next week. No one could do that. No one should do that! If you complete more than two chapters' exercises in a week, chances are they will be ineffective. One chapter per week or even per month is as fast as you need to progress. If you do, within fifteen weeks (or fifteen months) you will be accomplishing more extraordinary achievements and fulfilling more of your dreams than you would ever have imagined possible.

For your sake, and for the sake of those you love, my prayer is that you will flip your ignition switch on and blast off to the ride of your life. I hope you'll let me hear all about your ride and the dreams you achieve, and if you would like to be a part of my mailing list, you can write me at: American Telecast, 1230 American Boulevard, West Chester, PA 19382. Or you may join my mailing list by calling 1-800-246-1771.

May God bless you and your family, and grant that you achieve every worthwhile dream you ever pursue, regardless of how impossible it may appear to be.

POWER SECRET #15:
Flipping the Switch

1. IF YOU ARE like most readers of self-help books, there's a good chance you haven't yet started your notebook or Dream Conversion Journal. Without taking this first step of faith, it will be nearly impossible for you to cut the chains and ignite your engines. So if you haven't yet started completing the exercises at the end of each chapter, now is the time to create your notebook and Dream Conversion Journal. If you prefer to use a preprinted notebook with all of the exercises and a Dream Conversion Journal you may do so by calling 1-800-246-1771.

2. If you have started the exercises in this book, keep it up! Remember: one chapter's set of exercises per month is the slowest pace you should consider, and two chapters' exercises per week is the fastest you should go.

3. Although all of us have to regularly deal with the six anchor chains to one degree or another, a few readers may find some of the six chains more severely limiting than others. Prioritize the following chains according to your desire to overcome them. You may wish to then focus first on the exercises at the end of the chapters that deal with your highest priorities.

   _____Your programming for mediocrity
   _____Your fear of failure
   _____Your avoidance of criticism
   _____Your lack of clear and precise vision
   _____Your lack of know-how
   _____Your lack of resources

4. When working with your Dream Conversion Journal, remember that this is a lifelong project. Unlike your notebook, your journal will not be completed in a matter of weeks or months, so don't be in a hurry. Start with the most important dreams in the most important areas of your life, and simply work from there. With each year that passes, you will discard some dreams and add new

ones. The goal of your journal is to provide a clear road map and schedule for achieving each of your dreams—short term, long term, and lifetime. It's your map; it's your life. Take it seriously but have fun with it. If you do, it will become your genie in a notebook.

About the Author

STEVEN K. SCOTT is a cofounder of the American Telecast Corporation and its group of consumer-goods companies. In addition to creating ATC's marketing programs with sales of over $1 billion, he has written and directed countless award-winning television commercials and productions featuring celebrities such as Cher, Jane Fonda, Kathie Lee Gifford, Charlton Heston, Tom Selleck, Chuck Norris, Michael Landon, and more than seventy other world-renowed celebrities.

In addition to cofounding and building more than a dozen multi-million-dollar companies from the ground up, Steve has coauthored two best-selling books with Gary Smalley and coproduced more than twenty best-selling videos. His book *A Millionaire's Notebook,* published in 1996, is currently in its fifth printing. Steve is also a popular national speaker on the subjects of personal and professional achievement, and turning dreams into reality.